A CONCEPTUAL APPROACH TO MANAGEMENT

A CONCEPTUAL APPROACH TO MANAGEMENT

Lloyd R. Amey

PRAEGER

New York
Westport, Connecticut
London

Library of Congress Cataloging-in-Publication Data

Amey, Lloyd R.
    A conceptual approach to management.

    Bibliography: p.
    Includes indexes.
    1. Management.   2. Management—Methodology.
I. Title.
HD38.A5858   1986   658.4   86-91513
ISBN 0-275-92311-8 (alk. paper)

Library of Congress Catalog Card Number: 86-91513
ISBN: 0-275-92311-8

First published in 1986

Praeger Publishers, 521 Fifth Avenue, New York, NY 10175
A division of Greenwood Press, Inc.

Printed in the United States of America

The paper used in this book complies with the Permanent Paper Standard issued by the National Information Standards Organization (Z39.48-1984).

10   9   8   7   6   5   4   3   2   1

Contents

HD38
.A5858
1986

Preface

The purpose of this book is to provide those entering the study of management with an introduction to the key ideas or concepts that need to be understood in pursuing this endeavor. Some caveats should, however, be stated immediately. First, while some of the concepts are universally applicable to the management of all types of organizations, the book has been written more particularly with business organizations in view, especially private business organizations. Second, the intention has not been to list all the concepts that have been found to be useful in studying business organizations but rather to be parsimonious, selecting the minimal set of key ideas underlying the various aspects of management. The resulting set of concepts, it is hoped, constitutes a basic methodology of management at the time of writing.

The book was written primarily for beginning Master of Business Administration (MBA) students in university business schools, and secondarily for students seeking various business-related professional qualifications (such as accounting, banking) that require courses in management. To all of these the following justification of the approach taken in this book is offered. First, existing books on management, often titled *Principles of Management,* invariably take a functional approach. They describe the various functions that managers perform: planning, organizing, staffing, directing, motivating, controlling, decision-making, and measuring performance. In these usually lengthy descriptions (500 to 800 pages) of what management consists of the treatment of conceptual ideas is superficial and incomplete. Business management is both an art and a science; there are elements of both. In many areas of business, however, relatively few large enterprises command a disproportionately large share of trade, and in these large enterprises management is collective, impersonal, and more dependent on applied science in most of its functions. This tendency has received reinforcement from the increasing maturity of management as an academic discipline. In the past quarter-century or so, the pace of new developments in management science, statistics, finance, and accounting, originating in the business schools, has considerably quickened.

The second reason why a book taking a conceptual rather than a functional approach to management is needed is that, as a career opportunity, management has a very wide catchment area—just as many of those occupying senior management positions in large corporations are engineers, accountants, and scientists by training, so the composition of a beginning MBA class in many universities is likely to include more graduates in pure and applied science, arts, and social sciences rather than in economics, business administration, or commerce. To these students from disciplines remote from business, it is the underlying ideas and ways of thinking, rather than a description of what management does, that will be most unfamiliar.

This book is the first of which I am aware that attempts to provide, in one volume, an introduction to these key ideas, a short methodology of management. Our coordinated knowledge of any field that is at least in part a science (as is the case with management) is formed by the combination of two orders of experience. One is observational, formed by direct discriminations of particular observations. The other is conceptual, based on our general way of conceiving the universe. Observational knowledge is invariably interpreted in terms of a conceptual order, a system of ideas in terms of which we interpret the world around us. The question of the priority of one or the other of these generators of knowledge is idle; novel observations modify the existing conceptual order, and novel concepts sometimes suggest new possibilities of observational discrimination. These remarks are offered (a) as a general justification of the attempt herein to present a reasonably comprehensive conceptual order or system of ideas for management, and (b) to warn that the results should not be regarded as eternal verities, but as subject to further change and refinement. At the very least, however, they suggest that concepts merit an equal place in our attention with description (based on direct observation), although as Whitehead (1947) has noted, observational discrimination is not dictated by impartial facts; it selects and discards, and what it retains is rearranged in a subjective order of prominence (consider the observed facts in early stages of civilization that the earth was flat with a domed sky, or that the sun was the sole origin of light).

A conscious attempt has been made to present the key organizing ideas of management in the text with as little resort to mathematical symbols as possible. At the same time, most chapters are accompanied by a mathematical appendix at the end of the book. It is left to the reader to decide whether to read both, although it is hoped that most readers will do so.

The book contains nothing original, except the selection of topics to be accorded the status of key concepts. The extent of my indebtedness to other scholars is indicated by the references to their work.

Lloyd R. Amey

1

Introduction

This series of essays is concerned with the management of organizations. Our environment is heavily populated with organizations of various kinds: the family; business firms; labor unions and professional associations; and religious, educational, cultural and political institutions. Most of us belong to more than one of these organizations; and many organizations number other organizations in their membership. Our focus here will be more particularly on business organizations—private firms and government trading enterprises engaged in the production of economic goods and services—although many of the ideas to be discussed have relevance, with appropriate modification, to other kinds of organizations. To avoid confusion, it should be added that the organizations to which we are referring are formal organizations. In Chapter 7 we shall have occasion to refer to a further class of informal or "invisible" organizations based on widespread conscious or unconscious social acceptance rather than legal constitutions. Arrow (1974b, 26), who proposed this broader definition of organizations, would include in the latter category such things as moral and ethical principles and the market (price) system.

Without attempting to define "organization" more precisely, the main features of interest to us can be sketched in. Organizations are purposeful groups. Business organizations come into being to exploit the benefits of collective action (relating to the allocation of resources and uncertainty) in situations where such action is more effective than when production, buying, and selling are undertaken by a single individual. To be successful, many decisions require the expertise and judgment of more than one individual. The superiority of joint action springs from division of labor and specialization in all the activities involved: the directly productive, administrative, and informational. Bringing activities within

1

an organization rather than dealing in a number of markets avoids the costs of using those markets, may have certain informational advantages, and may also avoid situations in which the price system breaks down, that is, it fails to achieve an efficient allocation of resources between producers and/or consumers.

Under a combination of influences—new legal forms for companies (limited liability), new technologies (including modes of transport), and growth in population—business organizations have been growing in number, size, and complexity since the mid-nineteenth century. "Big Business" now includes giants economically more powerful than many national economies. Collectively, business organizations have the power to influence our lives in many ways; they may also offer us opportunities; and they compete for limited natural, human, and technological resources. These are reasons for a concern that they be administered efficiently and with social responsibility. That task falls to management, and to some extent to government in setting the conditions under which business is conducted.

What is involved in managing an organization? One way of answering this would be to list and describe all the things that managers do. This *functional* approach has been elaborated in numerous books bearing the title *Management* or *Principles of Management*. In them we learn that management involves planning, organizing, staffing, directing, and leading, (which in turn involve influencing, motivating, and communicating), and managing conflict, change, and stress. Other tasks of management are decision-making, controlling, and measuring performance. Such an approach serves a useful purpose, but judging from the literature, the result is more accurately characterized as descriptive rather than conceptual.

A sufficient reason for taking a different approach in this book is that in the past few decades the study of organizations and their management has gained a measure of maturity (which is not to say that all or even most of the problems have been solved).

The question this book addresses may be put as follows: Given our present state of knowledge, what are the basic notions, essential ideas, and ways of thinking needed in order to understand what is involved in the (effective) management of organizations? In attempting to answer this question, the intention has been to establish the mind-set, in the form of the minimum set of concepts or organizing ideas, and the methodology, needed for the study of management and the analysis of its problems. Some or all of these ideas underlie all management problems. An acquaintance with these ideas at the outset of studies in management, commerce, business, or public administration should make for a better understanding and integration of the functional areas. It is hoped that this will be of special benefit to graduate students of business administration whose previous studies have been in disciplines far removed from economics or commerce.

Organizations have been the subject of intense study and theorizing by researchers from a number of the social science disciplines, chiefly economics, psychology, sociology, and political science. More recently this multidisciplinary endeavor has been aided by contributions from the systems and engineering fields. For a very comprehensive treatment of most aspects of organizations and most of these approaches, readers are referred to the excellent book by Scott (1981).

2

Systems

The first concept to be discussed is also the most encompassing. It is the concept of *system* and, associated with it, the "systems approach" to problem-solving. In everyday speech we use the term *system* in describing all sorts of things (e.g., weather system, number system). In its technical usage, however, which has come into currency during the past fifty years, a system is a whole made up of a series of parts, at least two of which interact and modify each other's behaviors. Interrelatedness of parts is the essential characteristic of a system. The fact that (some of) the parts are interrelated means that the whole can behave in ways that none of the parts can: consider a human being and a single limb. We say the whole possesses certain "emergent properties"—the whole is more than the sum of its parts. The effect of this kind of parts–whole relationship (2 + 2 = 5) is sometimes referred to as *synergy* or *gestalt*.

Not all wholes are systems. A human being is a system because, to take one example, the body (via its sense organs) acts on the brain, which then acts on the body (say, the arms); the body influences and is influenced by the brain. The number 15, the sum of the integers 1 to 5, on the other hand, is a whole but not a system, because its components do not influence each other's values. The number 15 is merely an aggregate. The systems we encounter can be classified as concrete, composed of at least two different connected things (objects); conceptual, composed of at least two different ideas; and systems that combine these two characteristics (the human nervous system might afford an example). If the system components themselves consist of at least two different interrelated components, we call such components *subsystems*.

Before explaining what is meant by the systems approach, we need to

4

say a little more about systems. Let us henceforth concentrate on concrete systems, as the objects we shall be concerned with (human beings, organizations are systems of this kind). We have seen that a system X comprises a number (at least two) of parts, components, elements. We shall call these specific parts the *system's composition*. Some systems have an unchanging composition; in others, such as organizations, the composition may change over time. At a given time a system has a definite environment, consisting for the moment of everything that is not-X. Finally, there are all the relations of system components with one another and with the environment. We call this whole set of relations the *system's structure*. Note that this is not the same as *organization structure*, which refers only to the relations between system components. To be able to speak of a system at all we need to know at least these three things: composition, environment, and structure. And we must determine them in that order, because we must know the system's components before we can identify its environment and structure, and the environment must be known before the structure, because the latter includes relations with the environment. All this can be expressed by writing $X = \langle C, E, S \rangle$, where C, E, and S stand for composition, environment, and structure, and $\langle \, , \, , \, \rangle$ denotes an ordered sequence.

One point needs to be added. *Environment* was provisionally defined above by saying that it consisted of everything not-X. This is not very helpful, as an example will show. Let us take a specific system, X Company Limited. How should we define this company, regarded as a business system? In other words, where should we draw the boundary? Does system X consist of the corporate entity, its assets, and the claims against those assets; or does it also include all the people working for X? In fact it includes all of these things and more. If certain elements outside firm X significantly affect X's behavior *and are in turn significantly affected by X's* actions (i.e., these external elements and X *interact*), such elements form part of the composition and structure of X as a system. The boundary of system X must be drawn to include these elements within the system. What we are saying is that in its decision-making, the system should treat the interactive elements of the environment as variables to be explained, not as given. The environment of system X may now be defined precisely as those external elements that affect X but are not significantly affected by X. Thus in the case of the business system X Company Limited, the demand for its products should be regarded as part of the composition of X (and the feedback loop as part of its structure), if demand significantly affects X's production and sales and is in turn significantly affected by X's advertising. The interacting external elements are to be explained, not taken as given. (The argument for defining a system's environment as those elements that act on the system unidirectionally is the same as that for defining *exogenous variable* in econometrics according to the strict causal principle.) Of course, the parts of the external scene that significantly affect the system may vary from problem to problem, as may the reverse effects. And what constitutes "significant" effect is not precisely defined. If we are dealing with a problem in one division of a firm, it will be understood that "environment" may in this case include other parts of the firm which do not interact with the division. The boundaries of organizational systems are often extremely hard to determine, and change over time.

This last point about the need to define a system correctly is important because it is frequently not observed in the literature. A second example will therefore be given to emphasize it (this is reported in more detail in Amey and Egginton 1979, 555–57). A certain manufacturer was experiencing considerable fluctuations in his production, finished goods inventory, sales, and work force. The firm sold to other manufacturers in imperfectly competitive markets in which product reliability and delivery time were more important than price. Even relatively small variations in sales order rate generated wide swings in production, inventories, employment, and hence profitability. The firm attempted in various ways to smooth these fluctuations, to no effect. The swings in its customers' order rate, it believed, were outside its control. What in fact was happening was that the time at which customers placed their orders depended partly on the manufacturer's delivery time. Changes in delivery time affected the rate at which customers released new orders, which in turn affected the manufacturer's delivery time, forming a feedback loop not considered by the manufacturer. The lesson: it is a common mistake to draw the boundaries of a business system to conform with the boundaries of the firm. In the example, customers' ordering decisions were no part of the manufacturer's formal organization. Yet what was needed in this case was stabilization of the input to customers' ordering decisions, namely the delivery delay, which was within the manufacturer's control. In order to bring about this stabilization, the interactions between delivery period and customers' ordering rate had to be included in the business system of the manufacturer; the system had to extend beyond the boundaries of the firm.

From what has been said about composition, environment, and structure, it follows that in considering any system we should think not only of the system itself, but also of its parts and its environment, the larger system or systems of which it forms a part. Every system (except the universe, defined as the totality of systems) should be viewed as part of a three-tiered hierarchy, as shown in Figure 2.1.

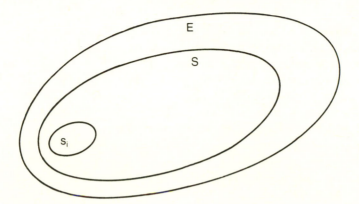

FIGURE 2.1. Three-tiered hierarchy of systems. E, environment; S, the system; s_i, $i = 1, \ldots, n$ = subsystems or components of S.

The systems approach

This leads us to the "systems approach" to problem-solving, or "systems thinking." This consists in recognizing that if we wish to understand the behavior of anything that possesses the properties of a system, we need to study not only the part–part and part–whole relationships, but also the system's relationship to one or more larger systems. This is based on the assumption that everything is part of some system, and every system except the universe part of some larger system.

Analysis, the breakdown of a phenomenon, problem, or thing into its parts, and trying to understand the whole from a knowledge of the parts, had been the traditional method employed by science to explain the behavior and properties of wholes. The systems approach is characterized by the *complementary* use of synthesis and analysis. Analysis is augmented by synthesis, the fitting of wholes into larger wholes. Thus to fully understand the behavior of a company, we need to know the relations between its various functions, departments, and divisions and their relation to the company (what they take from it and contribute to it), and its relations with other firms and with the economies and societies in which it operates.

The special value of the systems approach lies in the fact that the combination of analysis and synthesis leads to greater explanatory power than is provided by analysis alone.

The relevance of the systems approach to problems concerning the management of organizations has important implications for a number of the remaining concepts we shall be examining, notably objectives, information, value, cost, control, and performance.

The notion of system and the associated systems approach take us a large step forward in seeking to understand anything that has the properties of a system, including business organizations. Systems thinking has led to important new insights in the natural sciences (especially biology and physics), engineering (including communications and control), and the social sciences. Structural similarities began to be observed in very dissimilar systems, leading to the discovery of new laws and concepts of great generality that cut across many disciplines. As examples, the same modes of control are found in the human body, certain kinds of machines, and in accounting, while hierarchical forms of organization appear in physical, biological and social systems of great complexity (Boulding 1962; Simon 1962). At the same time, the grouping of systems into distinct classes by certain common properties helps to explain their behavior and evolution, and distinguishes these classes from one another.

Complexity

The first property of interest is the complexity of a system. Boulding (1956) has constructed a nine-tiered hierarchy of systems arrayed by degree of complexity. Beginning with (1) static structures (frameworks), it proceeds through (2) simple dynamic systems (e.g., clockworks), (3) cybernetic systems (systems with feedback) to (4) the most elemental living system (the cell), thence to (5) plants, (6) animals, (7) humans, (8) social organizations, and finally (9) transcendental systems (comprising "inescapable unknowables").

How are we to measure system complexity? One way would be in terms of the number of conceivable states a system may be in, the number of different kinds of behavior it may exhibit. Technically, this is given by the number of components of the system's state space. To illustrate, consider a human being. At any given time this person is in a certain state relative to the reference frame age, a certain state relative to the frame wealth, and similarly for other properties of interest (e.g., health, inputs, outputs, relations between components of the human being). If each of these properties is represented by a set containing all the conceivable values that property may take, the Cartesian product of all these sets of conceivable values (ranges) with the set of environmental elements with which the system is linked and the set of reference frames yields the conceivable state space of the system at a given time (Bunge 1977, ch. 3).

Such a measure would not be particularly useful, however, for several reasons. First, a given property (represented by a state variable) usually cannot take on all conceivable values, due to various kinds of constraints. Second, at least some of the components of a system are interrelated, and hence mutually restricted. They cannot take on all conceivable values as they could if they were independent. As a result, the conceivable state space (representing the conceivable variety of behavior of the system) is constrained to the degrees of freedom (actual variety) of the full variety of behavior. A better indication of a system's complexity is possible *in terms of* the system's degrees of freedom, an aspect of system states common to all concrete systems and familiar to the reader from statistics (statistical estimation). This alternative measure would say that "complexity" is given by:

the degrees of freedom of the system's states
minus values of the state variables excluded by constraints other than those due to interrelatedness of system components
plus values of the state variables due to emergent properties of the system (behaviors of which the system as a whole but not its parts is capable).

Why should we be interested in the degree of complexity of a system? System complexity measured in the way just indicated appears to vary directly with the levels in Boulding's hierarchy, a fact that has important practical implications for control. Thus a social system (organization at level 8) is able to adapt to and survive a wide variety of disturbances, environmental and internal. Human beings (level 7) can adapt to disturbances within somewhat narrower limits, while an ordinary machine (level 2), which can operate in only one fixed mode, cannot adapt at all— it either operates or ceases to operate. As we shall see later, system complexity appears to be related to some of the other system characteristics we will be considering, notably openness (directly), cohesiveness (inversely), and the system's behavioral characteristics.

Closed and open systems

A second grouping of systems that has proved very useful is the distinction between closed and open systems. This distinction rests on a property analogous to a thermodynamic property of physical systems, an analogy that should hold since all concrete systems are physical (wholes composed of at least two different connected things). While thermodynamics is concerned with the general laws governing heat-transfer processes, it provides a distinction that can be generalized to a wide range of processes. This is the distinction between processes of increasing and decreasing entropy. By entropy we mean the degree of disorder or randomness of the states of a system's parts, or the probability of the state of the system as a whole actually occurring. The second law of thermodynamics then asserts that concrete systems increase in entropy continuously until they cease to exist. Put another way, the second law says that concrete systems go from less probable to more probable states, that is, from less entropic to more entropic states. It so happens that there is a class of systems for which the second law does not hold, at least until such systems cease to exist (for all concrete systems eventually die), and this class of systems includes the systems of most interest to us, human beings and social organizations. We call systems that obey the second law *closed systems,* and those that violate the law *open systems.* Human beings and social organizations (indeed all living systems) are open systems. We shall see in a moment that all systems except the universe are in fact only relatively closed or open.

Now to explain this in a little more detail. It is not uncommon to find a closed system defined in the literature as one that does not exchange things (matter, energy, information) with its environment, or as a system without an environment, and an open system as one that engages in exchanges with its environment. This distinction is insufficient. It does not tell the whole story; in particular it tells us nothing about the behavior to be expected of a system. The real distinction between open and closed systems is due to Bertalanffy (1950), first published in German two decades earlier. Bertalanffy pointed out that the essential distinction between closed and open systems has to do with *entropy transfer.* An open system is one that is open to entropy transfer, a closed system one that is not.

This notion is best explained by an example. Consider first an ordinary machine (i.e., a machine without feedback), which is a closed system in the sense just described. The general course of events or evolution of a machine is constantly increasing entropy. The machine eventually wears out; all work stops, it becomes inert. In this state its entropy is a maximum. As with other closed systems the machine goes from less entropic (less probable) to more entropic (more probable) states. To anticipate, notice also that the machine, while it receives inputs from the environment, does not absorb any of these inputs into itself and use them for its own maintenance and survival. It is incapable of using the inputs it receives to reverse the entropic process.

Human beings and social organizations are examples of open systems. Like all concrete systems, including machines, these systems eventually run down and become inert. But, unlike the machine, the system in this case imports things (matter, energy, information) from its environment in amounts that make it possible to more than offset the increase in entropy going on within the system due to irreversible processes (wearing out). The system is able to produce negative entropy from these exchanges with its environment in amounts sufficient to arrest and reverse the process of increasing entropy. It has the capability of becoming *negentropic* (in a state of negative entropy). In other words, taking in more from the environment than it puts out *makes possible* a transfer of negative entropy from the system's environment. This is what is meant by "entropy transfer." As a result, open systems go from more entropic (less improbable) to less entropic (more improbable) states.

A word of caution is needed here, and is indicated by the words "makes possible" above. A system that makes exchanges with its environment, even one that imports more than it exports, does not thereby bring about an entropy transfer and become negentropic. Open systems need not all be negentropic. The net import of materials from the environment is necessary (it provides the means) but it is not sufficient. To become negentropic (and hence survive longer against the relentless process of running down) *the system must have the capability to organize and utilize the inputs from the environment for its own maintenance and self-regulation.* It must, in other words, be able to convert the net transfer of materials into negative entropy (i.e. use them to become more organized), reversing the tendency toward greater disorder. Expressing this somewhat differently, in closed systems the total change in entropy over time is always positive; in open systems it may be positive or negative, but is typically negative. We may thus speak of entropic systems and negentropic systems, the former evolving toward greater uniformity (increasing entropy, decreasing energy levels), the latter toward greater complexity or organization (decreasing entropy, a high energy level).

The sociologist Buckley (1967, 47) has given an example that clearly illustrates the point. When a person A speaks to person B in a language foreign to B, A is emitting only noise so far as B is concerned. There is no transfer or mapping of the structured variety of sounds or vocal energy from A to the repertoire of meaningful sounds in the mind of B. B lacks the ability to organize and utilize what she is hearing to convey meaning. She lacks the ability to convert the vocal energy emanating from A into negative entropy, or information. Even when the net import from the environment takes the form of information (rather than matter or pure energy), the recipient may not be able to harness it to reverse the inherent tendency toward increasing disorder. Open systems typically can, *but may not,* become negentropic.

Every system except the universe (the totality of systems) interacts with some other things (engages in exchanges with its environment), and thus the universe is the only system that is absolutely closed in all respects and at all times. All other systems are only temporarily or relatively closed (or equivalently open). Thus the ordinary machine in our earlier example is closed to entropy transfer, but all systems are gravitationally open. But openness to exchanges with the environment does not always imply openness to entropy transfer.

Why should the closed-open system distinction be important to us in the study of the management of organizations? The most important reason is that organizations, including business enterprises, are *not* to be regarded as closed systems, a legacy that dies hard in some areas of management study. Second, knowing that organizations and those who participate in them are open, *negentropic* systems tells us something about how we should expect them to evolve, and that this evolution will differ markedly from that of closed systems. Open systems, especially people and social organizations, are of primary interest to us, closed systems only to the extent that they generally play the role of tools used by open systems. Third, knowing that organizations are subject to environmental fluctuations, which may be threatening or beneficial, alerts us to the need to learn as much as we can about this changing environment. Unless the organization can change the environment in its favor, it must adapt to it in order to survive. This has important implications for, and affects our thinking about, several of the concepts to be discussed in later chapters, notably the way in which we should define objectives and performance, the importance we should attach to planning, and how we should approach the problem of control. It also places heavy emphasis on organization structure and information as having key roles to play in maintaining the viability of the organization.

Fourth, a body of theory, supported by observations of chemical and biological systems, suggests that the characteristic state of an open system, to which it tends and which it sets as its objective, is a steady state. This is attained when there is a constant ratio between the values of all system components, that is, a firm with constant rates of all inputs yields a constant rate of output, and holds to these rates over some time interval. (Mathematically, a system is in a steady state when the time derivatives of all or some of its state variables are equal to zero, and this condition holds for some interval of time, that is, the stationary values are stable in some sense. See the Mathematical Appendix for a formal treatment of steady state, state variables, state space.) When it is in a steady state the system is often working at its maximum potential. A property of open systems not possessed by closed systems is that if they attain a steady state they can do so in a number of different ways and from different starting points. The technical name for this property is *equifinality.*

As mentioned, these results were obtained by studying mainly biological systems. Some writers have asserted, without proof, that they apply equally to social organizations, a more complex type of system. Intuitively, it seems likely that organizations possess the property of equifinality, but less likely that they should set themselves the objective of attaining a steady state. Without proof, it would be unwise to accept without modification everything that has been found to be true of organismic systems (animals, humans—complexity levels 6 and 7) as being true also of organizations (level 8), because the increase in system complexity from level 7 to level 8 is large. There will be more on this in the next section, and on the appropriateness of steady state as an organizational objective in Chapter 4.

A behavioral classification

Another grouping of concrete systems into classes according to how their behavior is determined has been proposed by Ackoff (1971). Before commencing this discussion, we need to say what is meant by *adaptation* and *learning.* A system is adaptive if, in pursuing one or more of its goals, it takes action to offset any environmental or internal disturbance that would prevent its achieving that goal or goals. A system learns if it becomes better at adapting over time.

Ackoff's classification can be introduced by first making a broad distinction between anticipatory and nonanticipatory systems, that is, between systems whose behavior does or does not depend on the expected outcome of their actions, respectively. *Nonanticipatory* systems are either state-maintaining or goal-seeking. A heating system regulated by a thermostat is an example of a *state-maintaining* system. The behavior of such a system is completely determined by the changes (stimuli) in room temperature to which it reacts. Such a system can adapt, but it cannot act autonomously or learn. Its behavior is purely reactive. An automatic pilot on an airplane is an example of a *goal-seeking* system. In common with a state-maintaining system it acts on outside stimuli and adapts, but it differs from a state-maintaining system in having a choice of behaviors—it responds rather than reacts, by being able to produce a variety of behaviors in answer to a change in its environment *or internally* until it produces that particular state that is its goal. If it is equipped with a memory the system can also learn.

Anticipatory systems have the common property that they are expectation-forming. When undertaking an activity or contemplating some future act, they are capable of expecting reward or punishment and of preparing to obtain the reward or avoid the punishment. Engaging in some act, or an outside stimulus, leads the system to expect a future event (the outcome). The system has foresight, and this presupposes learning— in this case the ability to pair a particular act or stimulus while the system is in a particular state with a possible future event (outcome). So only learned behavior can be anticipatory, and learning means that the system must have memory. Learned behavior, as distinct from purely reactive behavior (state-maintaining system), is also motivated (by the expectation of attaining a particular outcome)—the outcome is expected to bring a reduction in motivation. Purposive and purposeful systems are two kinds of anticipatory system. Both are able to form expectations and prepare for future events.

A *purposive system* has all the properties of a goal-seeking system with memory. Like a goal-seeking system, it does not choose its goals, although in a slightly different sense. In a goal-seeking system the goal is "wired in" (i.e., set by someone outside the system). A purposive system can pursue different goals, all having the common property of the purpose, but the particular goal to be pursued is determined by an initiating event, not by the system. As an example, a pet dog begins to move its tongue and salivate at the mere sight or smell of food, in preparation for possible future digestion.

Thus a purposive system can adapt and learn and form expectations, and chooses means but not ends. A *purposeful system* goes one stage beyond this in being able to choose ends as well as means (ways of achieving them). The distinguishing feature here is that the system displays will—the system "has a mind of its own." Human beings and social organizations are examples of purposeful systems. All purposeful systems are (open and) negentropic, but the converse is not always true— only the higher forms of open systems, human beings and social organizations, levels 7 and 8 in Boulding's hierarchy, are considered to be purposeful. As an example of purposeful behavior, consider a firm that at time $t = 0$ is planning ahead to $t = 5$, and expects demand to cause a substantial increase in its product prices between $t = 1$ and $t = 2$. To do the best it can over the planning period the firm may decide to hold back sales and build inventories in the first period so that it can benefit more from the higher prices expected to prevail in the second period. This discussion is summarized in Table 2.1.

The reader should be made aware of the fact that the explanation of purposeful behavior is still controversial. On one hand, Ackoff and Emery (1972) contend that this kind of behavior is led by the end result (expected outcome) and thus is *future-determined*. This view, shared by some

TABLE 2.1. A classification of systems by type of behavior.

Type of System	Behavior Determined by	The System Can	
		Adapt	Learn
Nonanticipatory			
State-maintaining	Environment and system's previous state	X	
Goal-seeking	Environment and previous state	X	X (if it has memory)
Anticipatory			
Purposive	Environment, previous state, and expectations	X	X
Purposeful	Environment, previous state, expectations, and will (whereby the system sets its own goals)	X	X

Source: Compiled by the author.

philosophers (Braithwaite 1953), sees determination of present events by future events as an indirect process. First, expectations are formed, these lead to intentions, which start a chain of actions whose final stage is attainment of the goal. Bunge (1979a, 302 et seq.) has another explanation. He agrees that purposeful, and indeed any anticipatory, behavior, whether it is conscious (intentional) or unconscious, is not indifferent to the end result, and occurs *as if* it were *somehow* directed by the expected end result. What he takes issue with is the view that present behavior, anticipatory behavior, is *determined* by future events. In Bunge's view, what determines nonintentional anticipatory behavior is not the future, but the immediately previous state, the system's whole history of blind successes and failures, and its environment. And what determines intentional anticipatory behavior (such as purposeful behavior) is not the future, but an idea of the future thought in the present. Bunge would ultimately reduce ideas about the future (expectations) to concrete form (present neurophysiological processes). It is left to the reader to judge whether there is any substance in this argument or it is only a matter of semantics. Anticipating Chapter 12, however, it should be noted that Bunge's view does not preclude the possibility of "teleological" explanation ("teleology" is the study of goal-seeking and purposeful behavior). A teleological explanation is one in which a question about a particular activity is answered by referring to a goal to which the activity is a means.

Integration

Another system property having a bearing on the management of organizations is the system's degree of integration or cohesiveness (Bunge 1979b). Recall from the earlier discussion that a system is modeled in terms of its components, environment, and a structure consisting of the relations between components (inner couplings) and between system components and the environment (outer couplings). A system's degree of integration is then measured by the number and strength of the inner couplings relative to the number and strength of the outer couplings (from the environment to the system). The environment is often hostile, so the outer couplings measure the disintegrating forces acting on the system (although without them the system would be deprived of the means of survival and growth. In place of "disintegrating forces" a more appropriate expression would be "change signals indicating the need to adapt."). For physical, chemical, and perhaps biological systems it is possible to measure the degree of integration. Such a measure cannot, however, be generalized to systems where information links play at least as important an integrating role as energy forces, as is the case with social systems.

A few general remarks can, however, be offered. It would appear reasonable to believe that for any given kind of system in a given environment there is a certain minimum size (measured by number of components) below which the system is not integrated, and a certain maximum size above which the system becomes unstable and breaks down. It can be established empirically that the greater the complexity of a system, the lower, in general, is its degree of integration. There is an inverse relation between degree of complexity and degree of integration. A further inverse relation can be established between the integration of subsystems and that of the system. If the components of a system are themselves systems, the integration of the subsystems competes with that of the system.

All this has some relevance to the conditions necessary for successful adaptation. For a (open, negentropic) system to adapt, not all components should be as tightly coupled as possible. Rather, components whose activities are related should be well linked, while those with unrelated activities should not be. The links between components may be indirect, through the environment, rather than direct and internal. We can say, then, that successful adaptation requires independence (restriction of communication) as well as integration (communication). Care must be taken to avoid too much linkage between components, because this increases the time required for adaptation to occur.

How do human beings and social organizations rate in this respect? Both are highly complex negentropic systems, but they are not tightly knit throughout. While the number of couplings between components or subsystems may be very large, many of these may not be operating all the time. They may be temporary and conditional, one component or subsystem affecting another only under certain conditions, as when a certain variable remains unchanged except when the disturbance to the system exceeds a certain threshold value. Many environmental variables may likewise be constant over appreciable intervals of time. Thus these systems typically comprise a set of subsystems, within which components are tightly coupled but between which couplings are more restricted. If this is an accurate characterization it is fortunate, for otherwise adaptation would take an unconscionably long time.

One particular type of system (a system with feedback or *cybernetic system*) is of special interest in the context of control, and will accordingly be discussed in Chapter 9.

A final point to be stressed is an admonition not to fall into the common trap of assuming that everything found to be true of organismic or biological systems is also necessarily true of organizations. We have already seen that organizations have a greater number of degrees of freedom, and can survive over a wider range of disturbances, than organisms. Moreover, in organisms only the whole has will, and none of the parts has, whereas in organizations the parts as well as the whole have will. As a result, a number of problems are more severe or difficult in organizations, problems such as coordination, control, motivation, even the problem of determining objectives.

3

Types of Interdependence

In the previous chapter we saw that interdependence of parts was the most important distinguishing feature of a system. Interdependence is a common feature of many management problems, particularly in problems of planning, decision, and control. This chapter will therefore be devoted to describing the various kinds of interdependence that may be encountered, and setting out the principles that determine how we should deal with these interdependencies in formulating or thinking about a problem.

First we need to be quite clear about the difference between dependence and interdependence, for in the literature relationships are sometimes described as dependencies which are really interdependencies. Recall the distinction made in the previous chapter between relations and couplings. A relation might take the form $x > y$; a coupling involves one thing acting on another *and modifying the latter's behavior*. This might be represented as $x \rightarrow y$, where the arrow is here to be understood as standing for "influences the behavior of." Dependence, which is discussed more fully in Chapter 12, is a one-way, asymmetrical coupling such as "x acts on y," while interdependence is a two-way, reciprocal coupling: $x \longleftrightarrow y$, x acting on y, and y acting on x. According to philosophers of science, *many, perhaps most, cases we encounter involve interdependence rather than a one-way relation of dependence*; and this is particularly so when dealing with social systems, where dependence is often a one-sided approximation to interdependence (Bunge 1979a, 93, 156–57).

What needs to be done if the problem we are considering involves interdependencies? It depends on the strength of their effects, on how much behavior is modified. If the effects are small, we usually ignore them. In many cases, however, they are not. Unless we are assured that

18

the effects are small, the presence of interdependence means that none of the things that interact can be considered on its own. If entity (say department) A interacts with entity B, and the effects of the interaction are not likely to be insignificant, then A should take these effects on B into account when considering an action, and likewise for B.

How should interdependence be taken into account in formulating a problem? Broadly, in one of two ways: either (i) by considering the actions of A and B together as a set or, what amounts to the same thing, (ii) if A's and B's actions are considered separately, by each unit taking account of the effects of its actions on the other in reaching its decision. With certain exceptions, the first method is used when management is centralized (i.e., when A and B are under the same management), and the second method when management is decentralized (A and B are under different managers). An exception is where a *central* management uses the procedures of the second method, iteratively, to adjust the decision data of decentralized units (e.g., departments or divisions A and B), while maintaining a semblance of decentralization.

It is time now to take a closer look at the effects of two or more units acting on each other. Interdependencies give rise to *external effects,* called *externalities* or *external economies and diseconomies,* effects felt outside the decision-making unit. The importance of externalities is that they generally do not enter into the calculations of the unit whose actions brought them about, unless made to do so by law or some other non-economic force. Thus until fairly recently industrialists, in deciding to build a new plant at a certain location, did not take into account the costs it would impose on the community in the form of removing pollution or of seeing the quality of the environment deteriorate. An external economy (benefit) occurs when one person or organization, in the course of producing some product or rendering some service for which payment is made, incidentally confers benefits on other persons or organizations, not producers of like services, and the nature of these benefits is such that payment cannot be exacted for them.

In each case the amount of the externality, measured at the margin, is a measure of the cost (benefit) imposed (conferred) by one unit on another or others. Reverting to the earlier discussion, interdependencies need to be considered in formulating decision problems when the *marginal* externalities differ significantly from zero.

Significant marginal externalities may be seen at the level of a national economy or of a single decentralized firm. In the economy they are reflected in a divergence between social and private net products after the effects of all market imperfections have been eliminated. That is, the divergence of private and social costs and benefits is a wider problem than that of externalities. The latter are a technical matter, arising only when production functions or consumption functions are interdependent, and are not a monetary matter (e.g., they do not include price effects). When such a divergence occurs, self-interest will not tend to make the gross national product (GNP) a maximum, and certain specific acts of interference by government with normal economic processes may be expected to increase, not diminish, GNP. Similarly, if marginal externalities occur in dealings between the parts of a decentralized firm, taking them into account in decision-making (called "internalizing the externalities") may be expected to increase the achievement of the firm as a whole, which will not be as high as it could be if this is not done.

Interdependencies of various kinds are encountered in management, in managerial economics, finance, management accounting, and management science. These may usefully be classified in several ways. One way would distinguish between those whose effects are confined to a single period and those whose effects occur in different periods (those that involve *choices* over time). The latter are called *intertemporal interdependencies*. These can occur in production and consumption, but will be illustrated here in relation to investment, as the examples given are believed to be more common. There is, first, a sense in which all investment decisions relating to capital goods taken by a firm are interdependent (involve externalities). The benefits produced by assets installed now will be partly determined by the already existing assets of the business and by assets yet to be acquired (as well as by the environment). All of these act in combination. However, the generalized (or serial) intertemporal externalities here are supposed to be taken into account through property rights and capital markets. (The interdependence of choice through time and of production possibilities through time are reflected in marginal rates of time preference and the marginal productivity of capital, each of which in equilibrium equals the rate of interest. See Collard, 1973, for a fuller discussion.)

The timing of investment represents a more specific type of intertemporal interdependence called *dynamic interdependence*. Firms are frequently faced with the problem of whether to build a new plant or to introduce a new product now or later. These are out-of-phase, mutually exclusive alternatives; one cannot be considered without the other.

A more complex type of intertemporal interdependence is encountered in determining the optimal replacement policy for assets that deteriorate rather than fail outright. Most machines are examples of the former, electric light bulbs in city street lighting of the latter. Here the relationship is called *serial interdependence*. This is the only case where it is deemed to be necessary to take into account the generalized intertemporal interdependence referred to earlier between the earnings of assets acquired at different times in formulating the decision problem.

Asset replacement also involves dynamic interdependence (when to replace). The distinguishing feature of serial interdependence is that it arises from interactions between past, present, and future replacement decisions. The replacement of the machine in service by a new one now depends on when the existing machine was acquired *and* on when the present replacement will itself be replaced. The optimal length of service of the asset (the existing asset, its replacement, its replacement's replacement, etc.) is a variable in the decision. Consequently, there is a need to consider chains of replacements; replacements cannot be considered singly.

Another classification of interdependencies would be based on the location of the units or activities that interact. Recalling the previous chapter's discussion of systems, this list would include interdependencies between:

  (i) decision alternatives within a single part of a system
 (ii) different parts of a system
(iii) parts of a system and the system as a whole
 (iv) the system and its environment
  (v) parts of the environment
 (vi) miscellaneous types not falling in any of the above.

Interdependencies between decision alternatives

Division X of Z Corporation has two production possibilities before it in the third quarter of 1987. Each order, if accepted, must be completed within this period, and the division must produce the whole of an order. Due to resource limitations (money and other required resources) the division can undertake one of these orders but not both. The constraint renders the orders totally interdependent: acceptance of one precludes undertaking the other; it is an "either-or" situation. Or: A department of a certain firm must transport materials across a river at a certain location. Suppose the only feasible alternatives are to invest in a bridge or a ferry. The bridge and the ferry are *physically interdependent,* mutually exclusive investment projects. Deciding on one automatically causes the expected returns of the other to drop to zero.

A further example drawn from the field of investment would be whether to build a new apartment block and whether to add a shopping center to it. As they stand these two projects are not interdependent. The apartment block can stand on its own as an independent project; the shopping center is only viable if the apartment block is built. We call the apartment block the *prerequisite project* and the shopping center the *contingent project.* But if we consider the alternatives to be the apartment block with and without the shopping center, they become interdependent, mutually exclusive projects, as in the previous examples.

Interdependencies between parts of a system

One part of a firm may cause external economies or diseconomies to another part or parts. These externalities influence production, and may take two forms. They may result from *cost* (or *technological*) *interdependence,* where the cost (more precisely the marginal cost, and provided the products concerned can be produced in variable proportions) of one product depends on the quantity produced of another. Here the cost functions for different products are interdependent. This may occur within a single part (e.g., department) of a firm or in different parts. If the products are complementary in production (what the economists call *joint supply*), an increase in the output of one will lead to a fall in the cost of the other, an external economy; and if the products are competitive in production, an increase in the output of one will lead to an increase in the cost of the other (external diseconomy). Some means must be found to induce the producer of the product causing external economies to increase its output (by the "right" amount), and to induce a reduction in the output of the product, causing a diseconomy (by the "right" amount), otherwise the profits of the firm will not be maximized. In other words, the nonzero marginal externalities must be "internalized" in some way; to the marginal cost of each of the products as normally determined must be added an adjustment term reflecting the effects of its production on the other product.

A special case of cost interdependence occurs with *joint production,* where two or more products are produced from a common raw material or materials, as with lamb and wool from sheep or gasoline, heating oil, and so on from crude oil. In this case the costs of the joint products are always interdependent to some degree, depending on whether the products are produced in technologically fixed or variable proportions and on whether it is optimal to sell all that is produced of each product in a finished state (as against selling or disposing of some or all units in a partly finished state).

The other kind of externality influencing production is *demand interdependence,* defined as occurring when the quantity demanded of one product is influenced by the demand for another. Here the demand functions for different products are interdependent. As with cost interdependence, this may occur within a single part (e.g., a department) of a firm or between different departments, and it may take two forms. If the products are complementary in demand (e.g., cups and saucers), an increase in demand for one leads to an increase in demand for the other. If, on the other hand, the products are substitutes (e.g., beef and lamb) an increase in demand for one brings a fall in demand for the other. When demand interdependence exists, an additional term must be added to the expression for marginal revenue to reflect the interaction between the products. Cost and demand interdependence are both thought to be fairly common in practice. If both are present, the optimal outputs and maximum firm profit will be obtained by equating adjusted marginal revenues to adjusted marginal costs.

A further kind of interdependence falling under this heading is revealed once we view a firm as a governance structure rather than as a production function. (The neoclassical theory of the firm in micro-economics represents the firm by a production function, relating outputs to inputs per unit of time; the firm's objective is to maximize profits subject to its production function.) Viewing the firm as a governance structure draws our attention to its internal organization. This viewpoint has led most recently to regarding the firm as a set of contracts or agency relationships, under which one party (the principal) employs another party (the agent) to perform certain services on his behalf for a specified remuneration. This involves delegating some decision-making authority to the agent. The agency relationship may be between the owners of the firm (the common stockholders) and top management, or between top management and divisional or departmental managers. The whole subject is discussed at length in Chapter 10. For our present purposes we need only note that there may be *interdependencies in these agency relationships*. An agent's behavior may be influenced by what the principal does—the incentives she offers, the monitoring costs she incurs; and what the principal does in these and other attempts to limit dysfunctional behavior by the agent may be influenced by what the agent does. For example, the agent may incur "bonding costs" to ensure that he does not act contrary to the principal's wishes, or to compensate the principal if he does.

A final illustration of interdependence between parts of a system is provided by regarding customers as a system. The basic theory of consumer behavior in economics sees the consumer as ranking combinations of commodities consistently in order of preference, represented by an ordinal utility function that assigns a higher number to a more desirable combination. Consumers are assumed to seek to maximize their utility subject to a budget constraint expressing their income limitations. Interdependence in consumption is exemplified by *interdependent utility functions*, where the utility (more precisely, the optimal utility) of one consumer depends on the consumption of another. The desire to "keep up with the Joneses" is an example. Consumer Smith's satisfaction (utility level) is lowered (by envy) when consumer Jones buys a Ferrari, and vice versa. As in the production case, the externalities need to be taken into account at the margin if the utility of each consumer is to be a maximum, given the utility levels of all other consumers. If one individual's utility is affected by the welfare of others, and this is not taken into account, it is no longer necessarily true that we can consider one allocation of commodities between consumers better because one individual has more commodities and no others have less (e.g., if the rich become richer and the consumption of the poor is unchanged, the poor may nevertheless feel worse off and envious, and the allocation is not "Pareto-optimal").

Interdependencies between parts of a system and the whole

This kind of interdependency can be seen in the productive operations of a decentralized firm. Suppose a large corporation has several divisions and the objective of the corporation, and of each of the divisions, is to maximize profits. If each division succeeded in maximizing its objective this would not, except by chance, result in overall optimization. There are two main reasons why this will be so. First, under decentralization the separate divisions are encouraged to act as if they were independent units. But there are interactions between them, and the existence of these interactions is why the corporation as a whole has certain emergent properties that none of the divisions has (recall the Chapter 2 discussion of systems). Second, there are often corporation-wide constraints which, like their interactions with other divisions, are not taken into account by the divisions in their decision-making. Only if both are taken into account will divisional optimization be consistent with overall optimization. Part–whole interdependencies of this kind can of course be taken into account by the central management doing all the decision-making, but this would be a retreat from decentralization which, presumably, was only instituted because the corporation believed it to offer advantages over a highly centralized governance structure. In many, probably most, cases the interdependencies can be recognized and dealt with by decomposition procedures while preserving the semblance of decentralization (Baumol and Fabian 1964).

Interdependencies between a system and its environment

If readers will recall the discussion of Chapter 2 on how to define or specify a system correctly (where to draw the boundary), they will understand that strictly speaking, there can be no significant interdependencies of this kind between a system and its environment. If the system is correctly defined, the environment acts on the system unilaterally, while the system includes all significant interactions between the two. The interacting parts of the environment are treated as endogenous. At the same time it should be recognized that the boundaries, particularly of social systems such as firms, are elastic rather than rigid, due to the interactive elements of the environment changing their identity or force. Moreover, which parts of the environment are interactive and are to be regarded as part of the system will vary, depending on the problem being considered and over time. The boundary of an open system is only uniquely determined for a given problem at a given time.

So if we are speaking in strictly systems terms, the heading of this section is a misnomer; interdependencies between a system and its environment are really between parts of a system. The type of interdependence met with in the theory of oligopoly and the theory of games are examples of the latter.

Interdependencies between parts of the environment

Emery and Trist (1965) have drawn attention to interdependencies occurring within the environment. Organizational environments, they point out, differ in their "causal texture," processes through which parts of the environment become related to each other. These processes are among the determining conditions of exchanges between an organization and its environment, and some knowledge of these interdependencies is necessary in order to gain a comprehensive understanding of the behavior of an organization. These interactions between elements of the environment that influence the actions of an organization are not confined to the economic (the environment also includes a political system and a cultural system), and between all of these elements there are interactions that have a bearing, sometimes very strong, on the life of an organization in a particular society. Consider only the effects on a business system of some of the more pronounced interactions between political and economic systems at the international level in recent times.

Other types of interdependence

A type of interdependence that may occur in the first three and last categories is *statistical interdependence,* usually referred to as statistical dependence. This arises as a result of uncertainty. Two events are said to

TABLE 3.1. Methods of treating various types of interdependence.

Method of treatment	Type of interdependence
Consider all the interconnected elements together as a set (if the elements concerned are under different managers, this would mean a centralized solution)	Cost and demand interdependence, if the solution decided on is joint optimization, or merger, or is otherwise decided centrally (e.g., by decomposition procedure and iterative adjustments, or cost interdependence in joint production) Physical interdependence, in production or investment Dynamic interdependence, in production, consumption, or investment Serial interdependence (in optimal asset replacement)
Consider elements individually, make adjustments for externalities	Cost and demand interdependence, if the parties concerned can act independently of central management (decentralization) Consumption interdependencies (interdependent utility functions) Game-theoretic approaches to decision-making Principal–agent interdependencies Oligopoly (determination of output and selling expenditure)
Either method, unconditionally	Part–whole interdependencies between divisions and a firm as a whole

Source: Compiled by the author.

be statistically dependent if the probability of one's occurrence is not independent of the probability of the other's occurrence. Here it is the probabilities that are interdependent; as shown in the Mathematical Appendix, the (marginal) probability of event A occurring, $P(A)$, depends on the (marginal) probability of event B, the conditional probability of A given B, and the conditional probability of B given A. The (marginal) probability of event B is similarly described. A sufficient, although not necessary, condition for two events to be statistically interdependent is that they are mutually exclusive. An example of statistical interdependence related to the expected cash flows generated by an investment project appears in Amey and Egginton (1979, 359–61).

Method of treatment

Two methods were mentioned earlier for dealing with interdependencies, that is, for taking into account significant marginal externalities. These were either to consider all the interconnected elements together as a set or, if each element was considered separately, to make adjustments for the effects of one's actions on the other elements. Which method should be used in a particular case? The circumstances will usually suggest one method rather than the other. In a few cases, however, there may be a choice of methods. Table 3.1 relates methods of treatment to types of interdependence.

The foregoing should be sufficient to convince the reader that interdependence is a widespread phenomenon in management problems. It occurs in numerous forms, some of the most common of which have been noted. In many cases the interdependence is erroneously called dependence. The lesson to be drawn from this discussion is to watch out for interdependencies and to include their effects (externalities) in decision data whenever they are significant—at the margin, if the decision problem concerns a marginal adjustment (such as price-output decisions under profit maximization), in total, if the problem involves a nonmarginal adjustment.

4

Objectives

At first sight the reader might wonder why this chapter is necessary. What is there to say, of a conceptual nature, about organizational objectives? Does not a glance at the microeconomics and management literature show that the business firm is *presumed* to seek to maximize utility under conditions of certainty, expected utility under conditions of uncertainty? (What firms actually do, of course, might be something entirely different.) While these objectives may be given a bewildering variety of *interpretations* by different firms or writers—profit maximization, revenue maximization, management's utility maximization, maximization of the rate of return on capital, and so on under conditions of certainty, maximization of expected current profit or expected wealth maximization (i.e., maximization of the expected discounted value of future dividends or earnings) and so on under conditions of uncertainty— is there anything deeper involved? The answer is yes. In fact, the very notion of an organizational objective opens up some of the most difficult conceptual problems discussed in this book. Our limited purpose in this chapter will be to make the reader aware of their existence and nature.

To the fundamental question Do organizations have goals? the usual answer is that they do not, that only individuals have goals. It will be helpful to change the question to Who sets the goals in organizations? for in this way goals and power and influence relationships are brought together.

The most commonly held view (Cyert and March 1963) is that organizational goals are determined as a result of a bargaining process between members of a dominant coalition of participants in the organization. It should be emphasized, however, that not all share the "rational system" view of organizations with which this explanation is usually associated. The "natural system" school argues that organizations are not to be viewed primarily as means for achieving specified ends (goals) but as ends in themselves. They are, fundamentally, social groups attempting, like all other social groups, to adapt and survive (Gouldner 1959, 405), and if survival of the organization is in jeopardy, the pursuit of specific goals will always be sacrificed to it.

The third main school of thought about organizations, the "open system" view, contains elements of the previous two: organizations seek to achieve their own specified goals, and to maintain themselves as social units. The distinguishing characteristics of this view are that it sees organizations as highly interdependent with their environments and as evolving toward greater complexity. In addition, "information acquisition and processing is viewed as an especially critical activity since an organization's long-term well-being is dependent on its ability to detect and respond to subtle changes in its task environment" (Scott 1981, 319). According to this view, as we saw in Chapter 2, an organization is seen as seeking to achieve its own goals, subject to meeting the demands of its participants and of its environment at least minimally. In the case of market-based organizations such as businesses, the market in principle provides a mechanism for rewarding firms that best serve the interests of their external constituencies. But most markets are imperfectly competitive in varying degrees, and hence markets may be an ineffective sanction, and government regulation may not take their place.

Coleman (1974, 39) makes an interesting observation from an open system viewpoint. In a society composed of individuals and organizations, one person may lose without a compensating gain by another person. People as individuals can lose out to corporate actors, and the "society functions less than fully in the interests of the persons who make it up." A similar view has been expressed by Ashby (1968, 116). We can recognize the truth of this proposition with regard to business organizations—they are capable of imparting a bias in the direction that social and economic activities take, and of not being responsive to the needs of their various publics. In other words, the normative ideal of organizations as open systems may seldom be realized in practice.

Each one of these views draws attention to different relevant features of organizations. Some kind of synthesis of all three appears most appropriate, an eclectic view.

Another point of disagreement concerns the timing of goal-setting. The orthodox view (economics, decision theory) is that action alternatives are ranked according to a predetermined objective, and the most preferred alternative chosen. March, however, now argues (1976, 72) that action choices precede goals, that the former are as much a process for discovering goals as for acting on them. This view of organizational decision-making, known as the "garbage can" model, sees organizations as organized anarchies, and could be regarded as pushing the notion of a loosely coupled system to the limit.

For the remainder of this chapter, without disavowing the relevance and importance of the additional features included in the "natural system" and "open system" descriptions of what organizations seek to do, the discussion will be confined to the organization's own objective and some of the conceptual problems that arise over it.

An organization is made up of a number of individuals or other organizations (we may call them participants or stakeholders, and defer until later a more exact description). The organization's plans and decisions are usually made under conditions of uncertainty. It has before it at any time a number of alternative courses of action (including the alternative of doing nothing), with the consequence of its action depending on the particular alternative chosen and the state of the world. "State of the world" gathers together all the influences not under the organization's control (exogenous factors, or the environment) that may have a significant effect on the consequences of the actions. The state of the world is not known with certainty. The organizational objective calls for a ranking of the uncertain consequences of choosing the various alternatives, and their associated probability distributions, according to their order of preference, from the most preferred down to the least preferred, it being assumed that if the organization is "rational" it will choose the most preferred.

The first problem that arises is that under conditions of uncertainty (or, more strictly, of risk—we will assume that each outcome occurs with known probability) the expected monetary worth of the consequences (outcomes) is not always a reliable measure of the expected intrinsic or "true" worth of an outcome. This was demonstrated by Daniel Bernouilli in the famous St. Petersburg paradox. Indeed, an organization's objective may include certain things that are not reducible to money (e.g., employee morale, customer satisfaction, and the organization's reputation in the minds of investors and the public at large). As a result, we have to adopt another measure. It has been suggested that under uncertainty, the appropriate measure of the worth of an outcome should be the expected intrinsic worth of the monetary outcome. This intrinsic worth is called *utility*, a psychic magnitude (subjective value) in the mind of one individual. Outcomes can then be ranked in order of their expected utility, where utility is some function of monetary outcome. But see the Mathematical Appendix for a further difficulty: if the decision-maker is not risk-neutral, he may not always act in accordance with the expected utility measure. It is also questionable why actions should be based on the *expected value* of utility (Luce and Raiffa 1957, 19–21).

A second problem is how to measure utility numerically for the utility index. This would measure the strength of preferences. This can be done in a great many ways; consequently, the utility index is not unique. For example, if A, B, and C are three alternatives, A is preferred to B and B to C, *any* numbers such that $a > b > c$ would correctly represent this preference ordering. We cannot use such numbers as a cardinal measure of utility, representing the relative strengths of utility. The only meaningful property of such numbers is that they indicate an order. It is meaningless to add them together or to compare magnitudes of differences between them. This is because on the utility scale neither the zero nor the basic unit of utility (called a *utile*) is determined. (We could say that the utility indexes of individuals are unique *except* for origin and units of measure.) Hence, a cardinal preference pattern tells us nothing that an ordinal preference pattern does not already tell us.

The third and most difficult problem is how to combine the utilities of individuals to yield an aggregate ("social," in our context corporate or firm) utility function. More precisely, we need a means of making the utilities of different individuals dimensionally compatible and then a procedure for aggregating them. Both of these steps require a value judgment (Arrow 1951, 11). In this classic work, Arrow addressed the problem of characterizing the logic of collective choice based on the ordinal preferences of individuals. The problem is essentially to define "fair" (reasonable, representative, ethically acceptable) methods for combining individual preferences to yield a single group preference pattern for a business or economy composed of these individual participants—in short, to construct a social welfare (or utility) function. The transition from individual preferences to social preferences is, of course, met in practice by a number of different methods, of which voting, custom, authority, and market mechanisms are some. Not all of these are always considered fair and representative, however.

Arrow laid down five conditions to be met by an amalgamation of conflicting individual preference patterns to form an aggregate or compromise preference pattern for a collectivity, these conditions being chosen because they have a history of being regarded as "socially desirable," minimally acceptable, or reasonable. To explicate the conditions we first stipulate three or more alternatives, two or more individuals, and assume that each individual makes a weak preference ordering of the alternatives, and that preferences are transitive. By "weak preference ordering" we mean that alternative x is preferred or indifferent to alternative y, which we will write as xRy. By transitivity of preferences is meant that for three alternatives x, y, and z, if xRy and yRz, then xRz. That is, for all orderings of the alternatives considered, pairwise comparison will show one to be preferred to the other, or indifference. The relation R here denotes the aggregate social preference relation, which we will assume is derivable by some rule from the individual preference relations R_1, R_2, ...

The five conditions may now be stated.

1. As with individual preferences, social preferences must be completely ordered by the relation R (meaning "at least as well liked socially as"), and therefore must satisfy the conditions of completeness, reflexivity, and transitivity. Completeness means that for *any* pair of alternatives x and y, either xRy or yRx or both, that is, completeness applies when $x = y$ as well as when $x \neq y$. By the relation R being reflexive is meant that xRx, whatever x may be; and transitivity has already been defined (complete ordering).

2. If x is socially preferred to y for a given set of individual preferences, and individual preference orderings change so that some individuals raise x to a higher rank and none lower it, x must remain socially preferred to y. (social preferences responsive to individual preferences)

3. Social preferences must not be imposed independently of individual preferences. (non-imposition)

4. Social preferences must not totally reflect the preferences of any single individual. (non-dictatorship)

5. The most preferred alternative in a set of alternatives must be independent of the existence of other alternatives; for example, if the social preference is x to y to z, and alternative z is withdrawn, it must not be true that y is preferred to x. (independence of irrelevant alternatives)

Arrow (1951) has shown in his Impossibility Theorem that collectively these conditions are inconsistent—no group preference function exists which fulfills all these conditions. For example, suppose majority rule is the means of arriving at the group preference function. This satisfies the above five conditions if there are only two alternatives, but violates condition 1 if there are more than two (it leads to intransitivities). Consider three individuals (1, 2, and 3) and three alternatives (x, y, and z). Individual 1 ranks them x, y, and z, individual 2 ranks them y, z, x, and individual 3, z, x, y. A majority prefers x to y, y to z, and z to x; we have no clear transitive ranking.

How are we to get around this difficulty? Briefly, the answer is either by making the Arrow conditions less restrictive (e.g., for three or more alternatives majority rule meets all but one of the conditions); or dropping condition 3 (non-imposition) or 4 (non-dictatorship); or by putting up with a scheme that is only mildly socially undesirable (e.g., a scheme resulting in some intransitivities that are, however, regarded as tolerable). Since decisions *are* taken by governments and other public bodies affecting a whole society or community, and by business firms whose members or stakeholders may be presumed to have conflicting individual preferences, we may expect to see many examples of objectives that fail in varying degrees to reflect the preferences of constituents in a socially acceptable manner, as defined by Arrow's five conditions.

Consider, for example, the theory of the firm in economics. It was once customary (classical theory) to think of the firm as being run for the benefit of the entrepreneur, who provided or borrowed the capital and was top manager. The objective of the firm was then considered to be the objective of the entrepreneur. This violates condition 3 (non-imposition). A more recent example of the same kind is Williamson's managerial discretion theory of the firm, in which top management is seen as the dominant stakeholder in most circumstances, and the firm is run by top managers for top managers, instead of as stewards for the owners (Williamson 1963). Williamson sees the objective as maximization of (top) management's utility function. Besides violating condition 3, there is still the problem of combining the individual preferences of the top managers (assuming they are not all of one mind on every issue).

An example of living with unresolved conflict of goals is presented by Cyert and March (1963), who view a business as a coalition of stakeholders comprising managers, workers, stockholders, customers, suppliers, government, and so on. Members of the coalition are presumed to have substantially different preference orderings (individual goals). Any attempt to define a joint preference ordering for the coalition is misdirected, they claim, and contrary to what we find in practice, where there is agreement on objectives only if the latter are highly ambiguous, not constituting a clear joint preference ordering. Empirical studies suggest that firms appear to pursue different goals simultaneously, and the existence of unresolved conflict over goals is a conspicuous feature of business organizations, they contend. These different goals pursued by a firm at the same time can be viewed as a set of more or less independent constraints imposed through a process of bargaining among potential coalition members. In organization theory several studies describe goals as the result of a continuous bargaining-learning process that will not necessarily produce consistent goals. Active members of the organizational coalition bargain over their shares of the spoils, which take the form not only of money payments but of power, authority, status, and so on. Goals may change over time in response to environmental changes, but on the other hand they exhibit greater stability than might be expected from a pure bargaining situation, due to the existence of organizational slack and inertia. Most of these goals (constraints) are of a "satisficing" rather than an optimizing nature—they specify acceptable or satisfactory goals (shares).

According to Cyert and March, organizational goals arise in the form just described because the firm is a coalition of participants with conflicting demands, changing foci of attention, and limited ability to attend to all organizational problems simultaneously. Under many conditions the firm is able to operate (make decisions) with inconsistent goals by attending to different goals at different levels of the organization and at different times (i.e., sequentially), and by making adjustments in organizational slack. They cite an example of a department in a retail department store in which price and output decisions are independent, and taken at different times with different objectives (Cyert and March 1963, ch. 7). It will be noted that, in discussing this latest viewpoint, we have gone from a single organizational goal to multiple goals; more on this later.

Reverting to the earlier discussion, Arrow (1951) argued against trying to construct a cardinal (measurable) utility measure, a measure of the strength of preference, in combining individual preferences into group preferences, on the grounds that (1) Such a measure lacks uniqueness. If a course of action can be explained by a given utility function, it can be equally well explained by any other utility function that is a strictly increasing function of the first. (2) If measurable utility is not unique, one cannot make interpersonal comparisons of utility (it requires a value judgment to make the utilities of different individuals dimensionally compatible). (3) The proponents of measurable utility have not advanced a single proposition concerning economic behavior that could be explained in terms of cardinal utility but not in terms of ordinal utility.

We should, however, mention one development in utility theory that reopened the controversy over cardinal versus ordinal measures, although as we shall see, "utility" here has a different meaning than it had in classical utility theory. This is von Neumann and Morgenstern's *theory of games* (von Neumann and Morgenstern 1944). We are concerned here only with the patterns of preference of each individual, ignoring the game aspects of the problem, the fact that the individuals are in conflict with one another. It is assumed that the possible outcomes of a given situation are well specified and that each individual has a consistent pattern of preferences among them. But game theory departs from the mainstream of utility analysis in that the objects of choice over which preferences are held are not certain, basic alternatives as before, but every possible pair of gambles over these basic alternatives. (A "gamble" is defined as any situation in which two outcomes are possible and in which the probabilities of the two outcomes are known.) For example, instead of choosing between three basic alternatives x, y, and z, each with a certain outcome, preferences must now be expressed between the lotteries (x, y), (y, z), and (x, z), each with uncertain outcomes. Hence the ordering of preferences now involves risk as well as the basic alternatives. Decision-makers must be able to evaluate the desirabilities of probability distributions of outcomes, just as they evaluate the desirabilities of definite payoffs.

It is then shown that if each individual's preferences among alternative probability distributions of outcomes are consistent as defined below, they can be represented numerically by a utility function that is unique up to a positive linear transformation. This measurable utility has the important property that an individual will prefer one lottery to another only if the expected utility of the former is greater than that of the latter. The preferred outcomes are then those that maximize expected utility. For this to happen each individual must conform to the five consistency conditions (known as the von Neumann-Morgenstern axioms of rational choice under uncertainty) shown in the Appendix in expressing his or her preferences.

Several points should be noted about the use of measurable utilities, in the von Neumann-Morgenstern sense, to represent preferences. First, these measures have no significance as measures of what is ethically or socially desirable. Second, this utility index has some, but not all, of the properties of a cardinal measure. Utility differences and expected utility may be calculated, but interpersonal utility comparisons are still impossible. Third, the von Neumann-Morgenstern axiom system assumes that each of a set of possible outcomes of an action occurs with a definite probability which the individual knows, and that these probabilities are *objective* probabilities. This may be unreasonable. The probabilities assigned may be subjective in the sense that they vary from individual to individual. In that case, little is known about how such probabilities combine with one another, how they relate to objective probabilities, and how they react with utility values (Luce and Raiffa 1957, ch. 2).

The reader who is interested in exploring the work of Arrow and von Neumann-Morgenstern further could consult Henderson and Quandt (1980, chs. 2 and 11).

Having made the reader aware of the conceptual problems that arise in stating a firm's objective when, as typically, more than one person is involved, it should be added that in practice firms express their preferences over a set of basic alternatives in terms of monetary measures (profit, cash flow, cost), risk considerations generally being taken into account indirectly (e.g. by lowering revenue and/or raising cost estimates, by allowances for contingencies, by shortening the estimated life of a project, and so on). The process by which individual preferences are translated into group preferences probably varies from firm to firm, even from one class of decisions to another, and over time. It is likely that it involves a classification of organization stakeholders into active and passive groups and, within the former, the question of dominance (see Chapter 5). Thus, in addition to failing to result in consistent preferences in Arrow's sense, it usually involves modification and simplification of the problem, as discussed in the next chapter, in the interests of making it operational.

We go on now to discuss some other issues concerning organizational objectives. The first of these has to do with the fact that an organization, in particular a business firm, is an open system as described in Chapter 2. As such, it is part of a larger system or systems, and contains a number of subsystems. The lesson drawn in Chapter 2 was that we cannot consider the firm's own objective in isolation: to remain viable the firm must also consider its orientation toward its suprasystem(s) and its subsystems. Specifically, in attempting to achieve its own objective the firm should also consider the minimal demands, at the least, of its environment and of its participants. Regarding the first, economic theory and systems theory have very different views as to what the firm's environment consists of. Economic theory sees it solely as economic—essentially other firms or markets. Systems theory would see it as economic, social, political, and cultural. In practice, firms seem to be closer to the latter view. Statements by firms about their objectives, at least, reveal a mixture of economic, political, social, and ethical considerations. The systems view could be operationalized by subjecting the firm's own objective to the constraints of at least minimally meeting the demands on it by its participants and the environment. Another problem arising from viewing the firm as a system (i.e., of interrelated parts) will be discussed in a moment.

A further set of problems concerns how firms' objectives, in general, should be characterized—as optimizing, satisficing, or adapting. Do firms characteristically choose the best possible alternative (e.g., the one that maximizes profit, expected profit, or the expected present value of discounted cash flows), or are they content to settle for any outcome that they regard as satisfactory, without continuing the search until they find the optimal outcome? Adapting involves considerations distinct from optimization; it introduces behavior over time and the need for learning.

Simon (1957b, chs. 14 and 15) has argued that the "global rationality" attributed to managers in economics is completely divorced from reality, and should be replaced by the principle of "bounded rationality." The notion of "economic man" assumes that he is not only rational but also an optimizer, possessing complete information on all relevant aspects of the decision environment, a stable set of preferences, and the ability to analyze alternative courses of action. One study of the objectives of 25 U.S. corporations as described in public statements by their top managements suggests that reality is very different from the notion of economic man (Shubik 1961). Instead of optimizing behavior, Simon believes rational action should be defined in terms of behavior compatible with the computational capacity available to the decision-makers in their organizations, and with their skills in problem formulation. Rational choice then means satisficing rather than optimizing, which dominates the economics literature. In terms of the third characterization of objectives, Simon believes that organizations adapt well enough to satisfice, but that their adaptability falls far short of the ideal of optimizing. Satisficing has been characterized by Simon (1957a) as "intended rationality."

Adapting focuses on the dynamics of behavior under uncertainty. As an open system, we know that in order to survive a firm must constantly adapt to an ever-changing environment as well as to internal organizational disturbances. Economists sometimes subsume adaptation into a more general form of optimizing model that has adaptation and learning built into it. Adaptation becomes movement toward an optimum; the suggestion is that, although decision-makers may not be rational all the time, in the sense of optimizing some objective, over time they will learn the optimal rule. Based on a number of experimental studies, however, psychologists have concluded that (individual) learning is not in general efficient, that is, behavior does not converge to the optimum, or even approach an optimum, after a long series of trials (Estes 1954; Arrow 1958). They would therefore tend to argue that learning cannot provide the explanation for rationality understood as optimizing behavior.

Two remarks about this conclusion are: first, that for it to have any relevance to the present discussion there would need to be a presumption that what is true for individuals (the subjects of these experiments) is also true for entities composed of a number of individuals; and second, it is difficult to see how the conclusion would be affected once allowance is made for the fact that neither individual nor organizational learning depends only on inferences from one's own experience, but relies to a significant extent on observation of others' experiences. In other words, individuals and organizations learn from their environments.

Another comment relates to the horizon over which the organizational objective is defined. An objective is meaningless unless we attach a time duration to it. Should the outcomes of alternatives all relate to the short run (e.g., one year) or to a longer period (a number of years) and, if the latter, to how long a period? In practice a firm's plans and decisions often have different durations for different activities, including a duration of zero for some plans. Forrester (1975, ch. 14) has warned that the dynamic behavior of social systems, including private and public business enterprises, is often counterintuitive. The mental models we have of these complex systems are often fuzzy; the assumptions we make about their structure and the future consequences of actions often involve internal inconsistencies. He gives some striking examples from his own research of how actions taken to alleviate problems actually make them worse. In particular, he found there was often a fundamental conflict between the short-run and long-run consequences of actions. Actions that led to an improvement in the short run did the reverse in the long run. The upshot of this finding would seem to be that planning is an important activity for management to undertake, and that current decisions should be taken within the framework of (continually revised) plans with a long horizon, at least until we gain more understanding of the complex nature of social systems. A possible explanation of Forrester's findings is offered in Chapter 9.

In the foregoing discussion we began by referring to "organizational objective," but as we went along it became "objectives" from time to time. Evidence suggests that the latter is likely to be the rule rather than the exception. For example, in the previously quoted study by Shubik (1961), the goals most frequently cited by firms related to personnel, social responsibility, consumer needs, stockholder interests, profit, and quality of product, in that order; and most of the firms mentioned several of these. The problem of business objectives then typically has the following characteristics: (1) Firms have multiple conflicting goals (attempting, for example, simultaneously to maximize profits and market share). (2) Different priorities are placed on these goals (the goals are incompatible with one another and so they cannot all be fully achieved simultaneously). (3) The goals are incommensurable (some are economic, some noneconomic); indeed some may be quite abstract (e.g., social responsibility, consumer satisfaction and protection), and assigning these a numerical value might distort the problem.

Given these characteristics, how can the objectives be stated in a way that provides a framework for rational decision-making? Two methods have been proposed, both of which generally assume that all the mathematical relationships involved are linear (i.e., all relationships can be expressed as a sum of terms, each involving only one variable to the first power). Under the first method, called *multiple objective* (or criteria) *linear programming,* a composite objective function is formed by giving each objective a numerical weight and summing the weighted objectives. Starting from an arbitrary set, the weights are obtained from the responses of the decision-maker to a series of questions of the form, "Are you willing to reduce objective i by so much in return for an increase in objective j of so much and in objective k of so much?" The search for a solution is restricted to consideration of efficient, or undominated, solutions, an efficient solution being one that satisfies the constraints and for which an increase in the value of one objective can be achieved only at the expense of a decrease in the value of at least one other objective. Over this set of efficient solutions the weights are changed in response to tradeoff questions put to the decision-maker until she is satisfied with a solution. Hence the solution could be described as "joint satisficing." On this method see Cochrane and Zeleny (1973). Notice that we abstracted from the problem of multiple decision-makers.

The second method proposed is called *goal programming*. Unlike multiple objective programming, it is an ordinal solution method. Instead of being the sum of weighted objectives, the objective function here consists of the sum of the weighted deviations (+ and −) from individual goals. These deviations are analogous to the slack variables of ordinary linear programming. The weighted deviations are to be minimized, subject to given constraints. The weights represent the priorities the management attaches to the individual goals. In goal programming these priorities need only be stated ordinally (i.e., ranked in order of importance). The solution offers the nearest approach to attaining the goals in the prescribed order (Lee 1972–73; Ijiri 1965a, ch. 3).

We have seen that conflict over corporate objectives is a common feature of many firms, and how an attempt may be made to resolve the conflicts, as above, or to leave them unresolved and deal with them sequentially through different classes of decisions, which must therefore result in some inconsistency in behavior. Further instances of goal conflict arise within a firm between subunit and corporate levels, and between individual employees and subunits. The first is the well-known decentralization problem already mentioned in Chapter 3. Firms commonly find it advantageous to delegate decision-making, at least in part, to divisions and departments rather than do it all centrally. These subunits are encouraged to act independently as autonomous units, as though they neither affect, nor are affected by, the decisions of other subunits or of top management. Obviously, since the firm is a system, all three interact, and unless this is taken into account the pursuit of subunit objectives will not be consistent with achievement of corporate objectives. There are various ways in which subunit objectives may be modified to ensure congruence with overall corporate objectives; they vary only in how much seeming autonomy is left to the subunits. Essentially, the subunit objectives must be made to reflect the effects of interactions with other subunits and be made subject to company-wide constraints as well as subunit constraints.

Assuming that this problem is resolved, the other problem is that the people who work in a firm may have personal goals that do not coincide with the goals of the subunit and the firm as a whole. Accordingly, they must be encouraged in some way to internalize the organizational goals. The question of motivation and incentives is the subject of Chapter 10.

5

Choice Under Risk and Uncertainty

In talking about objectives in the previous chapter it was impossible not to refer to decision-making under uncertainty. There is thus some overlap between this chapter and the last. That there is still much to discuss on the subject of choice under uncertainty will soon become apparent, however. In what follows, attention will be confined to individual choice; no further mention will be made of group decision-making.

We will also be concerned with situations in which uncertainty is taken into account explicitly in formulating decision problems; the formal statement of the problem will involve probabilities in some sense. Now it is trite to say that virtually all decisions faced by business firms involve some element of uncertainty. Many, probably most, manufacturers produce in anticipation of demand, and when the farmer plants his crop he cannot know with certainty what the weather will be over the growing period. It does not follow, however, that these decision-makers will pose their decision problem in a probabilistic framework. Decisions that involve uncertainty can still be formulated deterministically (i.e., without introducing probabilities explicitly), sometimes by incorporating in the data arbitrary aggregate allowances for contingencies. When the U.S. government began building Polaris ballistic missiles in the late 1950s, for example, a project fraught with uncertainty because it was the first of its kind undertaken, it used a network technique called PERT (Program Evaluation and Review Technique) to exercise control over the time spent on the project. While this technique was apparently reasonably successful in its purpose (it was credited with saving two years in developing the missile), the actual time network it results in is deterministic, not probabilistic, although a particular class of probability distribution (a beta distribution) is assumed in arriving at the expected times to complete the tasks making up the project. As with the lump-sum allowances for contingencies, the element of uncertainty is recognized, but it is not introduced explicitly into the essential framework of the problem.

There are further ways of handling uncertainty without dealing with it explicitly. One would be to just go ahead and take decisions, and rely on rapid feedback of their outcomes to find out whether they were good or bad. This approach might not be unreasonable in the case of repetitive decisions, such as weekly orders for supplies, but would not be recommended for "one-off," nonrepetitive decisions involving large sums of money. Another obvious response to uncertainty is to eliminate it or lessen its impact before making the decision, rather than accept it and go to great pains to model it explicitly. Common observation reveals that many business practices are aimed at uncertainty avoidance. Some examples are long-term contracting, advertising and research and development expenditures, forecasting and planning, mergers with other firms, cartels and other associations of firms, joint ventures, interlocking directorates, and diversification of activities. With these few remarks, the remainder of this chapter will be devoted to decision problems in which the fact that exogenous influences ("state of nature") and hence outcomes are not known with certainty is given explicit formulation.

Before embarking on this it will be useful to have in mind some structuring of the approaches (decision models) to be discussed. Figure 5.1 presents such a framework.

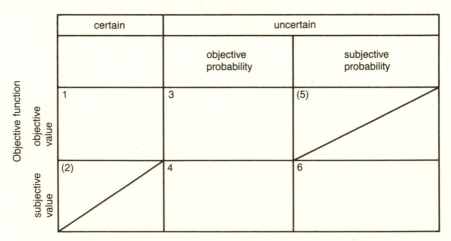

FIGURE 5.1. A classification of decision models.

The intention here is to show that we shall be concerned not only with cases where the preference ordering is over consequences expressed by objective values (such as dollar profits), on one hand, or by subjective values (utilities) on the other, but also to give notice that "probability" is not an unambiguous term. It may be understood as objective (usually as a limit of a long-run frequency, the ratio of favorable outcomes to total possible outcomes) or subjective (personalistic, judgmental, "probability" here understood as the degree of belief or degree of confidence an individual attaches to an uncertain event). The numbers in the cells indicate the order of discussion. After explaining the principal features of the approaches belonging in each cell of the table for a *single decision* (this will take up most of the chapter), the case of sequential decision-making will be discussed, the situation where the same kind of decision (e.g., ordering of materials) is repeated at intervals, and where uncertainty can be reduced by learning from experience or by otherwise obtaining additional information. The chapter ends with some brief remarks about two other interesting ideas related to choice under uncertainty: the concept of "dominance" stemming from the work of Wald (1950), and the concept of "possibility" and possibilistic decision-making (Zadeh 1977) related to an ordinal theory of uncertainty, in contrast to probability, which involves a cardinal theory.

In addition to the above classification of approaches to decision-making, we also need to introduce at the outset the basic elements of a decision problem. Unless a person makes decisions intuitively and is not overly worried about their consistency, we need to have information on the following:

(i) A choice must be made among a set of *acts* (decisions), $\{a_i, i = 1, \ldots, m\}$, which are believed to be worth considering and feasible, given various constraints on action.

(ii) The relative desirability (outcome, *consequence*) of each of these acts depends on which "state of nature" (event) prevails. The set $\{s_j, 1, \ldots, n\}$ of states covers all possibilities. These events, one of which will certainly occur, are mutually exclusive and exhaustive. Which one will occur cannot be predicted with certainty.

(iii) This information can be represented in a *payoff table* with acts shown by rows, states by columns, and consequences (c) in the cells (Fig. 5.2).

It will also be *assumed* that:

(iv) The decision-maker's *preferences* among the consequences (c_{ij}), and among hypothetical lotteries with these consequences as prizes, show

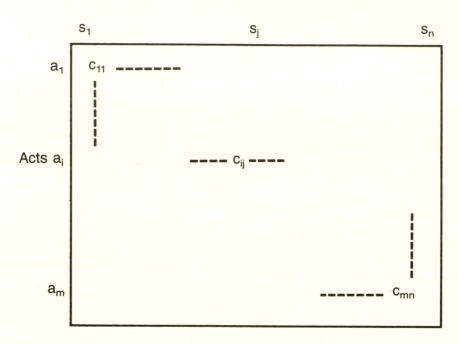

FIGURE 5.2. Payoff table.

consistency (i.e., obey certain reasonable conditions for rational choice), enabling them to be represented by a *utility function*. In other words, we assume that a utility value u_{ij} can be associated with every consequence (or act–state pair) c_{ij}.

(v) The decision-maker can express his *judgment* as to the chance of each of the states s_j occurring.

(vi) The utility function mentioned in (iv) reflects an indecomposable mixture of the decision-maker's attitudes toward (a) monetary payoff and (b) risk in any given decision situation. It is assumed, that is, that this function reflects the decision-maker's initial financial position and his attitude toward risk-taking.

The reader may have noticed that (v) is stated in the broadest possible way; there is no mention of the word "probability." This was done advisedly, so as not to preclude different definitions of "probability" being used, or even whether it is meaningful to talk about probabilities in all of the situations now to be discussed.

We will consider three situations: decision-making under certainty (included for purposes of comparison), under risk, and under uncertainty. The differences between risk and uncertainty will be explained as we proceed.

Decision-making under certainty (cell 1)

In this case the decision-maker knows with certainty that one particular state (say s_k) will occur: $p_k = 1$, where p denotes objective probability (and $\Sigma p_j = 1$). This narrows the search down to one column of the payoff table; each act leads to a single definite outcome in column k. The problem is then to find which act (i.e., which of the m rows) yields the greatest monetary payoff. If it is row i, the desired outcome is c_{ik}. All the entries in the table except those in common k are zeros. The neoclassical theory of the firm in economics and a typical linear programming problem afford examples of decision-making under certainty—problems where uncertainty, although known to be present, is not taken into account explicitly.

Under certainty there is no reason to introduce utility into the decision problem—the intrinsic worth of an act is accurately indicated by its monetary payoff. Hence cell (2) in Figure 5.1 has been crossed out, indicating that it is empty.

If we do not know with certainty which state of nature will occur, we can distinguish three possible situations, described as decision-making under risk, under uncertainty, and under a mixture of risk and uncertainty. The last of these has to do with the case where uncertainty can be reduced by acquiring additional information (or, in statistical decision problems, can be reduced at the cost of further trials or experimentation). This case will be discussed separately later in the chapter. For the moment let us concentrate on the first two.

The basis of the distinction between decision-making under risk and under uncertainty is that in the former case states of nature, and hence consequences of act–state pairs, are not known with certainty, but the probability of each state and consequence is known to the decision-maker. The term *uncertainty* is reserved for the case where not even the probabilities are known. We will assume in this case that the decision-maker is *totally* ignorant about the true state.

Decision-making under risk

This case falls partly in cell 3 and partly in cell 4 in Figure 5.1. Which situations fall in which cell we will now see.

In normal circumstances the way we would deal with this case, if $p_1, \ldots, p_n$ are the known probabilities associated with states $s_1, \ldots, s_n$, would be to calculate the expected monetary value (EMV) row by row of Fig. 5.2. For row i this would be $p_1 c_{i1} + p_2 c_{i2} + \cdots + p_n c_{in}$. We would then select the act that *maximizes EMV*. Cell 3 is the domain of such situations. While this decision rule would be a valid guide to action in most practical business problems described as decision-making under risk, there are some in which it would be highly misleading.

What are "normal circumstances," that is, when is EMV a valid guide to action? The answer turns on the amount of money at stake and the decision-maker's attitude to risk-bearing (see vi above). The point was explained in the first paragraph of the Mathematical Appendix for Chapter 4. When faced with two alternatives, one offering a certain return of $1,000, and the other a return of $0 or $2,000 with equal probability, most business people will choose the first, even though both have the same EMV ($1,000). More generally, we can say that maximizing EMV is a valid decision rule if the decision-maker in question would use this rule in choosing between an act with a certain monetary payoff and an act whose payoffs are the best and worst of all the possible payoffs of the actual decision problem being considered, with equal probability.

If this condition is not met we must assume that there is some way in which the decision-maker's preferences among the consequences of the various acts can be summarized by a utility function. In other words it is assumed that to each act–state pair (a_i, s_j) there can be assigned a measurable utility (u_{ij}), which obeys some consistency conditions regarded as reasonable. One such set of consistency conditions was stated in Chapter 4 (the von Neumann-Morgenstern conditions). The entries in Figure 5.2 are then changed from c_{ij}'s to u_{ij}'s, and the decision rule becomes the *maximization of expected utility* (EU), where the expected utility of act i is $p_1 u_{i1} + p_2 u_{i2} + \cdots + p_n u_{in}$. Cell 4 is the domain of risky situations in which EU maximization is the appropriate decision rule. It can be shown, incidentally, that when EMV maximization is the appropriate rule (cell 3), adoption of this rule will also maximize EU (Schlaifer 1959, 43–44, for proof).

We have not yet explained how the utilities are generated. The explanation, which is long and technical, has been relegated to the Mathematical Appendix, where numerical examples are also given to support the arguments. The method of analysis involves scaling the decision-maker's preferences and calibrating her judgments ("probabilities") by reference to a basic lottery whose consequences, $\bar{c}$ and $\underline{c}$, are respectively *at least* as attractive (unattractive) as the best (worst) possible consequence of the actual decision problem. The analysis results in the choice between real alternatives being replaced by a choice between surrogate reference lotteries by a rule that amounts to maximizing expected utility.

This technical analysis leaves a few questions unanswered. One general observation is that it focuses on a single decision in isolation from the other decision problems that the businessperson faces at the same time, and in the future. As we saw in Chapter 3, many decisions are interdependent, some over time, and this circumstance needs to be taken into account if it results in significant externalities. Note also that this procedure, by design, justifies the use of expected value (of utility) in representing the decision-maker's attitude to risk-taking, without questioning its appropriateness to such a task (e.g., might higher moments of the probability distribution of utility be relevant also?).

Before proceeding to decision-making under uncertainty, cell 5 of Figure 5.1 merits a brief comment. This is a virtually empty box— subjective probabilities are seldom associated with a choice criterion related to objective values; the two things are antithetical. In an *indirect* sort of way, however, such a combination is possible where a decision problem is essentially a case of decision-making under risk, but where (a) the probabilities are arrived at subjectively rather than in a relative frequency sense (cell 4), and then (b) these subjective probabilities are used to calculate an expected value using a standard (objective) probability distribution. This is the procedure used in PERT, a method used to exercise control over the time spent on projects, as mentioned at the beginning of this chapter. Thus we would say PERT (and cell 5) involves a combination of cells 3 and 4. Such instances are comparatively rare, and need not concern us further.

Decision-making under uncertainty

We come finally to cell 6, the domain of decision-making under uncertainty, and assume that the decision-maker is totally ignorant about the chances of the respective states obtaining. By the device of hypothetical reference lotteries, we can construct a table as shown in Figure 5.3 where, as in the last part of the previous section, we call the entries in the table utilities (u_{ij}), because we presume that the consequences are ordered, as in the case of certainty and risk.

As with the second approach to decision-making under risk, the aim is to choose a row of this table (an act) that is optimal in some sense. But in what sense? We can no longer follow the procedure adopted in the previous case. If the reader will look at the discussion of that procedure (decision-making under risk, EMV maximization inappropriate) in the

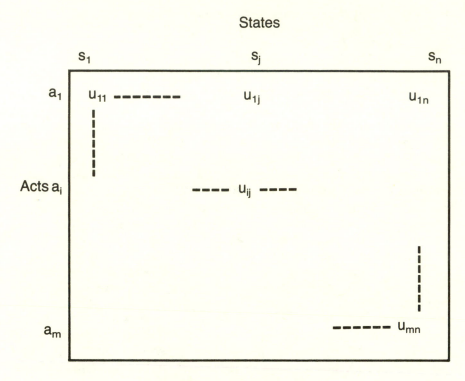

FIGURE 5.3. Utility table.

Mathematical Appendix, she will see that we can get as far as point 6 but no further, because we do not have probabilities for states. Hence we cannot use the EU maximization rule (points 7–9).

The big problem is to decide what should be the optimality criterion in this situation. A number of possibilities have been proposed: the "maximin" utility criterion, "minimax" risk (or "regret"), Hurwicz's optimism-pessimism index, a criterion based on the principle of Insufficient Reason (Jacob Bernouilli), and several axiomatic approaches which, like the von Neumann-Morgenstern axioms in the theory of games and Arrow's axioms for the formation of group preferences (referred to in Chapter 4), our intuition suggests are reasonable. As stated earlier, none of these criteria has gained general acceptance for all decision-making under uncertainty. Some criteria are valid in certain circumstances, some in others. Axiomatic approaches, by laying down certain conditions that must be met by all acts and preferences, restrict the class of potentially acceptable criteria. The interested reader who would like to learn more about these approaches is referred to Luce and Raiffa (1957, ch. 13) or to Baumol (1965, ch. 24).

A point worth mentioning is that there is a presumption that real decision-makers (e.g., businesspeople) usually fall somewhere in between, having no information and knowing the probability distribution of states (between complete ignorance and risk). Savage (1954) has shown that by teasing out this partial, vague information by asking the decision-maker a number of yes-no questions that force consistent answers, a probability distribution over states can be generated (a distribution of subjective probabilities) that can be used to make decisions. As a result of his axiom system this can be done in such a way that expected utilities reflect the decision-maker's true preferences. The problem is thus transformed from a problem of decision-making under uncertainty to decision-making under risk, and the criterion is to maximize expected utility. This approach may be applied to unique, "one-off" decisions to which the usual frequency theory of probability would obviously be inapplicable.

Some questions remain about this approach—for example, as to whether the decision-maker can always answer the questions that take the form of simpler hypothetical choices, and whether forced answers will always provide a reliable basis for real-world decision problems. Some further queries concerning Savage's subjective probability-utility approach are raised by Baumol (1965, p. 551).

Subjective probabilities, as defined by Savage, *in theory* have the same mathematical properties as objective probabilities. A subjective or introspective personal probability is a number p, $0 \leqslant p \leqslant 1$, that represents a person's belief about the likelihood of a particular state (or event) occurring, prior to its first occurrence. Revision of these a priori subjective probabilities in the light of experience (additional information) is governed by Bayes' formula (see the Mathematical Appendix). Subsequent decisions are then based on the revised probabilities. In practice, however, it is not certain that subjective probabilities will always add up to one; hence they may not qualify as measures in the sense of measure theory (Chapter 11). Another troublesome question concerns whether or not subjective probability and utility are independent, or whether they might interact (Edwards 1961).

There is a close affinity between decision-making under uncertainty and statistical decision-making; witness the titles of Schlaifer's and Savage's books. In effect, statistical inference and the theory of games together form the basis of what is called "statistical decision theory." Faced with uncertainty, the statistician conducts more experiments ("trials"), trying to gain additional information. So, frequently, does the businessperson, as was indicated at the beginning of this chapter. We will

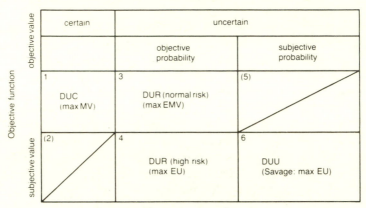

Fig. 5.4: Types of decision problems based on the information available.
and the associated decision criteria

Legend: DUC decision-making under certainty
DUR decision-making under risk
DUU decision-making under uncertainty
EMV expected monetary value
EU expected utility

FIGURE 5.4. Types of decision problems based on the information available, and the associated decision criteria.

have more to say about when to acquire further information in the next chapter.

To summarize the discussion thus far, Figure 5.4 is a fully clothed version of the skeletal Figure 5.1.

Sequential decision-making

All of the cases we have been talking about so far could be characterized as static decision theories, concerned with a single isolated decisions at a later stage. Choices occur in sequences rather than singly; ness, are not like this. They retain the risk or uncertainty feature, but they are dynamic rather than static. They are sequential in nature, that is, extended in time, with a decision at one stage having an effect on decisions at a larger stage. Choices occur in sequences rather than singly; information available for later decisions is contingent on the nature and consequences of earlier decisions in the sequence. The latter become initial conditions that affect the decision to be made at the next stage. So decisions become interdependent (Chapter 3). An example of a decision problem that is both sequential in nature and involves uncertainty would be the holding of inventories, where the beginning inventories for any period partly reflect decisions and events in the past. Information may also be obtained about the uncertain future if the increase in expected payoff justifies the cost.

The decision-maker's proper response to situations of this kind is to form a *policy* or strategy rather than a single decision made for all time—and theoretically the consequences of any truly sequential decision extend to infinity. A technique called *dynamic programming* (DP) has been developed for dealing with sequential decision problems; see Bellman and Kalaba (1965) and the Mathematical Appendix. The method consists, essentially, of abstracting from the full sequential (multistage) decision model a single-stage (proximate) decision problem formulated in such a way as to reflect some characteristics of the full sequential problem. At the first stage, for example, the decision-maker seeks the optimal solution to a problem with the information available to him at that time, with account taken of planned future decisions which impose constraints on what is possible in the future, the aim at each stage being to make decisions that will be optimal over the entire horizon or sequence. The same procedure is followed at each subsequent stage. There are some similarities between sequential decision processes and learning. For situations where the state-updating transformation (ϕ) referred to in the Mathematical Appendix is not completely known (uncertainty), there is a stochastic version of the DP model.

Dominance

The term *dominance* was used in connection with the preferences of various classes of stakeholders in Chapter 4. Of more direct interest in the present context were the references to weak preference orderings in discussing Arrow's conditions for consistent group preferences (also Chapter 4), and the idea of an efficient point in the discussion of multiple-criteria programming in the Mathematical Appendix to that chapter. The fundamental idea behind the dominance concept is that x dominates y if x is at least as preferred as y for a given class of utility function, U. As we have seen, if the decision is under certainty or falls within the decision-maker's "normal" range of risk, U will usually take the form of a monetary value.

If in a given decision problem there are two possible acts, a and b, a is said to *dominate* b if a is at least as preferred as b (i.e., $a \succ b$) under a given class of utility functions (i.e., for *all* $u \in U$). The symbol $\succ$ means "is preferred to," and $\sim$ means "is indifferent to." If a dominates b but b does not dominate a, then for *some* values of $u \in U$, a must be preferred to

b ($a \succ b$). a is then said to be more *efficient* than b (recall the vector maximization approach in multiple-criteria programming). This property may then be used to narrow down the set of available acts by eliminating those whose consequences (utilities) are less desired than those of efficient acts, and give explicit consideration only to these.

In practical problems there are usually more than two acts to choose between, and this procedure seldom has the desired effect of reducing the entire set to one efficient act. Other procedures must then be brought to bear to discriminate between the efficient acts. One such procedure, in conditions of abnormal risk or uncertainty, is to look at the probability distributions of consequences of the efficient acts (the probabilities having been generated by means of reference lotteries). Then if the decision-maker's choice criterion is expected utility maximization, he could make pairwise comparisons of the efficient acts, declaring a to be at least as desirable as b if and only if $F_a(x) \leqslant F_b(x)$ for all $u \in U$, where U is the decision-maker's class of (non-decreasing) utility function for money, x is the monetary consequence of an act, and F_i is the probability distribution function for x for act i. This is called first-degree *stochastic dominance*. If it is possible to further restrict the class of utility functions considered (by proceeding to second and higher degrees of stochastic dominance), it may eventually be possible to find the single most efficient act. For a fuller discussion of stochastic dominance see Whitmore and Findlay (1978).

The stochastic dominance approach to problems of decision under uncertainty can be extended to problems of choice over time, such as financial investment and capital budgeting (Ekern 1981).

Possibilistic decision-making

As we have seen, we do not have a universally valid decision rule for rational behavior under uncertainty. About the best that can be said is that different rules are valid in different circumstances. One relatively new concept is that of "possibility." A possibility measure differs from a probability distribution in that the former is based on ordinal information while the latter requires cardinal information. Both possibility and probabilities can be defined from subjective or objective information. The point is that possibility requires *less* information than probability theory. A theory of possibilistic decision-making has been developed that could prove useful in making decisions when the type of information available concerning uncertain states is not strong enough to make cardinal statements about the distribution. For example, the statement, "It is cold today" may be *some* guide to behavior. It restricts and orders possible states (temperatures) without specifying one or even a range, and without implying probabilistic information. Possibilistic decision-making uses the idea of a fuzzy set (see the Mathematical Appendix).

6

Information

We are living in an age of revolution in communications and information. In McLuhan's words, the world has become a global village; scarcely anything happens anywhere that we do not quickly hear about, a vast change compared with earlier times. A wide range of activities—education, research, publishing, the news media, forecasting—contributes in varying degree to the creation and dissemination of knowledge. Machlup (1962) estimated that the "knowledge industry" in the United States accounted for 23 to 29 percent of GNP in 1958 (this may have been an overstatement) and was growing at a much faster rate than GNP. Organizations of all kinds share in this informational activity. As systems, at least some of their parts are interrelated, that is, they communicate with each other. As systems high on the ladder of complexity (recall Boulding's hierarchy in Chapter 2), there are indications that a greater proportion of their energic inputs from the environment takes the form of information rather than matter or pure energy. To the extent that an organization is effectively adaptive, its behavior will reflect characteristics largely of its environment; the environment must be selectively mapped into the organization in the light of its goals (Simon 1969, 84–118). In other words, to adapt successfully the organization must constantly monitor its environment and quickly match its orientation to the state of a changing environment. In one form or another, of course, organizations collectively also put back much information into the environment. Organizations are information processors, or manipulators of symbols. Much of the information that is processed and communicated within organizations is recorded in some form, but some of it is verbal. Informational activities in an organization include collection, coding and decoding, processing, storage and retrieval, and communicating.

The breadth and importance of informational activities in the management of organizations require us to be more precise about what we mean by "information." If, as appears necessary, an attempt is to be made to manage the information flows through an organization, we need to say just what we mean by "information" and be able to measure it. There are at least three different measures of information, each based on a different definition.

Definitions of "information"

In communication theory and *information theory,* "information" means the degree of surprise or unexpectedness caused by the receipt of a message, unexpectedness being measured by the logarithm of the recipient's probability that a particular event (or particular value of a variable) will occur in the future, when the prior probability distribution is known. This is called the *entropy measure* of the expected amount of information in a message. "Amount of information" is here merely a negative measure of uncertainty. This measure is described formally in the Mathematical Appendix. Note that the measure applies to the message or signal itself; it expresses the statistical rarity or surprise value of the signal. It says nothing about the nature of the source or the receiver, or the conditions under which signals transmitted become meaningful information.

The second definition is the "semantic information" measure, or "content measure" (Bar-Hillel and Carnap 1964). Unlike the information theory measure, this considers the consequences of receiving information associated with the occurrence of an event or the value of a particular variable. "Information" is here defined in terms of the meaning conveyed by a message; and meaning will vary from one recipient to another (if A speaks to B and C in Esperanto, the meaning will be very different to B, who knows Esperanto, from what it is to C, who does not). For a message to have meaning there must be a particular relationship between sender and receiver. Semantic information involves a relational perspective; equal amounts of information (information theory) could convey quite different meanings to different people. This is still not the measure we want for management purposes, however. As Bar-Hillel and Carnap (1964, 252–54, 257) acknowledge:

> If a practically acting man bases his choice either on content measure alone or a probability alone [information theory], he will sometimes be led to choices that are clearly wrong . . . we should choose that action for which the expectation value of the utility of the outcome is a maximum.

The third measure of information, and the one with which we shall be concerned, is an economic one. This *information economics* measure is an outgrowth of the economics of uncertainty (rational choice under risk and uncertainty, discussed in the previous chapter) and statistical decision theory (individual decision-making) or the theory of teams (group decision-making). Recall that uncertainty manifests itself in the dispersion of (subjective) probability distributions over possible states of the world. Information then consists of events (such as the receipt of a signal) which change these probability distributions (Hirshleifer 1971). So in the economic sense information is the meaning derived from a signal *provided* that the recipient's probability distribution changes or the knowledge of the recipient is changed (Feltham 1972). Compared with the information theory sense, it is *changes* in probability distributions, not just probability distributions (a process, not a condition) that matter (Hirshleifer 1971). The information-economic approach develops a measure of the change in payoff (net benefit, value minus cost) resulting from the receipt of information or from a change in the information system (more on this later). Meanwhile, we will continue the descriptive and qualitative discussion by considering some of the many aspects of information in organizations.

Some aspects of information in organizations

Students of economics will know that the price system plays an informational role. It is a form of continuous referendum for reaching the best distribution of productive resources between different possible uses, registering the strengths of different demands in a common scale, and inducing adjustments to make these demands compatible with one another in the aggregate. At the same time it is well known that the price system fails to lead to an optimal allocation of resources in certain circumstances: where there are interdependencies among different processes, between firms or within a firm; where producers are subject to increasing returns to scale; or where there are indivisibilities in inputs or outputs.

As Arrow (1974b) has noted, organizations are a means of achieving the benefits of collective action in situations in which the price system fails. One particular failure of the price system in addition to those just mentioned and especially important in understanding organizations is the presence of uncertainty. Participants in a market do not know which state of the world is the true one. Theoretically, it is possible in these circumstances to conceive of conditional contracts (contracts to buy and sell a certain commodity if a specified state has occurred) instead of contracts to buy and sell fixed amounts, and attach prices to these conditional contracts. In practice, however, it would be impossible to cover all the possible contingencies by a contingent price system alone, or in combination with insurance contracts against the contingencies. A contingent price system alone would fail to allocate risk-bearing between market participants, due to the great complexity and cost of insuring against all conceivable contingencies, to the difficulty of distinguishing between genuine and non-genuine risks (the problem known as "moral hazard," discussed in Chapter 10), and to the possibility that parity of information (as to the prevailing state of the world) is lacking between the parties to a contingent contract (the problem known as "adverse selection"). We see this inequality of information ("information asymmetry," "information inpactedness") between the parties to a transaction very clearly in the relation between a principal and agent within a firm—they may possess very different bodies of knowledge. If we employ the term *information structure* to mean both the existing knowledge possessed by an economic agent and the possibility of acquiring additional relevant information in the future, inequalities of information structures between different participants strongly influence the possibility of allocating risk-bearing through the market (i.e., price system) in conditions of uncertainty. Hence organizations (firms) narrower in scope than the market come into existence partly due to the presence of uncertainty. Some transactions are carried out within organizations rather than through the market, partly as a result of the above-mentioned features of the network of information flows in existence. Of course, this does not eliminate the problem of allocating risk; it merely "passes the buck" back to individual organizations. Risk-sharing within an organization is one of the questions that will be discussed in Chapter 10.

A second aspect worth drawing attention to is the strong interdependency that exists between information structure and organization structure. This has been commented on by Feltham (1972, 19) and Simon (1961, 154). Feltham quotes from Fair (1960, 233):

if we are satisfied for our purpose to characterize an organizational structure as an assignment of the total necessary set of tasks to a given set of people, we can say that the required information flow is a function of the organization structure chosen. Further, reasoning that economy dictates fitting an information transfer system to a specific movement pattern of information, it follows that an economical information transfer system is dependent on the organization structure. There is no reason not to consider the converse, i.e., that of adapting the organization structure to an existing information transfer system, but it seems meaningless to attempt to discuss one without taking the other as given.

Simon (1961) makes the same point:

> Not only is communication absolutely necessary to organization, but the availability of particular techniques of communication will in large part determine the way in which decision-making functions can and should be distributed throughout the organization. The possibility of permitting a particular individual to make a particular decision will often hinge on whether there can be transmitted to him the information he will need to make a wise decision, and whether he, in turn, will be able to transmit his decision to other members of the organization whose behaviour it is supposed to influence.

As a number of writers have noted, in firms as in economies, this strong interaction between information structure and organization structure is probably the most important consideration in deciding between a highly centralized and a decentralized form of organization.

The last aspect that will be commented on here is the limited information-handling ability of both human beings and organizations. As it applies to individuals, this has been referred to extensively by Simon; see, for example, Simon (1957b, 196–206). Irrespective of the way information is accumulated and stored, and even when computers are used, the individual himself is the limiting factor. As Arrow states (1974b, 39), "Immediately or ultimately, the information must enter his brain through his sensory organs, and both brain and senses are limited in capacity." The individual's capacity for acquiring and using information is strictly limited. These limitations are partially overcome by organizations, whose function is to take advantage of the increased productivity of collective actions in situations where the price system fails, but at a cost. On the benefits side, a number of individuals pool their different information, and informational economies can be achieved by virtue of the fact that information received can be considerably condensed before it is communicated to decision-makers without losing value (i.e., without affecting the payoff of the decision). As Arrow notes (1974b, 54), the theory of sufficient statistics is an example of this. Not all the information received by a member of the organization has to be communicated to the central office, or to decision-makers elsewhere in the organization. But information is costly to acquire (it is assumed that all free information will be availed of), communication channels have to be set up and coordinated, and the use of coding reduces but does not completely offset the tendency of the costs of communicating information within the organization to increase as the scale of operations increases. In sum, organizations often possess information advantages over markets in the presence of uncertainty, and over a single individual. Economies can be achieved by reducing information acquired, much of it decision-irrelevant, to its essence before retransmission. In the end, however, since the cost of communicating information and coordinating its use tends to increase more than proportionately as the scale of operations increases, it is usually desirable to make some tradeoff between the payoffs from optimal actions and the information costs involved, by simplifying or modifying decision problems.

The economics of uncertainty and information economics

It is useful at this point in the discussion to introduce a distinction made in statistical decision theory between decisions to act and decisions to collect information. These are referred to as "terminal acts" and "experiments," respectively. Hirshleifer (1971) describes them as active and passive adaptations to the presence of uncertainty, where uncertainty is represented by the dispersion of individuals' probability distributions over possible states of the world. The economics of uncertainty (Chapter 5) considers the case where a terminal act represents merely adaptation to a given state of uncertainty; information economics involves going beyond this by gathering more information prior to terminal action. Generating more information prior to decision yields no direct benefits but is designed to serve the instrumental purpose of increasing the value of the terminal act (i.e., payoff). The argument that concluded the previous section may now be restated by saying that it will often be profitable, on balance, to select a suboptimal terminal act (a less than optimal payoff) in order to economize on internal communication and coordination costs.

Information decisions

With the foregoing as background, we are now in a position to consider the second type of decisions mentioned above, namely decisions about "experiments," or more specifically, about the value of an information system and choice among information systems—in short, the economics of information. Here information is regarded as an economic commodity, with associated benefits and costs and, as with other commodities, decisions about information must weigh the one against the other or compare the net benefits of alternative information systems.

It is important to note here that the "cost of information," represented by a reduction in the expected payoff of a terminal act, includes not only the cost of collecting data, but also the costs of all the subsequent informational activities. Malone (1964, 29), quoted by Feltham (1972), describes the cost component of information as follows:

> The cost [of decisions] arises from the utilization of scarce resources . . .
> —funds for collection of data, conversions of data into usable informa-
> tion, decision-maker's time and equipment in searching for alternatives
> and selecting a decision method, and analysis of the information so that
> an optimal course of action can be selected. Finally, communication,
> implementation and review of the decision are also required.

In addition to these, Arrow (1974b, 39–43) has pointed out that the individual is ultimately the chief input into any of her information channels. This is because, as stated earlier, the information must enter her brain through her sensory organs, and both brain and senses are limited in capacity. Psychological studies have shown the limits of the sensory perception abilities of human beings and their limits as informa- tion processors. For example, the data collected may be affected by the abilities and accumulated knowledge of the person or persons responsible for collection and screening. A hitherto unheard signal (such as a communication in an unfamiliar foreign language) is useless and does not transform the recipient's probability distribution; learning the foreign language involves an irreversible capital investment by the individual which should be considered part of the cost of information (e.g., via depreciation). And the effectiveness of internal communication is in- fluenced by the fact that individuals have different learning styles, and that they bias and counterbias data.

Excellent treatments of the problems involved in the economics of information have been available in accounting texts for more than a decade now (Feltham 1972; Demski 1972, 2d ed., 1980), and more recently in Demski and Feltham (1976, chs. 2 and 3); they have been slower to appear in economics texts (see Varian, 1978, who is one of the very few authors to include it). The analysis of these problems is rather technical, and little purpose would be served by describing it in words. A brief and simplified indication of the approach is given in the Mathematical Appendix.

Information structures to promote effective and rapid adaptation and learning

Recalling the discussion of Chapter 2, as open systems, organizations must selectively adapt to changing environments continually and quickly in order to survive. By "selectively" is meant adapting in the light of the goals of the organization, and "learning" means getting better at adapting over time. This calls for frequent detailed monitoring of the environment and the ability to match changes in the environment that may affect the organization's goals and selecting of appropriate responses. This selectivity of responses to feedback of information from the environment implies that to adapt successfully and quickly an organization needs to have a repertoire of responses on hand. According to Simon (1969, 97) this is built up from past experience and trial-and-error. Information about what he calls "stable configurations" (tried methods that worked in particular situations) is preserved and guides the process of adaptation. This is analogous to natural selection in the evolution of biological systems. Without it an organization's selectivity of responses would not be quick enough. In Chapter 2 we referred to this need to selectively map the environment into the organization, as structure (change the organization structure) or as information, as being what transforms an import of energy (including information) into negative entropy. This shows the need for organizations to have a memory; but the information stored must be the right information, in the right form, quickly retrievable and interpretable if it is to be of use in the process of adaptation and learning.

Common deficiencies of conventional organizational information structures

Against this background, the indications are that many existing organizational information systems are deficient when it comes to promoting adaptation and learning. One deficiency mentioned by a number of writers is described this way by Arrow (1974b, 50, 59). Consider the decision areas within an organization as divided into active, monitored, and passive categories. An active area is one in which experiments are performed, signals are received from them, and terminal acts are chosen as functions of these signals. In monitoring decision areas, some experiments are performed, but signals convey too little information to take terminal acts; but if appropriate signals are received, it is optimal to make further experiments that yield enough information to bring about terminal acts (i.e., move the decision area into the active category). In a passive area no experiments are being conducted, and no terminal acts are undertaken. The partition of decision areas into these three categories depends on the relative benefits and costs.

Arrow believes that, compared with individuals, organizations have a greater ability to monitor but a lesser ability to change from a passive to a monitoring or active mode, that is, to bring new items onto their agendas and act on them: "Short-run efficiency and even flexibility within a narrow framework of alternatives may be less important in the long run than a wide compass of potential activities." In other words, organizational information systems tend to develop rigidities; in the long run these lead to inertia and a reluctance to change, when the proper role of the information system should be to spot potential opportunities and threats, and promote experimentation, innovation, adaptation, and learning.

The same view is echoed by Hedberg and Jönsson (1978). They believe a *majority* of modern information systems resist change, and have made organizations more rigid rather than more flexible. This may be even more true of computerized information systems, which increase the role of programmed behaviors. There are also indications that organizational information systems tend to hamper search, and filter away significant amounts of relevant uncertainty, diversity, and change signals (Mowshowitz 1976). The result of these influences "has been that [organizational] decision makers often have faced unrealistically homogeneous and explained environments . . . information systems dysfunctionally add to organizations' inertia" (Hedberg and Jönsson, 1978, whose remarks are based on a number of empirical studies of Swedish firms). They conclude that very conscious and considerable design efforts are needed if information systems are to change the behavior of organizations by reducing their inertia and making them adapt more readily to change. Much more detailed monitoring of the environment would appear to be the first essential. Other evidence suggests that *informal* information channels are often more effective than formal ones in making best use of available information and improving performance.

7

Organization Structure

In Chapter 2, "organization structure" was defined as the inner couplings between the components of a system. In nontechnical language, the term is meant to convey the way work is assigned to parts of an organization. The main message of this chapter is that in studying the behavior of organizations, structure is an important variable within management's control.

Discussions of organization structure very often have in mind only the formal structure, as represented in organization charts and established authority-responsibility relationships in the organization. Thus a firm may be subdivided into divisions, operating departments, and service departments, including administration. In established firms, however, social relationships soon lead to the emergence of an informal structure. This informal structure has been variously described in the literature. Perhaps the best way to characterize it would be to say that the formal structure refers to job titles, the informal structure to particular persons. Certain behaviors might be associated with, or expected of, X in his capacity as head of department A. But because of special personal qualities, skills, and beliefs, X may exercise informal authority not appearing in the organizational "blueprint," in department A or in other parts of the organization (Scott 1981, 83). Various writers have suggested that the informal structure may serve useful functions, by increasing the ease of communication, correcting weaknesses in the formal structure, and leading to higher performance. In the previous chapter we referred to the strong interdependence between the information structure and organization structure. There will usually be an active informal communication network in addition to the formal one specified by the formal organization structure.

Markets and hierarchies

A natural starting point for the discussion of organization structure is to ask why there are such things as organizations. Why do organizations come into existence? Let us confine the discussion to commercial organizations, those that conduct transactions in goods and services, as exemplified by the modern privately owned corporation. Coase (1937) was the first to point out that firms and markets are alternative ways of organizing economic activities:

> Outside the firm, price movements direct production, which is coordinated through a series of exchange transactions on the market. Within a firm these market transactions are eliminated and . . . the entrepreneur-coordinator . . . directs production.

Coase later noted (1953, 331–51) that firms are established because there are costs in using the price system. Organizing transactions within the firm also involves costs, however, and a firm should be expanded to the point where the costs of organizing an additional transaction within the firm equals the cost of conducting the same transaction by an exchange in the market, or the costs of organizing in another firm.

This theme has been taken up and developed by Williamson, by regarding markets and organizations as alternative governance structures for conducting economic activities. In the neoclassical theory of the firm in economics the firm's internal organization is ignored; firms are classified according to the structure of their external markets. Essentially, the firm is regarded as represented by a production function. In a series of writings (1975, 1979, 1981) Williamson would augment the model of the firm as production function by including the concept of the firm as governance structure. Since many formal organization structures have been observed to be hierarchical in form, this literature has come to be known as the "markets and hierarchies" view.

According to this view, the firm should try to economize on transaction costs as well as on production costs (within an overall objective such as maximizing profits). By "transaction costs" Williamson means not only the ex ante costs of contracting, but also the ex post costs of executing and policing the contract. In other words, the costs of planning, adapting, and monitoring task completion are added to the conventional costs of production in the firm's optimization problem.

The bearing of all this on the question of organization structure is that it suggests a grouping of activities in subunits so as to economize on transaction costs. Williamson says there is a presumption that the evolving corporate structure over the past 150 years, from unitary form (highly centralized, "line-and-staff"), to multidivisional form (decentralized into operating divisions with a central office manned by top executives responsible for planning, strategy, and overall control), to conglomerates and multinationals was motivated by, and has had the effect of, economizing on transaction costs. No other hypothesis, he says, is able to provide a rationale for this succession of organizational innovations. Later in the chapter we will have more to say on the determinants of the form of governance (markets versus hierarchies) and of organization structure under this transaction cost view.

Three views of organizations and organization structure

Before getting more deeply involved in the implications of the transaction-cost theory for organization structure, it will be useful to examine three older views of organizations that have received a good deal of attention, especially in the sociology and organization theory literatures. These have already been referred to in Chapter 4 as the rational, natural, and open system views. Organization structure takes a different form under each view. The following elaboration is based on Scott (1981).

The rational system view of organizations is seen in its most extreme form in the neoclassical theory of the firm in economics. It focuses on the normative structure of organizations—the formal specification of goals, procedures, and roles—nothing more. The firm is seen as being oriented toward its input and output markets, and no account is taken of its broader social and cultural context. In particular, the rational system view virtually ignores the behavior of participants in the firm.

The natural system view is more concerned with the behavior of organizational participants and with the interactions between the normative and behavioral structures of organizations. It does not question the existence of highly formalized structures and official goals within most organizations, but argues that formal structures tend to be ineffective and become transformed by the emergence of informal structures. Participants share a common interest in the survival of the organization. Attention must be given to the maintenance of the system itself, not just to the attainment of specified organizational goals. The organization is first and foremost a social unit concerned with its own survival, an end in itself, and participants will engage in collective activities through informal structures to secure this end. Organization structure (formal and informal together) is determined partly by the environment and partly by the organization's functional needs, and these two are often in conflict—adapting to the environment may be in conflict with attainment of the organization's own goals (Parsons 1960). Most natural system theorists view the environment as hostile; Parsons is an exception. To him the environment is a stabilizing force, sustaining and legitimating the organization in pursuing its goals.

In this respect Parsons anticipated the third view, the open system school, which argues that open systems survive *because of* rather than despite the environment. The principal distinguishing feature of the open system view is that organizations and their environments are highly interdependent; external forces shape internal arrangements, and vice versa. In the short run, organizations individually try to adapt to their environments; in the long run, organizations collectively gradually transform their environments. Larger and more powerful organizations are likely to be able to influence their environments more than small organizations.

Other features of the open system view are that organizations, like other open systems, tend to evolve to higher levels of complexity (environmental complexity tends to become mirrored in structural complexity), and that unlike closed physical or mechanical systems their parts are loosely coupled. Less constraint is placed on the behavior of one part by the states of the others. Compared with systems of lesser complexity, organizations (and social systems in general) have a marked capacity for modifying and elaborating their structures.

Beyond saying that one would expect organizations, as open systems, to place greater emphasis on boundary-spanning and bridging activities (close monitoring of the relevant environment is an example of the former; a variety of uncertainty avoidance measures such as mergers, joint ventures, and interlocking directorates exemplify the latter), open system organization theorists are notable for the variety of their views.

One view that has received more attention than others is the *contingency theory* of organizations (Lawrence and Lorsch 1967). This theory says that organization design decisions are contingent upon environmental conditions. The design problem is to select a structure appropriate for the information-processing requirements of the tasks to be performed, and the latter depend on the degree of environmental uncertainty (Galbraith 1973). Organization structure cannot be decided once for all. The best design depends on the nature of the environment to which the organization must relate, and the environment is constantly changing. Besides, the structure must serve certain internal needs also. Contingency theorists assert that the more homogeneous and stable the environment, the more appropriate is the formalized and hierarchical form of structure.

Reality probably involves a combination of all three views—rational, natural, and open systems. The rational system view, with its emphasis on the economic aspects of organizations, should not be dismissed as some noneconomists suggest, particularly if one interprets "rational" as meaning that individuals act in an *intendedly* rational way in conditions of uncertainty and limited information-handling capacity. The natural system view reminds us that organizations are social as well as economic units, and that the behavior of people in organizations must be taken into account. An organization, as it were, has a behavioral structure in addition to a normative structure as portrayed in the rational system model. It draws our attention to the commonly observed appearance of informal structures and informal communication networks, and to the overriding interest of participants in ensuring the organization's survival. The open system view adds yet further dimensions by emphasizing the critical importance of organization–environment interactions and observing that, as complex systems, organizations tend to be loosely coupled, the links between their parts are rather weak, with each subunit acting more or less independently. This latter is the reverse of what is suggested by the rational system view.

Other influences on organization structure not mentioned explicitly in the foregoing are power relations within the organization, technology, size of the organization, the degree of uncertainty surrounding its activities, and the degree of interdependence of its parts.

More on hierarchies

Reverting to the markets and hierarchies discussion, Williamson (1981) means by "governance structure" the explicit or implicit contractual framework within which a transaction is located, the transaction being his basic unit of analysis. Uncertainty, frequency of exchange, and the degree to which transactions, particularly investments, are of a specific nature, are singled out as the principal dimensions for describing transactions (Williamson 1979). Markets are the main governance structure for nonspecific transactions, whatever their frequency; transactions tend to be organized within the firm as they become progressively more "idiosyncratic" (nonstandardized, specific), particularly if they are recurrent or of high value. Increased uncertainty also leads to a move away from market governance for idiosyncratic transactions. The objective in all these cases is to economize on transaction costs which, according to Williamson (1979), essentially reduces to economizing on bounded rationality while simultaneously shielding the transaction against the hazards of opportunism ("self-interest seeking with guile") by either of the parties to the transaction.

We turn now to a consideration of transactions that it has been decided, for whatever reason, to conduct within the organization rather than through the market. Now, organizations are highly complex systems (recall Boulding's ladder of complexity in Chapter 2), and Simon has frequently stated (e.g., Simon 1969) that complexity often takes the form of hierarchy, that the complex system has a parts-within-parts, nested, or stratified structure. Simon (1969) further argues that hierarchical structures consisting of both formal and informal relations have a strong adaptive and survival capacity to the extent that the subsystems represent "stable intermediate forms." In other words, hierarchy can be regarded as a decomposition principle by which strongly interdependent activities are grouped together in such a way that their interdependence is taken into account. Simon offers, as an illustration of what he means by "stable intermediate forms," the organization of the Arab revolt against the Turks by T. E. Lawrence during World War I. The revolt was limited by the character of Lawrence's largest stable building blocks, the separate, suspicious desert tribes. Simple systems evolve much more rapidly if they include stable subsystems, and the resulting complex system will be hierarchic.

These hierarchical structures, which are so frequently observed in nature and in social systems, tend to be loosely coupled. That is to say, the interactions within subsystems tend to be much stronger than those between subsystems. In a business, for example, there is generally more interaction, on the average, between two people working in the same department than between two people in different departments. Such a system is described as "nearly decomposable": the interactions within subsystems are strong, those between subsystems weak but not negligible. According to Simon (1969), many complex systems have a nearly decomposable, hierarchic structure; and this property helps us to understand their behavior. Before elaborating on this, it should be noted that Simon himself (1969) adds a qualification: "At least some kinds of hierarchic systems can be approximated successfully as nearly decomposable systems." Ouchi (1980) claims to have found one of the exceptions in the high-technology industries, which are characterized by activities subject to great uncertainty (associated with the technology) and a high level of interdependence between subsystems. In these circumstances, according to Ouchi, hierarchies are inadequate and give way to a clan type of structure in which members of a group form ties based on common internalized goals.

Much has been written about centralized versus decentralized forms of organization as exemplified, for example, in unitary and multidivisional modes of organization, respectively. At issue here is the question, "To what extent is it necessary for the efficiency of a firm that its decisions be made at a high level where a wide degree of information can be made available? How much, on the other hand, is gained by leaving a great deal of latitude to individual departments which are closer to the situations with which they deal, even though there may be some loss due to imperfect coordination?" (Arrow 1959). Simon (1969) took us a notable step forward when he considered the factoring or decomposition of problems and activities according to rational hierarchical principles. Arguing that division of labor is quite as important in decision-making as in production, Simon (1973, 270) states:

> [from] the information processing point of view, division of labour means factoring the total system of decisions that need to be made into relatively independent subsystems, each one of which can be designed with only minimal concern for its interactions with the others.

In other words, the object is to recognize the situation referred to as "near decomposability" in hierarchically decentralized firms.

Elsewhere, Simon has made an analysis of nearly decomposable systems (Simon and Ando 1961). An example of what is meant by "near decomposability" is provided in this analysis for a linear system. Suppose a dynamic system is represented by a system of equations of the form $y = \phi(x)$, x and y being vectors, and further suppose for simplicity that the y's are the values of the x's in the next period (i.e., the system is state-determined). If the relations are all linear, the function ϕ can then be written as a difference equation $x(t + 1) = x(t)P$, where x denotes the state variables, time is denoted by t, and P is a matrix of constant coefficients. The behavior of this system over time depends on the properties of the matrix P, in particular on the patterns of zeros or near-zeros in this matrix. We will assume that P is a square $n \times n$ matrix. The matrix would be (completely) decomposable, denoted here by P^*, if after an appropriate permutation of rows and columns it could be written in the form:

$$
P^* = \begin{bmatrix}
P^*_1 & & & & & \\
& P^*_2 & & & & \\
& & \ddots & & & \\
& & & P^*_I & & \\
& & & & \ddots & \\
& & & & & P^*_N
\end{bmatrix}
$$

where all the P^*_I's are square submatrices and the off-diagonal elements are all zeros. Diagonal dominance here reflects the fact that the system is made up of completely isolated subsystems. Suppose now that we change the matrix P^* to form a new matrix, $P = P^* + \varepsilon C$, where C is an arbitrary matrix of the same dimension as P^* and ε is a very small positive number which defines εC as weak connections. The new matrix P is nearly decomposable.

If the mathematical representation of an organization answers to the description of nearly decomposable, what does this mean in terms of how the organization should be structured? Principally it shows that the loose couplings (weak interactions) between subsystems give rise to dynamic behavior of widely different speeds. To effect conditions of near decomposability, the subunits represented by the diagonal elements should be constituted as almost autonomous units, almost independent of each other and of the off-diagonal elements in the linear system above. The diagonal elements represent the high-frequency, short-run dynamics of the system, which in the case of a firm would correspond to the production departments. These should be grouped in such a way that the interactions between departments are weak, and those within departments strong. A clear separation should be made between these high-frequency elements and the low-frequency elements representing the long-run dynamics of the system. The latter are represented by the off-diagonal elements (assuming that the slow motion has been removed from the diagonal elements), and correspond to the high-level "strategic" processes in the firm.

According to this "hierarchical decomposition principle" (due to Simon and Ando), a vertical slice through the organization should clearly distinguish the higher levels (strategy and policy formation, planning, major decision-making) from the lower levels (operations), setting up the latter as quasi-independent units. The short-run behavior of the organization, which is dominated by the high-frequency elements, may then be studied by regarding the operating units as isolated, approximately independent subsystems, as though the interactions between subsystems do not exist. A horizontal or longitudinal slice reveals the temporal effects of strategic decision-making undertaken at a high level in the hierarchy. The organization's behavior in the long run is dominated by the low-frequency elements. Simon and Ando's analysis reveals that a system that is weakly coupled in the short run may be strongly coupled in the long run, that even very weak interactions between subsystems may become significant over a sufficiently long time interval.

In other words, this way of factoring activities is right for the short run, but in the long run it is generally wrong. Simon and Ando go on to show how an organization's long-run behavior should be studied, using an aggregate model of the whole system in which each operating subsystem is represented by a single aggregate index, without regard to its internal interactions. Incentives should then be devised within and between subsystems to encourage subsystem behavior consistent with the organizational goals.

A nonmathematical discussion of the multi-time-scale behavior caused by weak couplings, and its implications for organization structure, will be found in Williamson (1981). The mathematical analysis of Simon and Ando has been extended to nonlinear systems in the engineering literature (Peponides and Kokotovic 1983); see also Amey (1984a).

Something like the structural decomposition proposed by Simon and Ando is found in decentralized organizations constituted in the multidivisional form (M-form), the purpose of which is to make a clear separation between high-level planning, strategy-making, and broad overall control on one hand and day-to-day operating decisions on the other. Most of the largest U.S. corporations have M-form structures. Observation suggests, however, that the hierarchical decomposition principle described above is not fully put into effect in these large corporations. Operating divisions have limited autonomy in matters related to their operations, incentive systems align divisional and corporate objectives very imperfectly, structure tends to be too inflexible for long-run adaptation, and planning fails to take account of the organization's system properties and gives insufficient attention to the long-run dynamics of the firm.

After studying a large number of organizations, Forrester (1975) concluded that social systems often behave counterintuitively over the long run. Actions taken to solve problems yield positive and intended results in the short run, but often make the problem worse in the long run. It is possible that at least part of the reason for this "devious and diabolical" behavior is due to the fact that social systems, which are weakly coupled, may exhibit behaviors of widely differing speeds, and that the "fast" and "slow" behaviors must be distinguished and their interrelationships understood if actions taken in the short run are not to prove dysfunctional, as Forrester claims to have found. (There are, of course, a number of other possible explanations of the counterintuitive phenomenon.)

Whether a particular organization can be characterized as nearly decomposable depends on how good an approximation one insists on. In the earlier representation of a linear system, this would mean how small ε is required to be. Simon (1969) maintains that almost all complex systems are structured hierarchically, that hierarchies have a property of near decomposability that simplifies their description and makes their behavior easier to understand, and that near decomposability is generally very prominent in biological and social systems.

Recognition that organizations that are nearly decomposable in form exhibit behaviors of different speeds, and that the "fast" local dynamics can be disconnected from the "slow" systemwide dynamics, has important implications for planning and for the design of control strategies.

Deciding on the organization structure and when to restructure are among the lower-frequency decisions that should receive adequate attention from the top levels of the hierarchy. If an organization is not loosely coupled—if the interactions between subsystems are not weak—it can often be made so by changing the organization structure, that is, by treating organizational design as a decision variable in the organization's optimization problem. For a profit-maximizing firm, Williamson (1981) sees the optimization problem as maximizing $\pi\ (Q,\ D;\ f) = P(Q,\ D)Q -$ production and transaction costs, where π denotes profit, Q output, D organizational design, f the existing design, and P the demand function.

Talking about loosely coupled systems reminds us of the discussion of a system's degree of integration in Chapter 2, where we saw that there is an inverse relationship between the degree of system complexity and the degree of integration. Some degree of integration and centralization is indispensable in order to secure the advantages of organization—coordination to maintain consistency of actions and a degree of stability, availability of expert staff with special expertise, and the bearing of ultimate responsibility. But against this must be set the costs of a high degree of integration and centralization—rigidities in the subsystems, lack of sufficient time for planning, strategy- and policy-making— because senior management is inundated with day-to-day problems. Provided that the high-frequency operating units are appropriately grouped, loose coupling and decentralization along multidivisional lines appear to offer a reasonably efficient tradeoff for many large firms.

In the previous chapter it was remarked that there is a strong interrelationship between organization structure and information structure. But we have seen that organization structure is partly (probably mainly) determined by the environment, and the environment is constantly changing. To adapt and survive, the organization's speed and direction of change must approximate those of the environment. This may require changes in organization structure. In practice, however, we find that firms change their organization structure only very infrequently. Consequently, a mismatch may develop between the information structure (decision structure) and the outmoded administrative structure. If this happens the organization can either be restructured and aligned with the information structure or, if the existing organization structure is retained, some means must be found to bridge the gap, a means of translating information from the decision structure format to the old administrative-bureaucratic format. This latter course results in substantially increased information costs. The former alternative is usually to be preferred, therefore, providing it justifies itself in cost-benefit terms. There may be situations in which sudden drastic changes in organization structure would lead to open revolt by employees. Therefore restructuring, if undertaken, usually has to be gradual. A further problem is that the organization structure that is most desirable for planning and decision-making may be less desirable for control, where something like the traditional administrative structure may be more suitable. Some relief from this formidable set of problems comes from the fact that restructuring is typically a gradual process, necessary only for long-run adaptation, and that it mostly concerns peripheral units of the organization, those at the interface with the environment, and less frequently the technical core (operating units).

Some conclusions

Although we still have much to learn about organizations and their functioning, a few conclusions may be drawn from the foregoing discussion. The most important of these is that organization structure should be regarded as a variable in planning and decision-making, not suppressed, as in the neoclassical theory of the firm in economics. As an open system, an organization's structure and information structure are largely determined by the environment, although both must serve internal needs as well. To have superior adaptive properties an organization must selectively map the environment into its information structure or its own structure. In the short run this mapping is probably for the most part into the information structure; in the long run the system's success in regulating itself and adapting critically depends on its ability to map the environment into organization structure. Anticipating Chapter 9, in control terms the law of requisite variety is limited to the short run; in the long run it is organization structure that is important (Sahal, 1982).

If an organization may be approximately described as nearly decomposable, the organization structure should effect a sharp separation between planning, strategy- and policy-making activities, and operating activities. The organization design should also reflect the functional and social needs of the system, and the need to coordinate subunits and to keep employee morale high. The existing organization structure may reflect power relationships within the organization, the effects of which may not always be to promote effective adaptation. Organization structure will be influenced by, and influence, the information structure. The latter may resist change or alert the organization to the need for change, which may take the form of restructuring. Both the information and the organization structures should be such as to encourage, within limits, individual initiative, experimentation, innovation, and allow a range of discretion to decision-makers.

8

Value and Cost

Many of the problems encountered in managing an organization, particularly a business organization, are economic, or at least have an economic dimension; and many of these problems call for the use of accounting data. Throughout economics, accounting, and finance the terms *value* and *cost* recur, with a variety of different meanings. This would be bewildering enough to the uninitiated, but to make matters worse, even professionals misuse some of the terms (e.g., speaking of "joint costs" when common costs is intended, or using "variable" and "indirect" cost interchangeably). Some preliminary guidance in this area is therefore desirable, even for students who have done some economics or accounting. The variety of different meanings of *value* and *cost* is recognized by putting these terms in quotation marks.

Value

It should be stated at the outset that we will be talking about *economic* values since ethics, for example, is also concerned with values in the sense of the relative desirabilities of various ends. Moral value, social value, and sentimental value are distinct from economic value, by which we mean the value of the *property* interests in things. Although it is seldom mentioned in economics texts nowadays (Debreu, 1959, is an exception, but this is a mathematically advanced book), the theory of value is the central core of economics. From believing initially that value (in exchange) was determined wholly by the relative cost of production (supply side), then wholly by relative marginal utilities (demand side), it fell to Marshall to effect a synthesis. Marshall showed that value is jointly

This chapter has benefited from access to an unpublished note by D. A. Egginton, to whom the usual disclaimer applies.

determined by *marginal* cost of production and *marginal* utility (i.e., by supply and demand). Marshall said, "We might as reasonably dispute whether it is the upper or the under blade of a pair of scissors that cuts a piece of paper, as whether [exchange] value is governed by utility or cost of production," adding that in general, the shorter the period considered, the greater the influence of demand on value, and the longer the period the greater the influence of cost of production (Marshall 1920). The "paradox of value," which had held up the development of economics from 1776 (Adam Smith) to 1870 (Jevons, a precursor of Marshall), arose because economists confused value in use (= total utility) with marginal utility, where *total utility* refers to the total satisfaction derived by an individual from the total stock of a good consumed or held, and *marginal utility* refers to the satisfaction obtained from the last unit acquired. Diamonds are higher-valued than water on most occasions because the marginal utility associated with additional units of diamonds declines less rapidly than the marginal utility of additional units of water.

It is not our purpose here to delve further into the history of economic thought. Marshall left some things fuzzy, and wherever relevant we will comment on these as we proceed. In this chapter, unless otherwise stated, we will be concerned with exchange value (= market price), determined by the interaction of large numbers of buyers and sellers in a market. It represents the price that goods would fetch or the price at which they could be replaced, providing in each case that the seller's/buyer's action has no perceptible effect on the price. Note that exchange value times the number of units of a good bought/sold does not represent value either in the sense of total utility or in the sense of the maximum price an individual would be prepared to pay. In Marshall's scheme all the data for the determination of exchange value are interpreted as objectively given: marginal utilities in the form of the demand functions of all buyers, and the cost of production of all producers in the form of money costs (what we shall later call "outlay costs"). This elimination of all subjectivity is, as we shall see, not possible in general.

Finally, it should be noted that it is difficult to make a clear distinction between "value" and "a valuation." "Value" is often used to indicate market-determined value (exchange value), although it is not invariably confined to this case. The two terms are often used interchangeably, and we will follow this convention here.

Value for what purpose?

The question, What is the value of good or property X? is quite meaningless. To give it meaning we have to ask the *purpose* for which the value is required, the *time and place,* and the individual or entity *for whom* its value is to be determined. For a more detailed discussion of value, readers are referred to Bonbright (1965), which is the standard work on this subject.

The same property may simultaneously have different values for different purposes. Thus the "value" of property X to its owner may differ from its market or exchange value, because only its owner is able to exploit the services of this property. It will depend on whether property X is held for resale or not, and if it is, on whether the sale would be made within a reasonable time or under "forced sale" conditions. Moreover, in some cases buying price (entry value, current replacement cost) rather than selling price (net exit value) may be appropriate. Property X will normally be worth at least the net market selling price to its owner, but there are exceptions even here.

Accountants normally "value" assets in a balance sheet at their acquisition cost (historical cost), less depreciation in the case of fixed depreciating assets. In many countries, however, inventories are valued at "the lower of cost or market," which means the smaller of historical cost and current replacement cost. It should be noted that there is no necessary equivalence between the value of a whole and the sum of the values of its parts. In a balance sheet, for example, the sum of the values of the separate assets is not a measure of the value of the firm because, for one reason, a certain value may attach to holding this particular combination of assets over and above the sum of their separate values.

The purposes for which property may need to be valued are numerous. Valuations may be required in order to assess damages from loss of property, or to determine compensation when a government exercises its rights of eminent domain (as when it takes over private land for a highway), for tax purposes, for determination of solvency, in corporate reorganizations and takeovers, to determine income, to determine whether a surplus is available for the payment of dividends, or for utility rate-making purposes. The determination of the appropriate value for each of these purposes has been further complicated by the fact that the courts have often not interpreted "value" consistently in a given type of situation. For example, whereas the courts have been willing to interpret the value of intangible assets, such as goodwill or franchises to the firm that has created them or to someone who contemplates buying them in terms of a capitalization of expected earning power, they have been far less willing to apply this concept of "value" to the tangible assets. In cases where some form of exchange value is the appropriate measure of value for a particular purpose it may, depending on the circumstances, be past or current exchange value, and either actual or imputed exchange value.

Value to whom?

As already stated, a particular property or good may have different values for different individuals. The same applies to a firm, the value of which to its owners (shareholders) will usually differ from the value of the firm regarded as an entity, its value from the viewpoint of management. To the individual shareholder, the value of his holding in the firm is the current selling price of the shares in the stockmarket times the number of shares held. This is not the case, however, if he is a very large shareholder, because the quoted market price is determined by dealings at the margin; it does not apply to transfers of large blocks of shares. As a result, share prices may be only a rough indication of the value of a holding in a quoted company to the shareholder.

From the firm's viewpoint, value is based on the total assets it owns less liabilities to nonowners. The central concept of value to the firm, regarded as an entity separate from its owners, is the present value of the expected future cash flows arising from its assets and nonownership liabilities. This is the firm's value in the sense that it represents the benefits that would eventually accrue to the shareholders in the form of dividends and adjustment of the market price of the shares *if* the firm's expectations prove correct. The present value of an asset is made up of the future exchange value of the inputs and outputs associated with its use, as estimated by the management, and the net exit value of the asset (its net resale or salvage value) at the end of its working life, all discounted to the present.

However attractive theoretically, this concept of value is impractical, involving as it does not only the estimation of future cash flows (theoretically over the entire life of the firm) and their distribution through time, but also the conceptually difficult problem of deciding on the correct rate of interest at which to discount these future cash flows. The present value concept is consistently applied in determining the "economic income" of a firm, another concept that is mainly of academic interest. But while this concept of value from the firm's viewpoint runs into formidable practical difficulties, and assumes that the firm is run solely for the benefit of shareholders (which is seldom entirely true), present value is useful in relation to other measures of value for determining what should be done with assets. This question is discussed later in the chapter under "Cost." We turn now to a consideration of some of these other more practical measures of "value."

Valuation of the firm in accounting

In their financial reporting, firms have to assign values to assets (property already acquired) and to (nonownership) claims against these assets. This must perforce be done on a basis that can be widely understood. The accounting profession and the law have interpreted this as meaning that there is a premium on objectivity; the question of the conceptual validity of the measure of "value" adopted (indeed whether it measures "value" in any meaningful sense at all) is thrown to the winds. Meeting this test of objectivity may put all of the value concepts mentioned in question, not just present value. For highly specific assets acquired some time ago there may be no current counterpart; and exchange value ceases to be objective when there is no active competitive market for an asset.

In practice the "values" that appear in balance sheets for various types of assets are based on conventions dictated by professional accounting bodies. In the main these values are current exchange values, either "entry value" (buying price, called *replacement cost* in accounting) or "exit value" (called *net realizable value* in accounting). The overriding valuation principle in accounting is past entry value (historical cost), less depreciation where relevant. Exit value may be used for inventories if it is less than historical cost (but not if it exceeds historical cost). The emphasis is on conservatism and financial prudence rather than on finding a conceptually defensible measure of "value."

Present purposes would not be served by exploring the vast subject of "value" more deeply; this task took Bonbright (1965) 1,198 pages to accomplish. It is sufficient if the reader remembers to be careful with this term, and that it only has meaning if we ask, for what, for whom, when and where?

Cost

If "value" is a highly ambiguous word, "cost" is no less so. Like "value," "cost" is not independent of the purpose for which it is required. "Cost" is also relative to rate of output, the time available to produce that output (an order for 1,000 units to be delivered by the end of the month will vary in cost from the same quantity produced over six months), and sometimes place. The relation of cost to the moment of decision is particularly important—"cost" before and after this moment are *conceptually* different things. To the student of business organizations, "cost" must be understood with more adjectives prefixed to it than "value." It seems hardly necessary to say that "value" and "cost" are two quite distinct concepts; yet, as we shall see, in one very important case, "cost" cannot be defined independently of "value."

Let us begin the task of threading our way through the multiplicity of meanings of "cost" by distinguishing between the use of the term in accounting and in economics. In accounting, "cost" is roughly synonymous with "expense" (under the usual accounting convention, "expense" is distinguished from "asset" in that the resources acquired are entirely consumed within the accounting period—usually one year—in the former case, whereas in the latter case something of value remains, although clearly it is difficult to fit certain items of expense, such as depreciation, to this definition). Accounting costs comprise outlay costs, those like labor costs that result in a cash outlay, and non-outlay or "book" costs, such as depreciation, bad debts. The influence of accounting conventions and taxation regulations results in some investment (capital expenditure) being treated as a current cost; examples are research and development expenditure and part of advertising outlays.

Cost ex ante

The distinction between "cost" in accounting and in economics cannot be taken further until another distinction is made, that between "cost" ex ante and "cost" ex post. *Cost ex ante* means estimated cost, cost before the moment of decision. These are *decision-determining* costs. *Cost ex post* refers to the actual cost incurred after a decision has been taken; these costs are *decision-determined*.

Returning now to the accounting and economics viewpoints, there is no essential difference between the two with respect to cost ex post, except that accounting convention and practice fails to make a clear distinction between current costs and investment expenditures. The difference concerns the meaning of cost ex ante. In accounting there is a tendency (particularly among professional accountants) to define "cost" in the same way ex ante and ex post, and irrespective of the purpose for which the cost is required. The accountant is also prone to include in ex ante cost items called "sunk costs," expenditures associated with the action now being contemplated which have already been incurred and which now cannot be avoided. In a more generous interpretation, accountants sometimes take ex ante costs to be the costs that appear in their budgets. There is a subtle difference here between budgeted costs and the costs that are decision-determining or decision-relevant. For while the costs that appear in accounting budgets, once they are finalized, are still ex ante in the sense of being "before the event" (they are still only estimates of costs which have not been incurred yet), these costs are decision-determined rather than decision-determining. They refer to the estimated expense of carrying out some action that has already been decided on (subject, of course, to possible revision of the budgets before the costs are incurred). We could call them *ex ante post-decision costs*.

To the economist, "cost ex ante" means *opportunity* (or alternative) *cost,* the highest-valued alternative foregone by choosing a particular course of action. That is, to be worth pursuing, the benefits minus outlay costs from choosing one alternative must not be less than the net benefits given up by not selecting the next best alternative. An example will make this clearer. Suppose I am considering whether to use certain resources to do A or B or nothing at all. The resources, consisting of materials and labor, required to undertake A may be acquired in the market for $\$c_A$, and those required for B for $\$c_B$. If used for A, the output can be sold for $\$r_A$, and if used for B for $\$r_B$. Market prices are accepted as an approximation to the opportunity costs of resources acquired through the market (see Amey, 1973, as to why they are only an approximation). Suppose the net receipts from doing nothing are zero, and that $\$(r_B - c_B)$ is positive. Then it will be worth selecting alternative A if $\$(r_A - c_A)$ is greater than $\$(r_B - c_B)$, or $\$[r_A - c_A - (r_B - c_B)]$ is positive. This can be stated as follows:

economic cost ex ante = opportunity cost

$\qquad\qquad\qquad$ = avoidable outlay costs + the implicit opportunity costs of any resources not represented by outlay costs

where the avoidable outlay costs of A for materials and labor are c_A, and the implicit opportunity cost of choosing A rather than B or zero is $(r_B - c_B)$. Both $(r_B - c_B)$ and c_A are opportunity costs; we could call c_A the explicit opportunity cost of choosing A. The first is subjective, the second objective. The implicit opportunity cost is subjective because it exists only in the mind of the decision-maker and is not objectively observable. It is what *he* takes to be the next best payoff. The implicit part of opportunity cost may be positive, negative, or zero.

A moment's reflection should assure the reader that inclusion of implicit opportunity costs in the data of a decision problem is a matter of convenience, not of necessity. We would obtain the same result (select the same preferred alternative) if we arrayed all the (feasible) alternatives in terms of objective quantities (receipts and avoidable outlay costs) and chose the alternative that maximizes $(r_i - c_i)$, $i = 1, \ldots, n$. (This statement is not quite true. To make it general we would have to remove the word "avoidable" before outlay costs, in the above statement and in the definition of economic cost ex ante in the previous paragraph. This modification is necessary to allow for the explicit introduction of uncertainty into the formulation of the decision problem, as discussed later.)

The conceptual difference between costs before and after the moment of decision, referred to earlier, lies in the fact that the first component of opportunity costs, outlay costs, will eventually become ex post costs, but the second component, implicit opportunity cost, vanishes at the moment of choice. It is only a cost ex ante.

Decision-relevant costs

The costs that determine choices merit a section of their own because not all ex ante costs are decision-relevant. Ex ante costs may be pre- or post-decision, as already noted, and of course only the former are decision-relevant. Thus decision-relevant costs are a subset of ex ante costs. *Pre*-decision ex ante costs are exemplified by the correctly specified costs for decision purposes, including what is meant by "cost" in the neoclassical theory of the firm *in the long run* ("cost" here includes implicit opportunity cost). Examples of *post*-decision ex ante costs are the costs appearing in accounting budgets and in the neoclassical theory of the firm *in the short run* (the argument here is that the short-run theory is a predictive theory, not a theory of choice; see Amey, 1986, ch. 5, for a fuller discussion). A second reason for treating decision-relevant costs separately is that it is necessary to discuss the role of "fixed" costs in decision-making. Do decision-relevant costs include "fixed" costs or not? The term "fixed costs" is used here in a broader sense than that used in accounting, where it means those costs that are constant in total over some relevant range of output. As used here, *"fixed"* or *shared costs* means costs that are constant over all the alternatives being considered. The constancy may thus relate to a time interval as well as an output interval. To avoid ambiguity it will be better to refer to these costs hereafter as *shared costs*. In this sense shared cost is the opposite of incremental cost. There may be receipts as well as costs that are shared by all alternatives. The question arises as to whether these shared costs and/ or receipts should be included in the decision data.

The answer to this question depends on whether or not the decision is subject to uncertainty, more precisely on whether uncertainty is recognized explicitly in formulating the decision problem. In conditions of certainty the alternatives will be identically ranked and the same alternative chosen whether we consider incremental amounts alone (the costs and receipts that would change if we chose the alternative in question) or total amounts (incremental plus shared amounts). The difference arises when the decision is subject to uncertainty. Dillon and Nash (1978) conclude that in conditions of uncertainty, the total approach should be used if (i) the decision-maker's attitude to risk is explicitly represented in the decision problem in the form of a utility function (decisions under certainty are independent of the form of the utility function); (ii) the utility function, reflecting the decision-maker's risk preferences at different levels of monetary return, is nonlinear; and (iii) the size of the shared costs/receipts is large enough to expose significant nonlinearities in the utility function. Conditions (ii) and (iii) together cause the addition/subtraction of a constant to/from a given dollar amount to bring a significant change in utility.

Dillon and Nash's three conditions as to when shared amounts should be included in the decision data are not quite the whole truth. A more rigorous analysis has been made by Ekern and Bøhren (1979). The nature of the problem may be displayed by letting x_i, y_i, and z be random variables expressed in money such that $x_i = y_i + z$ holds for all decision alternatives, where x_i is the total amount (of costs, benefits, or net benefits, as the case may be); y_i is the incremental amount; z is the shared amounts, constant over all alternatives; and i identifies decision alternatives ($i = 1, \ldots$).

In essence, the problem is to find the cases in which a ranking of alternatives based on distributions of x_i is consistent with a ranking using marginal distributions of y_i. If the decision-maker's utility function is linear in money (implying risk-neutrality), an expected monetary value (EMV) criterion may be used without fear of distorting the rankings. If the utility function is nonlinear (implying risk-aversion or risk-seeking) an expected utility criterion is appropriate and EMV will usually be inappropriate.

Ekern and Bøhren show that:

(i) Rankings of decision alternatives based on total and incremental amounts may, in general, be inconsistent under uncertainty
(ii) The incremental approach is correct if the utility function is linear in money *and* the shared amounts are constant within states
(iii) The total approach is needed if
   (a) The utility function is linear but the shared amounts are not constant within states, or
   (b) the utility function is nonlinear, and the incremental and shared amounts are not statistically independent, and if inclusion of the shared amounts exposes significant nonlinearities in the utility function
(iv) Both approaches yield consistent rankings if
   (a) the utility function is linear and the shared amounts are constant within states, or
   (b) the utility function is nonlinear, the incremental and shared amounts are statistically independent, and inclusion of the shared amounts does not expose significant nonlinearities.

An example illustrating case (iii) (a) appears in the Mathematical Appendix.

An excellent treatment of decision-relevant costs from an information economics standpoint appears in Demski and Feltham (1976, chs. 3 and 4).

Costs in relation to output

Costs may also be described according to their behavior in relation to changes in output. *Variable costs* are those that remain (approximately) constant per unit with changes in output, *fixed costs* those that are constant in total over the relevant range of output. Fixed costs are a subset of the more general category of shared costs. In accounting, variable costs are those that vary in (approximately) direct proportion to output; in economics the term *variable* does not necessarily imply linearity in this relationship. Another category, called *separable fixed costs,* are fixed costs that become discontinuously variable at output zero, as when some segment of the business is closed down.

The role of ex ante fixed costs as just defined in decisions concerning the determination of output (or price) or any other decision involving a change in output parallels that of shared costs as already discussed. Under certainty, fixed costs are not decision-relevant, or rather it makes no difference whether they are considered or not. Under uncertainty, when a number of output alternatives are being considered, costs that are constant in total over the relevant range of output are the same for all alternatives (i.e., they are shared costs). As such their decision-relevance is governed by the rules listed above.

Besides also being shared costs in decisions involving output changes, fixed costs in the accounting sense may be described as unavoidable costs. That is, these costs are the same in total whether, say, 1,000 units or 10,000 units are produced per period of time. It is worth noting that it is not only in relation to changes in output that certain costs are unavoidable. Some costs may be unavoidable in relation to a time interval; for example, a certain expense may result from a commitment (such as the terms of an employment contract) that makes the expense unavoidable for three months, say, but avoidable thereafter. Other items of expense may be unavoidable if an order has to be produced very quickly, say within a month, but avoidable if the order may be produced over a longer period.

A further category of "fixed" costs is the case of *joint costs.* Joint production refers to the situation where several different products are produced from the same raw material or materials. Oil refining is an example. Crude oil is partially refined (jointly processed); then further processing may be undertaken to convert this intermediate product or feedstock into gasoline, heating oil, petrochemicals, and so on. All costs up to the point ("split-off point") at which a decision must be taken on whether to finish the first final product in the production sequence are called *joint costs* (although there may be more than one split-off point). They include the costs of materials and joint processing, and are incurred for the benefit of all the joint products. Figure 8.1 illustrates this situation.

A different kind of example of joint production which will not be discussed here is the case of production over time, in which investment in productive capacity is the counterpart of a common raw material. The production in different time periods can be regarded as the joint product of this productive capacity; see S. C. Littlechild (1970) for further discussion.

Joint costs are "fixed" (unavoidable) in a special sense. To explain, suppose each unit of material that is jointly processed to the split-off point is sufficient to yield (after further processing) two units of product A and one unit each of B and C. The joint costs are "fixed" in the sense that the cost of A (or B or C) can only be avoided by not producing *A, B, and C.* Hence they are subject to the above rules concerning the decision-relevance of shared costs. Joint costs may include costs that are variable or fixed in relation to output.

The decisions that arise with joint production are (i) whether to operate the joint process; (ii) at what level to operate it to achieve the firm's objective (such as profit maximization), and (iii) once the process has reached the split-off point, whether to finish each of the joint products. Under certainty, the joint costs are decision-relevant in the first two cases, and usually irrelevant in the third (at the split-off point they are "sunk" costs). In (ii) and (iii) a further condition is that a product should be finished only if the additional costs beyond the split-off point are less than the additional revenue from sale of the finished product over selling or disposing of the intermediate product at the split-off point. Under uncertainty, the rules for shared costs stated earlier apply in decision (ii); in (i) the joint costs are decision-relevant (the criterion there is that total revenue must exceed total costs, or its expected utility equivalent); in (iii) they are usually irrelevant because they are "sunk" costs.

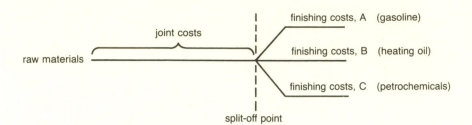

FIGURE 8.1. Joint production.

An exception to the conclusion that joint costs are irrelevant in (iii) under certainty or uncertainty will now be noted. It arises from the fact that it will not always be optimal to finish and sell joint products in the same technologically determined proportions in which they are produced. In this situation the joint costs will be decision-relevant (i.e., part of the additional costs) in (iii) for the product that (most) exceeds its production proportion. The last unit of material jointly processed is in this case processed solely for the benefit of one product; the joint costs are no longer joint. The additional costs of finishing the last unit of this product stretch right back to the beginning of the joint process. In this situation it will be optimal to sell or dispose of some units of the other products at the split-off point. For a fuller analysis of joint product decisions with worked examples, see Amey (1984b, 1985).

Some writers misuse the term *joint costs* to mean what we later refer to as indirect, overhead, or common cost. The two cases are different and should be distinguished. In the former case the cost cannot be avoided unless production of *all* products is stopped; this is not necessarily so with overhead costs.

Other cost terms that appear frequently in the management literature, usually in relation to ex ante costs, are:

(i) *total, average,* and *marginal cost:* If C is total cost and q denotes number of units produced, average cost is C/q and marginal cost dC/dq. Marginal cost may also be described as the avoidable cost of one additional unit. A nonmarginal change in costs is called incremental cost (ΔC).

(ii) *standard cost:* Predetermined costs used as benchmarks against which actual costs are compared at short intervals (costing periods) for control purposes. The standards usually reflect what management expects costs to be in the year ahead if all work is performed with reasonable efficiency and prices do not behave unpredictably. Although normally established ex ante in practice (i.e., before the events to which they relate have occurred), we could also think of ex post (or hindsight) standards being set at the end of a period. Standard costs are sometimes used in decision-making rather than actual costs.

(iii) The distinction between private costs (those expenses regarded as costs by the firm itself) and social costs has already been referred to in chapter 3.

In estimating costs for planning and decision-making purposes, account may need to be taken of the *learning effect*. In performing a new task or in repeated performances of an old task, workers often increase their efficiency over time, leading to a reduction in the average time required to produce a given output. Average and marginal costs may both increase as output increases beyond a point for other reasons, but the learning effect works in the opposite direction. This reduction in average and marginal cost due to learning is often quite significant and should be taken into account in estimating. Notable examples of the learning effect not being taken into account have occurred in "cost-plus" defense contracting by private firms. For a fuller discussion of the learning effect see Bierman and Dyckman (1976, ch. 10).

Cost ex post

Ex post or actually incurred costs are of interest for performance measurement, control, financial reporting, and as a *guide* to future costs in planning. Several new cost concepts are used in discussing ex post costs.

The variable/fixed cost distinction continues to be useful with respect to ex post costs. In exercising control, if the costs for a particular part of the business are expected to vary with the level of activity, as would be the case with many components of production cost, it is desirable to have a budget (flexible budget) that reflects the expected behavior of costs at the realized activity level. In order to do this it is necessary to divide costs into variable and fixed. If these were indistinguishable in budgeted cost, a comparison of actual with budgeted cost would give a misleading idea of changes in cost due to variations in output.

In practice, accountants often use approximations to the variable cost of a process or unit of product. The usual approximation is *direct cost,* those costs that can be identified with (traced to) the process or product at reasonable cost. The remainder, called *indirect costs,* those that cannot be so traced, are accumulated separately before averaging over processes/units of output. Indirect costs may include some variable costs as well as fixed costs, and are also called *overhead costs.* Terms are used rather loosely, however, and both economists and accountants are inclined to treat overhead costs as fixed costs. Direct plus indirect cost per unit of product is called *total cost.*

The allocation problem

Cost allocation, in its most common usage, refers to the assignment of certain costs to segments of a firm and/or to products as a means of calculating average (and full) product cost. Less commonly the term is also used to include the assignment of costs to time periods; for example, various formulae are available for spreading the acquisition cost of depreciating fixed assets such as machines over their estimated working lives. This latter use of "cost allocation" is a means of giving effect to the accountants' "matching" principle (matching costs against the revenues that they help to generate period by period).

The current costs that are the subject of allocation are indirect costs. These are predominantly costs that are common to a number of products (e.g., the lighting and heating of a factory) and are therefore sometimes called *common costs.* Joint costs are an extreme case of common costs in that, since one joint product cannot be produced (at least up to the split-off point) without the others, it is illogical from an economic point of view to allocate the joint costs to individual products. However, it may be rational to do so for other reasons. For example, if production of the various joint products is the responsibility of different managers, by making the appropriate allocation of the joint costs it is possible to decentralize production in such a way that each of these managers, acting independently, will be led to do what is best for the firm as a whole. The appropriate allocations are obtained as a by-product of the firm's optimization problem. See Amey (1984b, 1985) and Kaplan (1982, 402–404) for demonstrations.

Cost allocations take two basic forms. Allocation of costs between production centers is termed *proration* of costs, and is based on proxy measures of benefits received (e.g., floor space occupied in the case of lighting). This is preceded by allocating all service center costs to production centers. The second stage is termed cost *absorption,* and consists in assigning costs to products in proportion to some measure of activity within the production center (e.g., direct labor-hours or machine-hours spent on the product). Cost absorption involves making an assumption about the expected rate of activity for the year. This is often what accountants call the "normal capacity" of the production center. (Other measures of expected rate of activity are "practical capacity" or budgeted production.) The expected annual indirect costs are then divided by "normal capacity" to form a predetermined cost rate with which indirect costs are loaded onto products. Over- or under-absorbed costs at the end of the year are adjusted in the income statement. Under *standard costing*, which uses predetermined costs (direct as well as indirect) for control purposes, the end-of-year differences between actual and predetermined costs are treated in a similar way.

Controllability of costs

Another classification of ex post costs made for control purposes is that of *controllable* and *noncontrollable costs*. Assignment of costs to production centers is the first stage in the calculation of average (i.e., unit) product cost in a multiproduct firm, but these costs are often used for control purposes also. In this context the production centers are called *responsibility centers*. Consequently, the performance of responsible managers might be judged on costs that include allocated (prorated) costs. But the fact that they are allocated means that the responsibility for incurring them lies elsewhere. The conventional view in accounting is that performance should be judged on controllable costs only, those over which the responsible manager has a significant, although not necessarily complete, degree of control.

This view may be challenged on several grounds. The first is the difficulty of implementation. A cost is the product of price per unit of some input times number of units used. Responsibility for purchasing the input and for deciding how much is used may lie in different responsibility centers. A second reason why such a treatment may not be desirable would be if senior management wishes to use the charging of costs to responsibility centers as a motivating device. Provided the subordinate has control over the quantity of the input used, the inclusion of allocated costs in performance reports and the allocation method would then depend on the desired influence on the behavior of the subordinate.

The question of controllability is bound up with principal–agent relationships, and hence with questions of incentives and risk-sharing (Chapter 10). Under certain contractual arrangements it can turn out that the optimal contract between principal and agent involves introducing a noncontrollable outcome and cost into the agent's incentive function. But unless it is believed that part of the agent's duty is to share the risks of the owners or the senior management, this point is debatable. Kaplan (1982, 612) argues that managers are not typically hired for their desirable risk-sharing abilities, and that it is only in situations of a single principal and a single agent that the agent needs to share risks as well as make decisions. Zimmerman (1979) has offered the rationale that the allocation of noncontrollable costs could be regarded as a lump-sum tax to reduce the discretionary spending of the agent. Readers should also note that "controllability" as used here in the accounting sense is not the same as controllability in the modern control theory sense (Chapter 9).

Costs and values in financial reporting

In the reporting of financial position and income by firms (in balance sheets and income statements) we find a mixture of costs and values and of time viewpoints (past, present, future). Costs and values may also be expressed in nominal or in real terms or somewhere in between, that is, they may be adjusted for changes in the general price level and/or for specific price changes.

Like classical economics, the traditional and most pervasive basis of valuation used by accountants is cost-based; it is also related to the past. At least in financial reporting outside the firm, the most commonly used valuation principle is *historical cost*, the outlay for which an asset was acquired. Fixed depreciating assets that yield benefits over several accounting periods are depreciated or amortized by charging the expired portion of their cost against revenues year by year in calculating income. While historical cost is economically indefensible as a valuation principle (except possibly at the date of purchase), accountants are reluctant to give it up. They justify their position by pointing out that it has the virtue of objectivity and verifiability, and accountants are much more vulnerable to lawsuits over their results or the financial statements they give their seal of approval than are economists. Moreover, in most legal jurisdictions, realized income (essentially the difference between historical cost and revenue) provides the fund available for permissible dividend distribution.

Even among its most ardent supporters, the historical cost convention does get modified in practice, however. Thus recognition is given to losses, but not gains, on current assets in the common rule of the "lower of cost or market value" for valuing inventories. The unamortized cost of fixed assets is usually amended only when there is a significant change in the estimated life of the asset (due, for example, to technological change), although in periods of rapid inflation many firms recognize the appreciation of fixed asset values in the accounts.

The widespread and continuing inflation that has occurred since the 1970s has dramatically highlighted the inherent weaknesses of historical cost as a valuation principle. The most widely adopted substitute is *replacement cost* (also termed *current cost*) accounting (RC), the price at which an asset could currently be replaced, a present entry exchange value. The use of this basis of valuation is not without difficulties, however. For example, should it mean the cost of replacing the actual asset held, or of acquiring a technologically improved asset capable of producing the same volume of output, or one capable of producing the same value of output? There is also the problem of obtaining replacement cost data for assets that are no longer traded, or are traded rarely or in different form. Another school of thought advocates adoption of a selling price valuation system. This is called *net realizable value* (NRV), and represents the estimated price at which the asset would currently sell, less any expenses of sale.

Economists would use *present value* (PV) as the basis of asset valuation in financial reporting. This is the highest value of the estimated discounted net cash flows arising from all alternative future deployments of the asset. Many accountants would regard the subjectivity of PV as inappropriate in published accounting reports, and there are problems in disentangling the cash flows to determine the PV of a single asset employed in combination with other assets.

Thus we see that in financial reporting, especially reporting outside the firm, the approach to valuation is a peculiar mixture of costs and values and of time periods.

In addition to their use as surrogate valuations in financial reporting, ex post costs may also be relevant in decisions concerning the disposition of assets (sell, hold, use, buy). The six possible relationships between the three valuation principles discussed above (RC, NRV, PV) and their implications for decision purposes and asset value to the firm are summarized below:

Relationship	Decision implication	Asset value to the firm given by:
NRV > PV > RC NRV > RC > PV	Buy for resale	RC
PV > RC > NRV PV > NRV > RC	Buy to use or hold	
RC > NRV > PV	Sell and don't replace	NRV
RC > PV > NRV	Retain	PV

It should be noted that RC is not a consistently reliable indicator of value to the firm in all circumstances. There is also the question of alternative deployments of an asset within the firm, and in this respect Keynes (1949) made a distinction between what he termed *user cost* and *retainer cost*. The latter includes the costs of owning an asset and holding it idle (e.g., a certain amount of physical deterioration occurs even if an asset is not used; there may also be obsolescence); the former includes the costs of using the asset (running costs, maintenance, repairs). In choosing between alternative uses of an asset, that use which yields the greatest excess of net receipts over user cost should be chosen. Variations in the rate of use of an asset in different periods affect estimates of the asset's economic life and should in principle affect the amount of depreciation. In practice, however, depreciation tends to be related entirely to age of the asset (which implies retainer cost), although the equally arbitrary assumption of relating depreciation entirely to use is sometimes adopted. Nevertheless, accountants usually regard depreciation as an entirely fixed cost.

9

Control and "Performance"

In this chapter we will be concerned with the "performance" of an organization and its parts—with what it means, and how to measure it—and with coordinating its activities to ensure that they are effective and/or efficient. This is generally referred to as the area of performance measurement and control. Before discussing these topics it is worth noting certain relations and interrelations between performance and control and other organizational activities or features. In chapters 6 and 7 it was noted that an organization's structure and information system are strongly interrelated. The literatures of agency theory (Chapter 10) and markets and hierarchies (Chapter 7) draw attention to the interdependence between information, structure, and control. These relations will be discussed in this and the following chapter. Information and performance are also mutually related—an organizational information system does not merely report on performance; it shapes it, and is in turn shaped by it (Lawler and Rhode 1976). Finally, control and performance may be interrelated, although not all forms of control are related to performance. Actual performance often determines the control measures taken, while the form of control system in operation and the mere fact that participants' actions are observed frequently affect performance. But this tangle of interrelationships cannot be discussed further without stating precisely what we mean by "performance" and "control." We begin with "performance."

"Performance"

As with a number of other words, the use of the term "performance" in the literature is sloppy, its meaning often treated as synonymous with "observed results" of actions or even with work effort. The first thing to note therefore is that "performance" is a relation, the relation between observed results and desired or expected results. This relation is sometimes expressed as a ratio (engineering), sometimes as a difference (accounting). The "performance" relation may also be defined either as a measure of effectiveness or as a measure of efficiency. By the first is meant the relation between observed results and some predetermined task. "Efficiency," on the other hand, implies a principle of economy: that activity is most efficient which, at a given level of operation, requires the least expenditure of money on inputs per unit of output. It is a relation between inputs and outputs. As an example, if the task is to build a stone wall in one week, the budgeted cost for which is $500, and at the end of the week the wall is 75 percent complete at a cost of $300, "performance" is efficient but not effective. "Performance" can be effective and/or efficient.

"Performance" also means different things to different people. Consider the performance of a business enterprise. In accounting this is measured in relation to internal norms—desired results in the form of budgets or standards set by management. To an economist, "performance" is judged by reference to an external norm. A firm is considered a failure if its realized results fall short of those expected to be available elsewhere, after making appropriate allowance for differences in risk. It is a failure in the sense that, had this been foreseen, the firm would not have been established or kept in operation. By contrast with the accounting and economic viewpoints, in a general financial and legal sense "performance" does not involve expectations. A business is a failure if it is unable to meet certain claims on it to pay money and has become involved in certain legal consequences (i.e., the firm is insolvent). A firm may be a success (failure) in the economic sense without being a success (failure) in the financial sense, and good "performance" in the accounting sense may not be good in the economic sense.

Frame of reference

But all of these ways of defining "performance" are narrow. Ultimately, what we mean by "performance" must depend on how we view the organization, and here we return to the three ways of looking at an organization discussed in Chapter 7: the rational, natural, and open systems views. Our point of departure here is that many different constituencies have an interest in the "performance" of an organization. No single measure can reflect how well each of these different constituencies considers the organization is doing, and different constituencies will have different criteria for organizational effectiveness. Each of the three ways of regarding an organization results in multiple criteria for assessing "performance"; it cannot be captured in a single measure.

The rational system model views the organization as an instrument for the attainment of specific goals. Performance criteria would here include measures of output and sales, product quality, productivity, efficiency (cost per unit), and profitability in relation to the corresponding goals, which would usually be internal norms determined by management ex ante. The natural system model views an organization as seeking to achieve specific goals but also undertaking activities required to maintain itself as a social unit. To the rational system criteria, this view would add a set of support goals. These would include measures of the satisfaction and morale of participants—measures of whether the inducements offered by the organization are sufficient to call forth contributions from participants sufficient to ensure the survival of the organization as a social unit: the interpersonal skills of managers, and survival itself (Scott 1981, 318–21). Under the natural system view, these support goals take precedence over the rational system goals whenever the two are in conflict; the overriding goal is survival of the organization. The open system model adds the further perspective of interdependence of the organization and its environment. This emphasizes the importance of system-elaborating activities, such as information acquisition and processing, and changes in organization structure designed to detect and respond to changes in the environment. Additional criteria for this view would call for measures of flexibility and adaptability.

It is clear, then, that the meaning of "performance" will vary with the frame of reference, depending on whether we focus on an organization's impact on individual participants, or on the organization itself, or see it in relation to systems external to itself, recalling from Chapter 2 that any system should be viewed as part of a three-tiered hierarchy—the system, its parts, and its environment. Ideally, all three should be taken into account in measuring organizational "performance"; we should combine the rational, natural, and open system views.

Accounting measures of "performance"

To the layperson, businessperson, and student of business administration, accounting measures of "performance" are the most familiar. These take the form of incurred cost of operating a department or process in relation to standard cost, indirect costs incurred in relation to standard or budgeted cost, and profits in relation to budget, either in absolute terms or as a rate of return on capital employed. The first kind of measures apply to "cost centers," the last to "profit centers" and "investment centers" (see Chapter 8), depending on whether the manager of the responsibility center has the authority to incur costs, earn revenues and incur costs, or undertake limited capital investment in addition to these.

In their role as plans, budgets establish the framework within which decisions are subsequently taken and act as a coordinating device. (In practice, plans are seldom revised as circumstances change, and are frequently ignored.) The same budgets frequently act as performance targets for control purposes. If the planning budgets and control budgets are not identical, the differences between the two are resolved by introducing "budgeted variances" in the income statement. The control budgets form the basis of the accounting technique known as *budgetary control*. If a firm employs standard costing as well as budgetary control, the standards are usually incorporated in the budgets. The two techniques of budgetary control and standard costing have the same essential purpose, namely of predetermining costs or revenues, comparing incurred (realized) costs (revenues) with the predetermined amounts, analyzing the deviations (called "variances") between the two, and either taking action to minimize significant unfavorable variances (more on the interpretation of "significant" later) or revising the predetermined amounts if such corrective action is not possible. In practice, standard costing is usually confined to cost items, although the technique is equally applicable to revenue items (sales revenue).

Which costs are the subject of budgets and which of standard costs depends on whether the costs in question are "engineered" costs or "programmed" or managed costs. *Engineered costs* refers to items in respect of which it is possible to determine fairly accurately what the "right" amount of expenditure should be. Direct production costs usually qualify, and standards are established for these. *Programmed costs* refers to activities where it is difficult or impossible to determine the "right" amount of expenditure in a given period—items such as advertising expenditure, research and development expenditure, or public relations. A programmed budget is established by a senior executive periodically making a judgment as to how much should be spent on these items. The programmed budget will include most nonmanufacturing overhead costs and may also include manufacturing overheads.

In both budgetary control and standard costing, then, "performance" is measured in terms of differences—the deviations of observed from predetermined results. It is fairly obvious that the significance of "performance" measured in this way depends crucially on what the predetermined performance targets represent. If they have been determined optimally, the performance measures derived from them will be measures of efficiency. In practice, the targets are not of this kind, but usually represent what results (output, costs, revenues) should be if work is performed with reasonable efficiency, and unforeseen events do not supervene. Such targets are described as "currently attainable" in accounting, and the measurement of "performance" against them is in no way to be taken as a measure of efficiency. It is possible that control systems based on the "principle of exceptions" may give too much attention to the dispersion and not enough to the mean, the control target. As Arrow (1964a) has observed, "Dispersion is not bad in itself; it is only bad because it may and usually does indicate a policy which will also lead to intolerably low average characteristics. But we must not overlook the more fundamental importance of the average characteristics."

The traditional accounting method measures "performance" as the difference between actual (observed) results and those shown by plans drawn up before the events of the period occur (i.e., ex ante plans). The standards in a budgetary control system then serve two purposes: as targets for subordinates to strive for, and as an evaluation yardstick in measuring "performance." Demski (1967) has argued that the latter purpose would be better served by comparing observed results with what he calls "ex post standards." That is, after all the events of the period have occurred and their outcomes are known, ex post or hindsight plans would be drawn up, showing what actions should have been taken and what should have been accomplished if the firm had possessed perfect information at the beginning of the period and had acted optimally on it. The argument here is that if the firm wants to encourage adaptive behavior, part of the task of adapting is to foresee opportunities and threats and prepare for them in advance. The measure of "performance" should include this forecasting and planning aspect of the firm's activities.

Critique of accounting performance measurement

A strong case can thus be made for measuring performance against ex post standards. The resulting measure reflects the ability to predict and plan as well as to implement the plan. The feedback of performance data measured in this way should, over a number of periods, facilitate learning and motivate people to adapt more successfully because they will associate their actual results with a fully adapted standard. There can be no doubt that the overriding purpose of performance feedback should be to encourage adaptive behavior. The determination of ex post standards, incidentally, is intended to be in addition to, not a substitute for, conventional ex ante standards. These would still be required in order to coordinate activities and delegate authority.

While accepting the spirit of the proposal to use ex post standards, some reservations may be mentioned. As one of their advocates notes (Itami 1977), in practice the setting of ex post standards may be too costly, or even impossible. Use of frequently (and systematically) updated ex ante standards might be a reasonable compromise. Second, use of ex post standards suggests that the earlier an organization obtains perfect information and acts on it optimally, the more successful it will be in adapting. But acquisition of additional information does not necessarily lead to more accurate prediction; it may merely increase a decision-maker's confidence in his or her original estimate or judgment. Nor does it necessarily lead to adaptation and learning. Constraints in the form of rigidities in the organization structure or in decision modes may prevent this from happening, or decision-makers may simply not act appropriately on the information. On closer inspection, the whole notion of an (optimal) ex post standard is somewhat ambiguous. If one looks back over a past period and asks, "What should I have done, if I had known then what I know now?" the optimum that could have been achieved with an ideal forecasting method is not the same as what could have been achieved if one were omniscient, because one's freedom of action would always be constrained to some extent in the former case. The principal advocates of performance measurement against an ex post standard (Demski 1967; Itami 1977) put the whole weight of adaptation on getting more information sooner (and acting on it optimally). But adaptation may require restructuring of the organization, a variable not considered.

Moreover, if the measurement of performance against ex post standards were to be put into effect with the frequency with which costs are reported (i.e., by costing period, as distinct from aggregate performance of the firm over the accounting period), as suggested by these writers, then under the usual accounting procedure for analyzing "variances" from standard cost this would fail to take account of interdependencies between different organizational units and different time periods, both of which would frustrate effective adaptation by the firm as a whole.

The proposal also focuses on the performance measure as the single motivator. But what motivates people to achieve is a vexed question that is not yet well understood. Besides the nature of the performance target (how adapted it is, and how difficult to achieve) we would need to consider certain characteristics of the performance measure (whether it is complete, objective, influenceable by the employee (but see Chapter 10), and the speed and frequency of feedback communication. Particularly if rewards are tied to performance, inappropriate responses to a few of these questions may lead to a failure to motivate or to dysfunctional behavior. Other motivators include organization structure (is it compatible with adaptation?), participation in standard-setting and in performance evaluation (Lawler and Rhode 1976), and various forms of rewards. This raises the problem of the proper mix of intrinsic and extrinsic motivation, of what kind of reward is most important to a particular employee.

Other questions raised by performance measurement against ex post standards are whether these measures would be timely enough for control purposes, whether success in adapting can be measured over an interval as short as the typical costing period (one month or less), and whether the role of employee participation would be affected by these arrangements.

To sum up on this argument, all we can say is that, if it is possible and not too costly, performance measurement against hindsight standards is a move in the right direction, provided it is not seen as the only or main vehicle for bringing about adaptation (because the accounting system has a narrow focus and performance measures are only one among several motivators), and provided it does not interfere with the operation of other adaptive mechanisms in the organization.

Beyond the reservations noted above about performance measurement against ex post standards, there are some more general criticisms of the accounting approach to performance measurement. A major weakness is that in practice the same set of targets is often used for planning purposes and for control. It is very doubtful whether they can be equally effective in both roles, because the two functions (planning and control) are quite different, even though they are often related. For a full discussion of the reasons why the different purposes served by budgets may be incompatible, see Amey and Egginton (1973, 559–60), Hopwood (1976, 41–45, 63–65); Stedry (1960, 4); and Steiner (1969, 42). Anthony (1965) speaks about the "conformance fallacy," that is, he states that it is a mistake to ask people to conform to the conventional ex ante standards, because conditions have usually changed by the time plans are implemented and made them irrelevant. This is only true, of course, if plans (and control targets) are not revised more or less continuously, as they should be but seldom are.

From a system's point of view, all accounting attempts to measure "performance" are revealed as having a number of weaknesses: "performance" is measured narrowly in relation to the firm's own goals, not as the performance of a system that is part of a three-tiered hierarchy of systems. The latter would require "performance" to be measured as the system's success in meeting its own goals, subject to satisfying the demands of its participants and of the environment at least minimally. Moreover, the accounting system is a very coarse and incomplete mapping of the system's state vector, all components of which should be reflected in an ideal performance measure. And finally, accounting performance measures in the form of deviations from budget or standard do not take account of interdependencies—between different organizational units, different causes of deviation (e.g., interactions between changes in price, quantity, mix), and different time periods. Successful adaptation in the short period may, as a result, be at the expense of adaptation over a longer period. The last point raises questions about the frequency of reporting on observed results (or, better, on the state vector) and the frequency of taking corrective action. (These questions will be discussed under "Control.")

The first point, concerning interactions between different organizational units, was referred to in the Mathematical Appendix for Chapter 4, where it was pointed out that failure to take these into account leads to a lack of goal congruence in decentralized organizations. Top management can attempt to coordinate the various units before they make their own decisions (pre-decision intervention), based on a prediction of the behavior of the whole system and of the environment; this is part of the planning process (see the later discussion of feedforward control). Without this intervention the decision problems of the various units are not well defined. After units have made their decisions, top management intervenes (post-decision intervention) iteratively to influence them to change their subsequent actions, if this is necessary in the interests of goal congruence (Mesarovic et al. 1970, ch. 2). The problem of how the organization can best keep its members in step with each other to maximize the organization's objective function is discussed by Arrow (1964a, 398).

Other problems in "performance" measurement (including the question of whether performance reports should be confined to those aspects of work that are in some sense controllable by the person or persons receiving the report) and behavioral considerations are more conveniently discussed in the next section under "Control," but the main discussion of issues to do with motivation, the form of incentives, and risk-sharing between principals and agents appears in Chapter 10.

Control

The most serious problems in the coordination of social systems, according to Mesarovic et al. (1970, 62), are due largely to the difficulties in *implementing a solution* that is found to be good on the basis of technical, economic, and other considerations. (In other words, the performance targets are assumed to have been appropriately set on a variety of grounds.) This problem has become particularly acute in the second half of the twentieth century with the emergence of very large corporate enterprises and government bureaucracies.

In the most general terms "control" is concerned with how to affect an organization from within so as to improve its operation and "performance." Some influence is exerted on the results of operations of the organization in order to achieve a desired result. More specifically, control has two functions: first, to regulate or stabilize operations and "performance" around certain norms (predetermined usually) in the presence of uncertainty stemming from environmental and internal disturbances; and second, to design and impose constraints on decentralized units of the organization and to coordinate their interactions so that the overall objectives of the organization are served and dysfunctional behavior prevented. The second purpose is implicit in the first, but warrants special consideration.

Methods of control

There are several different ways of attacking this problem of control. One would be to install some compensating device that would offset the effects of disturbances. This method is called *open-loop control* and operates on inputs to the organization. A cutback in the rate of production next period if inventory build-up has been excessive in the current period is an example. Another way would be to eliminate disturbances by insulating the organization against its environment. Various forms of uncertainty avoidance fall in this category. A number of activities are aimed at making the environment more stable and predictable: long-term contracting, advertising and research and development expenditures, forecasting and planning, mergers, diversification, various forms of association with other firms, and interlocking directorates. What Cyert and March (1963) call "organizational slack" is another example: large firms frequently accumulate a margin of resources over and above what is required to ensure the effectiveness of the organization. This reserve is built up in good times and run down in bad.

A third method is to allow disturbances to impact the organization, and then in response to feedback information, to attempt to equalize deviations of observed results from predetermined norms (desired results). This method, exemplified by the accounting techniques of budgetary control and the analysis of deviations from standard cost, is called *closed-loop control,* and is the most familiar type of adaptive mechanism. It operates on the system transformation, more specifically on an error signal that can be regarded as the result of randomness in the environment. A feedback control system consists of two subsystems: the controlled system (the organization) and the controller. The controller observes the controlled system only, not the environment.

Finally, feedforward control is the method that embodies, in addition to the system to be controlled and the controller, a model of the environment. The controller monitors the environment as well as the controlled system. The current values of certain environmental variables, thought to correlate with some future value of the state of the controlled system, are monitored. These correlations are built into the controller, which can then modify the control variables (e.g., the control budgets) in accordance with the current values of the environmental variables and the system state to maintain some function of the latter constant. Compared with feedback control, this type of control introduces two new features: a model of the environment, and prediction (or choice of some future desired state of the system). Unlike feedback control it operates on perceived or assumed regularities in the environment, as represented by the correlations referred to, rather than on randomness of the environment. And not being tied to an error signal (deviation), control is more direct and timely than feedback control. Both feedback and feedforward controls may be equipped with memory.

Feedforward would offer a superior means of control (and control systems with memory are better than those without) *if* organizations could develop sensors for monitoring and understanding the significance of environmental changes that are as effective as those evolved by human beings and some animals. Until that happens, the feedback mode is likely to predominate. If it involves forecasting rather than mere extrapolation of past plans, planning may be regarded as anticipatory, feedforward control. Rosen (1975) believes that it is particularly in the area of anticipatory control that social adaptations are singularly defective. This argues for the increased importance of planning—not conventional planning, but planning based on forecasting that fully recognizes an organization as an open system. In all this it goes without saying that it is very important to define correctly the system to be controlled, the organization or the firm (see Chapter 2)—both feedback and feedforward controls contain a model of the controlled system (at least if the control process is deterministic or stochastic; see below).

Feedback control systems may be classified in terms of the nature of the control process. In a deterministic control process, complete knowledge of the characteristics of the process being regulated is assumed. In a stochastic control process, uncertainties are present in the process or in the inputs to the process, but the probability distributions are known. An adaptive control process (as the term is used in control theory) is one in which even the probability distributions are not completely known. It is then necessary to make observations and gain further knowledge of the process while it is in operation. A learning control process is an adaptive control that has the added capability of being able to improve its behavior over time. One can think of an adaptive control system as incorporating a "pattern recognizer," which adjusts feedback in response to estimated changes in the system's variables, while a learning control system would include, in addition, a "teacher," which would train the pattern recognizer to make better recognitions. Adaptive control requires two feedback loops and learning control, three.

A distinction needs to be made at this point between classical and modern approaches to control.

Classical control theory

Feedback control is based on servomechanism theory. This is now referred to as *classical control theory*, and is to be distinguished from *modern control theory*. The most important difference between the two is that classical control operates on the outputs of the control system, whereas modern control operates on system states intermediate between control inputs and outputs.

The basic idea of control through feedback is simple. Deviations between observed and desired results are fed back and included in the control inputs. The act of control itself comes, not from the feedback of information, but from the corrective or amplifying action it triggers—the response to the feedback. The feedback is described as negative (positive) if it opposes (amplifies) the forward transformation describing the work done by the controlled system. A system with feedback is called a *cybernetic system*, and there may be more than one feedback. Essentially, such a method of control ignores the system's environment, acting only on the *effects* of disturbances, and attempts to regulate a system that is specified only in terms of input–output relationships, *input* here meaning control instruments or variables (e.g., budgets in the case of accounting control). In the Mathematical Appendix the way negative and positive feedbacks operate is explained.

The feedback form of control is very common in engineering systems, biological systems (e.g., the human body), and social systems (e.g., large corporate enterprises and government agencies). Of interest are the conditions under which the classical control model is valid and effective, and whether there are limits on the degree of control exercisable by such means.

Regarded as an adaptive mechanism, the classical (input–output) control model is, as stated earlier, inferior to the feedforward mode of control, but unfortunately, in our present state of knowledge the latter cannot be developed for social systems. Feedback systems have certain inherent limitations: the delay in operating the feedback loop, and the ease with which such systems can be "fooled," due mainly to the fact that they do not monitor the environment directly. For example, a thermostat that monitors water temperature and is designed to prevent water from boiling will fail if the pressure of the water is lowered. Equally important, the implicit assumption that it is always possible for a control system, specified only in terms of input–output relationships, to alter the dynamic characteristics of the system being controlled in such a way as to achieve an appropriate response, may break down when applied to very large and complex systems (such as large business enterprises), even if the number of control variables is large. Servomechanism theory was really designed for single input–single output systems. Its extension to multivariable feedback systems, where a number of outputs are measured and a combination of their deviations used to adjust a number of control variables, raises difficulties. For example, it may not be possible to adjust all the control variables simultaneously when this is what effective control demands. A further possible limitation of feedback control, if it has external validity, is that laboratory experiments by psychologists strongly suggest that in probabilistic learning situations (these include virtually all learning tasks outside the laboratory and are tasks where there is no uniquely correct response), provision of outcome feedback, that is, feedback of actual outcomes or of the deviations of actual from desired outcomes as in accounting controls, may have negative effects (lead to worse control and performance). Instruction and training in the task requirement without any feedback of results usually lead to better performance than outcome feedback alone (Amey 1979b, ch. 8; Hammond et al. 1973).

The *law of requisite variety* (Ashby 1956, ch. 11) states the maximum amount of control achievable by a feedback system. *Variety* means the number of distinct elements in a set; for example, the set (a, b, c, b, d, a, c, e) has a variety of five, and corresponds to expected amount of information (H) minus redundancy (R) in information theory (see Mathematical Appendix for Chapter 6), where $R = 1 - H/H_{max}$. The law says that for a given variety of disturbances affecting the system, there is a lower limit to the size to which a subset of possible outcomes may be reduced. For example, if environmental disturbances introduce a variety of 50 "bits" into outcomes, and if an acceptable degree of control (i.e., those outcomes regarded as acceptable) demands that outcomes be restricted to 10 "bits," the control system must be provided with a variety of *at least* 40 "bits." The controller must have available a repertoire of responses with a variety of at least 40 "bits" to confine the effects of the disturbances to 10 "bits." The variety of outcomes achieved will be an absolute minimum when each different disturbance evokes a unique response. A formal statement of the law of requisite variety appears in the Mathematical Appendix.

Organizations are, however, capable of achieving a degree of control greater than that indicated by the law of requisite variety for at least three reasons. First, response to disturbances (or adaptation, if it is effective) requires an organization selectively (i.e., in the light of its goals) to map the environment into itself, either as information *or as structure.* In the short run, adaptation usually takes the form of acquiring additional information (in the case under consideration the deviations from desired results brought about by environmental and other disturbances) and trying to make appropriate responses to that information. In the long run, adaptation more often requires the environment to be mapped into organization structure, so that the organization is restructured to match the changed environment. A second point is that, as we saw earlier, an organization is not restricted to the feedback method of control. It can undertake various forms of uncertainty avoidance, institute standard operating rules to buffer parts of the organization (particularly the operating departments, the "technical core") from environmental uncertainty, and so on.

Finally, the law of requisite variety essentially regards an organization as a closed system. It shows the maximum amount of control achievable when regulation is direct. But in an open system regulation may also be indirect, in the form of learning from the environment. An example will illustrate. Suppose a child wishes to discover the meanings of English words and his father has only ten minutes to spare. The father has two possible modes of action. He could tell the child the meanings of as many words as possible in that time. This is the direct method. Clearly there is a definite limit to the number of words that could be explained in ten minutes. The indirect method would be for the father to spend the ten minutes showing the child how to use a dictionary. At the end of ten minutes the child may not have added a single word to his vocabulary, but in the future the number of words the child can understand is no longer bounded. When the information about meanings comes through the father directly, it is limited to the amount that can be transmitted and understood in ten minutes. By the indirect method the information comes partly from the father and partly through another channel, the dictionary. Likewise, in the context of control, learning from the environment amplifies the degree of control achievable. But feedback control ignores the environment; it is sensorily deprived.

The validity and effectiveness of the classical control model depend also on a number of technical considerations, which will be mentioned only briefly. All transformations in the model (v and r in the Mathematical Appendix) must be linear or linearizable; the system must be stationary (time-invariant), that is, its behavior must not be explicitly dependent on time; there must be no constraints (such as thresholds on acceptable values) on the system variables to be controlled; and the system must be "completely controllable" and "completely observable," two conditions that will be described shortly.

Modern control theory

The modern control theory approach, developed in response to the limitations of the classical approach especially when applied to large, complex systems, specifies the system not in terms of input–output relationships but in terms of state description. The notion of "state" is explained in the Mathematical Appendix for Chapter 2. The state of a dynamic system is the minimum amount of information required to determine both the output and the future states of the system when its inputs are known. Thus defined, the state of a system such as a business enterprise or government agency cannot be described solely in terms of accounting variables. A system's state is described by a set of state variables located between inputs to the system (control variables) and outputs of the system (outcomes). Control variables are those that the controller (or decision-maker) is free to specify arbitrarily within the limits imposed by constraints. The control problem is to choose values of the control variables so as to achieve the control objective (desired state).

In modern control theory the system to be controlled is represented by equations in its state variables. One equation relates the state variables to the control variables, and a second relates state variables and control variables to outputs. A further equation or equations relating control variables and output would be added if the system has feedback control(s). The general form of these equations is shown in the Mathematical Appendix.

Under the classical approach the system dynamics (the changing relationships within the controlled system) remain a "black box" (unknown). Under the modern control theory approach, control is exercised by trying to achieve complete "controllability" (to be defined in a moment); complete "observability" is a prerequisite of full system specification in this approach, as evidenced by the second system equation shown in the Mathematical Appendix. These two terms were mentioned earlier and will now be explained. Note that in the control theory sense, "controllable" does not mean the same thing as it does in accounting. In responsibility accounting the "principle of controllability" states that a performance report should contain only data relating to activities over which the person whose performance is measured has a significant (although not necessarily total) degree of control. In control theory, "controllability" refers to the ability of the controller to move each of the state variables from given values to other values by manipulating the control inputs (e.g., by changing the budget program in the case of accounting control). A system is said to be completely controllable in the control theory sense if it is able to do this in a finite time. That is, controllability requires every state of the system to be affected by the input (a control instrument or instruments). A system is completely observable if measurement of its output over some finite interval of time contains sufficient information to enable the system's state to be completely identified. In other words, observability requires that every state of the system shall affect the measured output. These relationships are displayed in Figure 9.1.

If they can be achieved, complete controllability and observability tell us much more about what is going on inside the system than the classical approach does. Under the input–output approach, large dynamic interactions may be occurring within the system that would not be evident from the measured outputs. The only type of system that will be accurately represented by transfer functions is one having complete controllability and observability, as shown in Figure 9.2. In order to achieve complete controllability and observability there remains the problem of choosing the appropriate inputs (control instruments) and observers (to measure outputs). See Amey (1979b, ch. 5) for further discussion of the state–space model, controllability, and observability. It is now well established that the state–space approach is much more suitable and effective than the input–output approach for application to very large and complex systems. This has been demonstrated in engineering, biology, and economics.

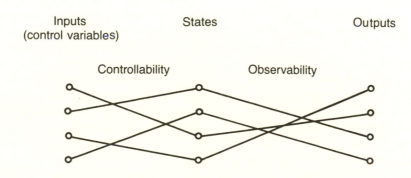

FIGURE 9.1. Controllability and observability.

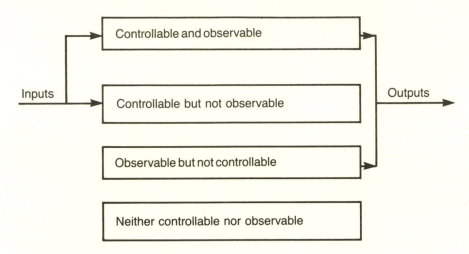

FIGURE 9.2. Classification of system characteristics.

Control criterion

The control criterion in error-controlled feedback systems is, in general, to minimize the deviations from desired results. In accounting this usually takes the form of seeking to minimize *significant unfavorable cost* deviations. There are other possibilities. Thus instead of trying to keep the error small we could try to minimize the squared error (which increases the penalty for being out of control whenever the error is large) or the integral of the error (this would impose a penalty for the whole time the error persists). These last two alternatives are examples of nonlinear feedback.

Under the modern control theory approch, the control *criterion* could become the minimization of cost subject to the system equations and initial conditions by a suitable choice of control variables at each point in time. "Cost" would here comprise the cost of operating the control system (the costs of effecting complete controllability and observability and of operating any feedback controls) and the cost (opportunity loss) of being out of control, both of which would be largely determined by the behavior over time of the state and control variables. A formal statement of the problem is given in the Mathematical Appendix. This criterion is only appropriate if we ensure that the benefits obtained outweigh the costs. The problem could alternatively be stated as maximizing benefits minus costs, subject to the same constraints. However, as it is stated (in terms of cost minimization or net benefit maximization), the problem subsumes others, such as the problem of convergence time (the time needed to get the system back in control) and the optimal frequency of control responses (how frequently the values of the control variables should be changed).

The control *objective* (as distinct from criterion), the desired state, will depend on what the system regards as its objective, and this will vary according to whether it takes a rational, natural, or open system view of itself.

Further comments on accounting controls

Considering only accounting controls, several other actual or possible weaknesses should be mentioned. The first is that these controls apply only to the *formal* organization—to divisions, departments, and more generally, "responsibility centers." These are the structure and relationships shown on an organization chart. In large organizations, whether corporate enterprises or government agencies, there exist networks of informal relationships whose influence is often significant, sometimes more significant than the formal relationships. This informal organization is not subject to the accounting controls. A number of other methods of control are of course employed by organizations in addition to accounting controls and those mentioned earlier under "Methods of control": supervision, statistical control (e.g., quality control), project control through networks (applied to construction projects, research and development), and standard operating rules (e.g., "when inventory falls to x units, reorder").

Another limitation of conventional accounting controls is that they are applied only at the tactical (operations) level of the organization. Organizations, in common with other types of open systems, evolve to ever more complex forms. According to Simon (1969), complexity frequently takes the form of hierarchy; the structure is pyramidal, consisting of different levels, with each level subordinate to the next higher level. For present purposes it is sufficient to collapse the various levels into two groups: strategic and tactical. *Strategic* is here used in a broad sense to comprise *all* senior management activities, such as planning (predictive adaptation), strategy-making, top-level decision-making, changes in organization structure in response to environmental changes, overall control of operating activities and the interactions between them, and in general all the factors that are critical to the long-run survival of the organization. Decisions at the tactical level are then taken within the framework of, or subject to, strategic decisions so defined.

Simon (1969), Simon and Ando (1961), and Ashby (1960, 192–96) have further stated that systems that are hierarchical in structure are weakly coupled, such that interactions within subsystems are (in the short run) much stronger than interactions between subsystems. This conclusion has already been referred to in discussing organization structure in Chapter 7. A weakly coupled system is formally described as nearly decomposable. Simon and Ando have shown that weak coupling gives rise to behaviors of quite different speeds. The system as a whole exhibits multi-time-scale behavior, which can be viewed as the superposition of the behavior of a number of "fast" subsystems and a single "slow" subsystem. The fast subsystems are modeled by terms representing interactions between variables within the subsystem, and the slow subsystem by terms representing interactions between subsystems, with each subsystem represented by an aggregate variable. Over a relatively short period the first group of terms dominates the behavior of the system, and as a result each fast subsystem can be regarded as approximately independent. Over a longer period the second group of terms dominates the system's behavior; the system as a whole slowly drifts under the influence of the couplings between subsystems, which in the long run are not necessarily weak. In other words, the fast variables describe local dynamics, the slow variables the systemwide slow behavior due to the weak couplings between subsystems. The ratio of strength of interactions between subsystems to that of interactions within subsystems determines the ratio of the speeds of the slow to the fast behaviors.

This line of research has been continued by Williamson (1981) and, in a control context, by Amey (1986, Appendix to ch. 4). In a business enterprise, the fast subsystems are identified with the tactical level (the production departments), the slow subsystem with the strategic level in the organization. Conventional accounting controls are confined to the tactical level and the short run. What seems to be missing, therefore, is some means of exercising control at the strategic level if long-run adaptation is to be ensured. Many, although not all, of the activities undertaken at this level eventually result in actions at the tactical level, but by that time it is usually too late to control them. Considering the nature of strategic activities, the control problem is formidable, but it needs to be faced. This research draws attention to a weakness in accounting control applied to hierarchical systems.

Other weaknesses of accounting controls are apparent when they are looked at from a behavioral point of view, namely, from the viewpoint of their effect on those whose performance is measured and who are subject to the controls. Lawler and Rhode (1976) discuss how the characteristics of information and control systems affect motivation, dysfunctional behavior, and decision quality, and find that many of the same characteristics that produce a maximum amount of motivation (toward high performance) produce a minimal amount of dysfunctional behavior.

Some characteristics, however, lead to high motivation and a high incidence of dysfunctional behavior, creating a conflict in designing systems. As noted earlier, performance should be based on measures that are complete, objective, and that can be influenced by the person being evaluated. If this is not possible, extrinsic rewards (such as monetary payments and promotion) should not be tied to performance because they may lead to a high incidence of dysfunctional behavior or to no motivation. In general, participation in setting performance targets and in evaluating performance by the person being evaluated is advocated by researchers in psychology. Rewards (whether intrinsic—those that originate with, and are felt by, the subject—or extrinsic) should follow performance evaluation closely in time.

In particular, four common ways are mentioned by Lawler and Rhode in which control systems may have dysfunctional effects. They may cause people to behave in ways that look good in terms of the control system measures but are dysfunctional in relation to the goals of the organization. "Rigid bureaucratic behavior" and "strategic behavior" fall in this category. Second, employees may report false data, either on what can be done or on what has been done. Third, control systems may for a number of reasons meet with strong resistance from the people who are affected by them. The controls may be perceived as significant threats, for example, by automating or computerizing jobs considered to require expertise; by creating new "experts" and giving them power; by people believing that objective data on individual performance will put them in a less favorable light; by changing the social structure of the organization and breaking up established social groups; or by reducing opportunities for intrinsic need fulfilment, such as the amount of autonomy the employee enjoys.

This is only a very brief and incomplete discussion of the behavioral aspects of control. Readers are referred to Lawler and Rhode (1976) and Hopwood (1976) for a fuller treatment. Looming large among the behavioral aspects is the matter of motivation, a discussion of which cannot be completed without considering rewards (in particular, the form of extrinsic rewards or incentives) and risk-sharing within the organization. These questions are taken up in the next chapter.

10

Motivation, Risk-Sharing, and Incentives

The previous chapter on performance and control suggested that the discussion of those matters was incomplete without a more detailed look at the question of motivation. By motivation is meant the problem of directing activity toward a goal. Assume that a business has a goal or goals that are translated into performance targets for individual workers or groups of workers. These workers are not will-less; they have some freedom as to how they carry out orders. Unless the firm is operating in perfectly competitive markets for its inputs and outputs, workers have no automatic incentive to carry out their orders with maximum effort (for fear of dismissal). They must be persuaded to do so (Amey and Egginton 1979, 566–67). The problem is further complicated by the fact that a worker's personal goals may not coincide with the firm's, and the worker may have risk attitudes different from those of his superior. There may also be information asymmetries between superiors and subordinates. On a psychological level, workers have differing potentials and aspiration levels (the levels of performance they set themselves). What motivates them also varies from one person to another. In addition to the various forms of administrative controls present in most firms (e.g., standard operating rules, budgets and standards), members of an organization are in a social relationship with one another, leading to further pressures to conform to or to resist the performance targets set by the firm. Ultimately, however, both the administrative and social controls must be internalized by members of the organization if they are to influence personal attitudes and behavior (Hopwood 1976, ch. 2). The source of motivation may be extrinsic, intrinsic, or some combination of the two, varying from one individual to another; and extrinsic motivation may be created by pecuniary or nonpecuniary rewards and punishments (such as not offering a reward or deferring it) applied by the organization. The emphasis on extrinsic rewards, particularly money, may vary from one culture to another, being perhaps stronger in North America than elsewhere, as may an individual's preferences for income and leisure.

Sources of motivation: Behavioral theories

Research on motivation to greater achievement in the workplace divides roughly into the motivation theories of psychologists and other behavioral scientists purporting to explain the sources of motivation and the effects of various kinds of controls and incentive schemes, and the work of economists whose fields of interest include theories of the firm on the role of motivation in explaining how people behave in organizations and how dysfunctional behavior might be prevented. The behavioral studies could be characterized as qualitative in the main, and the economic studies as quantitative. But there is some overlap between the two approaches.

Because of the sheer volume of behavioral studies and because no consensus appears to have been reached yet, little would be gained in reviewing this literature. Even though they seldom agree among themselves, however, these researchers have added greatly to our understanding of individual and group behavior in organizations. In these studies motivation has been variously linked to an individual's preference for attainment versus nonattainment of a certain outcome, such as a performance target ("valence"), her subjective probability of achieving this outcome ("expectancy"), the extent to which she believes her actions influence the outcome, the type of performance measures and controls employed, the extent to which work satisfies various personal needs, and which needs are dominant for her, her desire for income versus leisure, and so on.

A selective survey of the main currents in this debate over the sources of motivation to achieve, and some reviews of the whole field, would include the work of Argyris (1952, 1964); Herzberg, Mauser, and Snyderman (1959); Maslow (1960); McGregor (1960); Stedry (1960); McClelland (1961); Katz (1964); Vroom (1964); Cofer and Appley (1964); Vroom and Deci (1970); Hofstede (1972, ch. 3); Atkinson and Raynor (1974); Madsen (1974); Hopwood (1976); and Lawler and Rhode (1976).

Evolution of the role of motivation in theories of the firm

The part of microeconomics known as the theory of the firm is concerned with the role of business firms in the resource allocation process in market economies. Over the years, different theories have been advanced to explain the behavior of firms, and with each new theory the conception of the role of motivation of those working for the firm has changed. The main line of development of thought proceeds from the classical theory through "behavioral" or managerial theories to the property rights approach and agency theory. Research in the last-named is now a flourishing industry in economics, accounting, finance, and management science.

In the *classical theory* the firm was run by an entrepreneur, whose objective was profit maximization in perfectly competitive markets. The entrepreneur provided or borrowed money capital, and his functions were managing and risk-bearing. He was supposed to safeguard employees who provided productive services against all uninsurable risks; he bore the residual risks. The sanctions of competitive markets ensured that employees had an automatic incentive to work with maximum effort. That is, strong motivation was provided by fear of dismissal for poor performance. There was no need for the firm itself to offer any incentive beyond the ruling wage. Any conflict of goals between entrepreneur and employees was resolved in favor of the entrepreneur (Cyert and March 1963, ch. 3).

The *neoclassical theory* recognized the prevalence of imperfectly competitive markets, but in other respects continued the tradition of the classical theory; the economic behavior of firms was still guided by the single objective of profit maximization, and although Berle and Means (1932) had shown that the typical firm was incorporated (limited liability company) and characterized by the divorce of ownership and control, the implications of this development for goal formation, motivation of managers, and risk attitudes were not explicitly addressed.

Widespread dissent from the view that the behavior of firms was guided by a profit maximization objective led to the appearance of *"behavioral" and managerial theories* of the firm (Penrose 1958; Simon 1959; Baumol 1959; Cyert and March 1963; Marris 1964; Williamson 1964). These theories are reviewed in Alchian (1965). The new theories had in common that they replaced or supplemented the neoclassical theory of the firm, which was primarily a theory of markets, with an inward-looking theory of the behavior of decision-makers within the firm under conditions of uncertainty. In other words, these were the first attempts to develop positive economic models of the firm. The concept of an entrepreneur and profit maximization (sometimes even optimizing behavior of any kind) were rejected. Once decision-making in the firm is seen as being undertaken by managers who are not (major) stockholders of the firm, and all markets are no longer assumed to be perfectly competitive, problems of control, motivation, and incentives arise. More attention is given in these theories to managers acting in their own self-interest.

But while the theories speculate about what the motives of managers might then be, many pay little attention to the problem of motivating managers to act in the interests of the firm. In Cyert and March (1963) the conflicting interests of members of the organizational coalition (comprising all the major stakeholders in the firm) are brought into rough agreement on organizational objectives by offering pecuniary and/or nonpecuniary side payments to the active members of the coalition. The analysis did not extend to enquiring into the circumstances in which particular forms of incentives were likely to lead to goal-congruent behavior, and there was no consideration of risk-sharing.

The two most recent developments have much in common but occurred independently. The first is known as the *property rights* approach (Coase 1937 and 1960; Alchian and Demsetz 1972), which is reviewed in Furubotn and Pejovich (1972). According to this view the firm is a set of (implicit or explicit) contracts among factors of production. *Property rights* refers to the relations, not between people and things (resources) as the term might suggest, but to the permissible behavioral relations between people arising from the existence of things, and relating to their use. Specification of these rights determines how costs and rewards are allocated among members of the organization. In other words, the property rights approach purports to show that the content of contracts between members of the organization affects the allocation and utilization of resources *in specific and predictable ways*—it assumes that systematic relations exist between property rights and the economic choices of members of the organization.

It is important to note that the unit of analysis is no longer the firm. Nor are the interests of those holding ownership rights given exclusive attention. Rather, the focus is on individual participants, including the owners, each of whom is assumed to be a utility maximizer acting in his/her self-interest, subject to the existing organization structure and to ensuring survival of the firm. Participants in the organization adjust *individually* to the economic environment, and the behavior of the firm is explained by observing these individual actions. This approach is characterized by emphasis on the interconnectedness of ownership rights, incentives, and economic behavior. The presumption is that property rights influence incentives and behavior, and that once human motivations are known the allocation and utilization of resources by the firm can be better understood.

The implication of a number of alternative property rights assignments, and of changes in the content of property rights, for motivation and resource allocation decisions have been studied. As viewed by the perfect competition model of the classical theory, for example, one set of property rights covers the use of all resources, and the entrepreneur possesses the ownership rights and arrogates to himself the entire direction of the firm. There are no transaction costs, and no control problem exists; the cost of exchange, and the costs of policing and enforcing cooperating (contractual) activities, are zero. The property rights approach departs from this view in recognizing nonzero transaction costs in most cases of interest, the possibility of discretionary behavior and shirking by managers, and hence the need for control. Like the behavioral theory of the firm of Cyert and March, the property rights analysis builds on the traditional (neoclassical) theory of the firm rather than replacing it completely.

The final development, known as *agency theory,* has an already extensive literature, of which some of the main contributions and reviews are Wilson (1968, 1969), Ross (1973), Jensen and Meckling (1976), Mirrlees (1974, 1976), Harris and Raviv (1978, 1979), Demski and Feltham (1978), Shavell (1979), Holmström (1979), Groves and Loeb (1979), Jennergren (1980), Fama (1980), Gjesdal (1981), Christensen (1981), and Baiman (1982). Discussion of this development will occupy the remainder of the chapter.

The basic agency model and its assumptions

As in the property rights approach, agency theory is concerned with contracts (agency relationships) under which one party (the principal) engages another party (the agent) to perform certain services on her behalf. The agency relationship may be between the owners (the stockholders acting through the board of directors) and top management (or the chief executive officer), or between top management and divisional or departmental managers. The firm is seen as a set of such contracts. Performance of the service in each case involves the principal delegating some decision-making authority to the agent. Certain assumptions are made about the objectives of principals and agents, about their preferences (e.g., their relative preferences for pecuniary and nonpecuniary rewards), their beliefs about the state of the world, and their attitudes to risk-bearing.

It is not usually possible, without incurring some costs, for the principal to ensure that the agent always acts in the best interests of the principal. By introducing appropriate incentives and by incurring monitoring costs, the principal attempts to limit dysfunctional behavior on the part of the agent. The agent, for his part, may in some circumstances also incur costs ("bonding costs") to ensure that he does not act contrary to the principal's wishes, or to compensate the principal if he does. Together with any residual loss the principal bears due to the failure of the agent to fulfil his part of the contract, the costs mentioned above are collectively called *agency costs* (i.e., all the costs except the cost of the incentives). Agency theory differs from the property rights approach in quantifying these costs. In what follows we will assume that the payoff from the agent's actions (denoted by x) is always expressed net of all relevant costs except the cost of the incentives themselves. In particular, we assume that the payoff is net of agency costs (monitoring, bonding, and any residual loss) and the costs involved in performance evaluation and in operating the incentive scheme. The normative agency literature is not very specific on this point, which only surfaces in the positive agency theory literature (e.g., Jensen and Meckling 1976).

In what has come to be known as the basic agency model, a single principal and a single agent are each assumed to act in their own self-interests, which is interpreted as seeking to maximize their own expected utility (EU). That is, uncertainty is introduced explicitly. The basic agency model spans a single period. The principal's utility function is defined over wealth alone (monetary payoff less the agent's fee), while the agent's utility function is defined over wealth and action (or "effort"), the latter term being intended to subsume all the agent's nonpecuniary benefits (e.g., leisure, consumption of perquisites on the job, congenial working conditions). The principal is generally assumed to be weakly risk-averse (i.e., risk-neutral or risk-averse), the agent to be strictly risk-averse and effort-averse (i.e., the agent experiences disutility from increased effort). It is further assumed that the agent's utility function is separable into utility for wealth and disutility for effort. That is, it is assumed that the agent's utility for nonpecuniary benefits is always on balance negative, a disutility.

The principal's problem is to choose an incentive scheme (called a fee schedule) such that her own EU is as large as possible when the agent maximizes his own EU by choosing a particular act (effort level). The fee schedule must also satisfy the condition that it yields the agent a certain minimal EU, that of his opportunity wage, otherwise he might leave the firm. If the agent takes action a (supplies effort level a) and the state of the world, the realized state occurrence, is θ, the monetary payoff is x; that is, $x = x(a,\theta)$. The fee schedule may be a function of the payoff, the realized state, and the action taken (effort expended), $f(x, \theta, a)$.

Only things that are jointly observable by both parties to the contract can be included as arguments in the fee schedule. These jointly observable variables define the principal's monitoring capacity. The employment contract specifies the fee schedule and the monitoring system to be used. The principal is assumed always to be able to observe the monetary payoff; she may or may not be able to observe the realized state occurrence or the agent's effort level. Principal and agent may have homogeneous beliefs (identical subjective probability distributions over states of the world) or there may be an information asymmetry between them. The agent is seen as choosing that act that maximizes his EU, given the fee schedule and monitoring system selected by the principal. The latter maximizes the EU of the monetary payoff less the agent's fee.

A relationship of the kind described has the characteristics of a noncooperative game: both parties seek only to serve their self-interest, but their utility functions differ in their arguments, the agent having a disutility for greater effort. Consequently the self-serving action of the agent may not be in the best interests of the principal. In other words, there may be disagreement between principal and agent over what constitutes a proper level of effort (or a good act) if the two parties have different risk attitudes, or different beliefs, or if the principal cannot directly observe the level of effort applied by the agent. If the principal can observe only the payoff and not the agent's effort level, the agent could supply a level of effort that is less than optimal from the principal's point of view and blame the poor result (payoff) on an unfavorable state of the world. This is the problem of *moral hazard.* It can be avoided if the agent is risk-neutral (Harris and Raviv 1979).

Another problem that may arise due to uncertainty (which, like moral hazard, may lead to a divergence between noncooperative and cooperative behavior) is one that may occur even if the principal can observe the agent's effort directly and base the fee schedule on it. If the agent has private information that he does not reveal to the principal, the latter is unable to determine whether the observed effort was appropriate, given the agent's instructions in the contract and the agent's private information. The problem of *adverse selection* arises if an agent is motivated to misrepresent his private information in order to take an action different from that desired by the principal.

Both of these problems (moral hazard and adverse selection) are the result of ex post uncertainty, that is, uncertainty that remains after actions have been taken and the results have been realized. Both can be avoided by the principal employing an information system that removes all ex post uncertainties, concerning the agent's effort level, his private information, and the realized state occurrence. As we shall see, complete information on what actually happened (for any given level of ex ante uncertainty, i.e., uncertainty at the time actions are taken) leads to the most efficient sharing of payoff and risk between principal and agent. In fact, even imperfect information on the agent's action may increase the EU of both principal and agent (Holmström 1979).

Reverting to the basic agency problem and assuming the principal is weakly risk-averse and the agent strictly risk-averse, if the principal can observe the monetary payoff and the agent's effort level, the fee schedule could be made a function of both, or $f(x, a)$. In fact, there is no need to do so in this situation, for the principal can employ a "forcing contract," making the agent's fee a dichotomous function of x only; for example

$$f(x) = \begin{cases} (bx \mid 0 < b < 1) & \text{if } a \geqslant \text{some acceptable level } a_0 \\ 0 & \text{otherwise} \end{cases}$$

The fee schedule in this case is therefore more correctly stated as $f(x \mid a)$. This fee schedule can be set in such a way that it ensures that the agent will take the appropriate action (or supply the amount of effort expected by the principal) even when the fee schedule is chosen without regard for the agent's self-interest. It does this by penalizing dysfunctional behavior—the agent receives a certain fee if the desired effort level is forthcoming and incurs a severe penalty if it is not.

The solution offered by the forcing contract is called a first-best solution in that it leads to efficient sharing of both payoff and risk between the parties (risk-sharing is here Pareto-optimal, *provided* the agent supplies the desired effort input). It imposes a cooperative solution. *Efficient* is to be understood to be synonymous with Pareto-optimal. The criterion of Pareto-optimality is the weak optimization criterion that calls a solution optimal if no one can be made better off without making someone worse off. It is a weak criterion in that it cannot judge between cases where one party is made better off and another worse off. Pareto-optimal risk-sharing means that it is not possible to make one party bear less risk without making the other bear more than he prefers to bear, given their respective risk attitudes. In the case being discussed here P-optimality requires most of the risk to fall on the principal, who is weakly risk-averse (i.e., risk-averse or risk-neutral). But even though the agent is strictly risk-averse, some of the risk will fall on him, since the outcome of his action depends partly on the realized state occurrence, which is uncertain: $x = x(\theta, a)$. The notion of P-optimality can be operationalized by saying that it will be the result of maximizing the principal's EU subject only to the agent's EU being not less than that of his opportunity wage.

Now consider the case where only the payoff is jointly observable, so that the fee schedule must be $f(x)$. In this case the problem is as just stated, but subject to the additional constraint that the agent will choose his act (or effort level) to maximize his own EU. This is a noncooperative situation between two self-seeking individuals. A first-best, cooperative solution which results in P-optimal risk-sharing, a P-optimal fee schedule, and P-optimal EUs is no longer possible because it would ignore the motivational problem of preventing the agent, acting in his own self-interest, from under-supplying effort. Any attempt to get the agent to provide the effort level desired by the principal would be unenforceable given this (first-best) fee schedule. The solution, taking into account the agent's self-seeking behavior, is a second-best solution. The contract must be made self-enforcing (i.e., it must incorporate the game theory notion of a perfect Nash equilibrium). In other words, there must be some tradeoff between incentive and risk-sharing to induce the agent to take the correct action (supply the desired amount of effort). The agent is offered greater incentive (a larger share of the payoff than in the first-best solution) but in return is made to share the risk of the uncertain payoff with the principal. Such an arrangement may result in a welfare improvement to both principal and agent—both may have larger EUs than in a first-best cooperative solution. Risk-sharing, however, will no longer be P-optimal, because the risk-averse agent will be required to bear some of the risk. The source of the divergence between first- and second-best solutions is the moral hazard resulting from asymmetry of information between principal and agent. The agent knows what his effort level is, but the principal is unable to observe it, either because it is impossible or prohibitively costly.

The idea that the EUs of principal and agent can be greater under a second-best solution than under a first-best solution is counterintuitive and calls for further explanation. It may seem implausible that when the principal cannot observe the agent's effort, the (second-best) solution can yield a P-optimal fee schedule *and P-optimal EUs,* even though risk can never be shared P-optimally when the fee schedule depends only on the payoff, unless the agent is risk-neutral (a lengthy proof of this last point appears in Shavell 1979). The reason why this may seem implausible is that both monetary payoff and risk preferences are embedded in the utility functions. The explanation is that if the principal appropriately alters the (risk-averse) agent's fee schedule, offering the agent an increased share of the payoff, this added incentive will induce the agent to bear more risk than he would otherwise be prepared to and still be better off (in terms of his EU) than when the risk is shared P-optimally. The principal, for her part, is willing to enter into such an arrangement because although she takes a reduced share of the payoff, she bears less risk, and she also is better off in terms of her EU than when risk is shared P-optimally.

A formal description of the basic agency model appears in the Mathematical Appendix.

Limitations of the basic agency model and the agency approach

Agency theory offers important new insights into the use of ex post (i.e., post-decision) information to motivate members of a firm and to share risk between them. It shows that evaluation of a member's performance may involve risk-sharing as well as motivational considerations, and that these are interrelated. Motivation of a member who is in the position of agent will in most cases (unless the agent happens to be risk-neutral) be influenced by the amount of risk he is called upon to bear. He will, for example, respond differently if his monetary compensation depends on the actual outcome of his actions than if it depends on the expected outcome. Moreover, providing an agent with ex ante (pre-decision) information that enables him to revise his beliefs about the uncertain state of the world may have the effect of making it less risky for him to shirk, thus reducing his motivation (Baiman 1982, 180). In short, agency theory views in a new light the questions of information system design and the uses to which information is put within a firm. The results thus far derived from agency theory research would appear to have implications for management accounting, the economic organization of the firm, and finance/financial accounting (the stewardship role of published financial reports in capital markets).

Nevertheless, there are some questions that agency theory, in its present state of development, does not tackle or leaves open to debate. Some of these spring from the assumptions of the agency model, others come from taking a broader view of the whole agency approach. It is not suggested that these present limitations are necessarily insurmountable, although the last one to be mentioned does raise fundamental questions about the whole agency approach.

The restrictiveness of some of the model's assumptions has been noted by Baiman (1982) and by Tiessen and Waterhouse (1983), among others. Thus the model assumes that both parties to the agency relationship are rational utility maximizers. Simon (1978) has questioned the validity of this description of their behavior. The agent's utility function is usually considered to be separable into utility for wealth and disutility for effort. All nonpecuniary *benefits* are supposed to be subsumed under "effort." While this separation is theoretically convenient, it may be questioned whether this is usually possible, and whether all nonpecuniary benefits are (a) measurable and (b) taken into account. Nonpecuniary benefits have to date received cavalier treatment in agency models.

Furthermore, the situations considered for the most part are confined to a single principal and a single agent. This leaves open to question whether the results of the analysis still hold when the "agent" is a group, particularly a large group, raising the possibility of coalition formation and collusive behavior. It also raises questions about how to develop a group utility function for multiple principals (such as a board of directors) or groups of agents, and of whether a series of contracts with individual agents will succeed in taking into account the interactions between them (unless "forcing" contracts are used all around, which may not be possible or economic).

Again, the basic model considers only a single period. Extension of the model to multiperiod situations appears to be theoretically tractable, by generalizing the solution concept of a perfect Nash equilibrium (Kreps and Wilson 1981). Confining the analysis to a single period of course introduces such questions as the role of "track record" and loyalty in incentive contracting, the possibility that short-run maximization may be at the expense of long-run maximization and survival of the firm (Kaplan 1982, ch. 16), and what effect multiperiod incentive contracting would have on the incidence of moral hazard.

Technical issues that the basic agency model raises include the fact that the labor market that determines the agent's opportunity wage (and thus his minimum acceptable EU) is treated as exogenous (i.e., given, not determined or influenced by the analysis), that the set of P-optimal fee schedules does not allow for the possibility of randomized fee schedules, and (in some versions of the model) that a solution to the agent's problem of choosing the act that will maximize his EU, given the fee schedule, exists and is unique. This last problem is referred to in the Mathematical Appendix.

Some versions of the basic agency model regard the information system as costless or give a shadowy treatment to costs other than the cost of the incentives themselves. As stated earlier, these costs are relevant to the agency problem, and include the costs of operating the incentive scheme, of monitoring the agent's activities (effort) and the environment (state of the world), of determining the principal's and agent's utility functions and their beliefs about the state of the world. The model presented in Baiman (1982) at least implicitly takes these costs into account, with the principal's and agent's subjective probability distributions made conditional on the information system used as well as on the agent's actions (effort).

A further set of questions comes to mind in viewing the whole agency theory approach from a distance and relating it to the real world. For example, the second-best (noncooperative) solution to the agency problem when only the payoff is jointly observable involves imposing additional risk on the agent. Kaplan (1982, ch. 17) justifiably observes that managers are not generally hired to share risk with their principals, but rather for their expertise and decision-making abilities. Casual observation also suggests that many employment contracts relate to positions (job titles) rather than to individuals by name, completely ignoring the individual's utility function, beliefs, and risk attitudes. Moreover, the terms of employment in many contracts do not refer to the duration of the contract (simply that it may be terminated by x months' notice on either side) and do not safeguard the employee against the risk of a cut in pay or a change in place of employment. For many jobs there is no written contract at all; in non-unionized work a written contract in which *all* the terms of employment are specified is the exception, not the rule. The usual assumption of agency theory, that the agent has a disutility for extra effort, is also unlikely to be an accurate description of all classes of agents (e.g., professionals). Indeed, is "effort" measurable in the case of senior managers?

Another kind of doubt about the agency viewpoint, noted by Baiman (1982) and Tiessen and Waterhouse (1983), stems from the markets and hierarchies (or organizational failures) literature referred to in Chapter 7 (Williamson 1975b). According to this view, hierarchies (multilevel organizations) supplant markets as a means of mediating transactions when the costs of writing and enforcing contracts in a market become too high. Organizations that are hierarchical in structure, in this view, cannot be analyzed by following the set-of-contracts approach adopted by agency theory because hierarchies are set up for the express purpose of mediating exchanges in situations where complete contracts cannot be written or enforced. In particular, the markets and hierarchies literature suggests that when the uncertainty surrounding the tasks delegated within the organization becomes pronounced due to ex ante environmental uncertainty or complexity, so that a premium is placed on adaptive behavior, the information necessary to write highly detailed contracts will not be available to both the contracting parties. In such circumstances no contract will be well specified. As work tasks become more uncertain, moreover, information tends to become highly impacted (i.e., information asymmetries tend to increase), and this private information can be used strategically (i.e., opportunistically) to serve an agent's self-interest.

In these circumstances, so the argument goes, market contracting tends to be replaced by an internal labor market that possesses advantages over an external market in reducing opportunism and information impactedness. The pricing and allocation of labor is handled in this internal market by *administrative rules* rather than directly by economic forces (Doeringer and Piore 1971; Williamson et al. 1975). Internal labor markets are described in this literature in terms of an enforceable social contract that *imposes* a cooperative solution on the employment problem. Internal labor markets typically attach wages to jobs rather than to individuals; there are administrative rules for appeals or arbitration in the case of wage disputes; positions are usually filled by internal promotion; remuneration consists of a fixed fee, with merit increases and promotion based on performance histories. (In the agency theory analysis, payment of a fixed fee offers no incentive at all, and hence fails on motivational grounds.) In the typical employment situation for middle and senior managers, extrinsic motivation is provided by bonuses and promotion based on record of achievement along several dimensions and on other personal attributes rather than by an incentive contract based on expected or actual payoff and/or effort.

The agency view also makes light of intrinsic motivation, the reward given by individuals to themselves, for example, the self-motivation to perform well for its own sake. In agency theory, nonpecuniary benefits are gathered together in the variable "act" or "effort." Disutilities are emphasized to the virtual exclusion of the utility of intrinsic nonpecuniary rewards. Also, in practice agents bear none of the state occurrence risk directly, except when part of their remuneration consists of some form of stock bonuses whose value is determined by the stock market or is related to profits or earnings per share, subject to some threshold value. External and internal labor markets must obviously be interconnected, but the suggestion is that the links are few, due to imperfect information on alternative employment opportunities or to nontransferable specialization of the employee to the operations of a particular firm.

All in all, then, the markets and hierarchies view, with its concomitant of internal labor markets subject to general administrative rules, is a far cry from the view espoused by agency theory. It is too early yet to attempt to adjudicate between these opposing views, except to say that the former seems to conform more closely to reality. This does not mean, of course, that it is necessarily better. But one has to question whether agency incentive contracting with many agents over many acts would really be administratively feasible.

Some implications of agency theory

The concept of the firm as being composed of a series of agency relationships has important positive implications for some established procedures in accounting, and for the theory of finance, as well as for the economic theory of the firm. We look first at the accounting and information system implications.

If the agency theory view of the firm is valid, one important result concerns the choice and design of information systems. It has shown how to order information systems whose signals are used solely for performance evaluation (i.e., motivational and risk-sharing) purposes, and to a lesser extent how to evaluate and order pre-decision information systems whose signals are used solely for belief revision purposes. For example, Holmström (1979) demonstrated that imperfect post-decision (monitoring) information about an agent's effort (a) leads to a strict Pareto-improvement in the EUs of principal and agent only if it contains information not conveyed by the payoff (x). This result is quite general, whatever the beliefs and preferences of principal and agent. Agency research into the value of information may thus provide useful insights into the implications of *choice and design of monitoring systems.*

Another implication concerns the management accounting practice known as *responsibility accounting.* This practice involves partitioning the firm into "responsibility centers" (cost centers, profit centers, investment centers), and holding the agent in charge of the center responsible only for outcomes over which he exercises control. "Control" is usually interpreted in terms of outcomes over which he has significant, although not necessarily complete, control. As we have seen, agency theory suggests that if the principal is weakly risk-averse and the agent strictly risk-averse, and only the payoff is jointly observable, the P-optimal employment contract would call for some risk-sharing, although the agent is never called on to bear all the risk. Consequently, the agent's performance evaluation report and his remuneration optimally depend not only on how well he performs the tasks for which he is responsible, but also on the realized state of the world, over which he has no control. We raised the question earlier as to whether it is practicable to reward managers on the basis of their risk-bearing ability as well as their task performance. Agency theory may or may not also provide a justification for the common practice of *allocating overhead and joint costs.*

Other implications of agency theory for management accounting include specifying the conditions under which *budget-based incentive contracts* will be P-optimal, and when *participation* by agents *in budget-setting* will lead to a P-improvement in EUs (the agency approach focusing, not on the motivational effect of participation per se, but on the opportunity it affords for the principal to extract from the agent private information which can then become an argument in the fee schedule). There has also been some attempt to characterize *optimal performance standards* in the agency context (e.g., should standards be very tight, "currently attainable," etc.?) (Demski and Feltham 1978). Finally, the question of when deviations ("variances") of actual cost from standard cost should be investigated has been examined in the light of agency theory. The agency approach recognizes that the decision about *when to investigate a deviation* (and more generally what kind of investigation policy to choose) is not unaffected by the particular policy chosen. This policy has motivational and risk-sharing implications. Baiman and

Demski (1980a) found that the use of policies based on statistical quality control (investigate if the deviation $x \leqslant x_L$ and/or if $x \geqslant x_U$, the subscripts denoting the lower and upper control limits) could be P-optimal within an agency context.

Agency research has also addressed the question of whether (cost and contribution margin) variance analysis in accounting (i.e., the use of standards, as discussed in Chapter 8, the computation of variances, and the isolation of the variances assignable to an agent) offers any advantage *from a motivational point of view* over basing an agent's compensation on the actual outcome, without disaggregation. Of course, to base the agent's compensation on the standard outcome alone rather than on the aggregated or disaggregated actual outcome would force the principal to bear all the risk, the standard outcome usually being defined as the expected outcome.

To illustrate, denote the actual outcome by $x = pq$, where p and q are the actual price and quantity variables, respectively, and let the optimal fee schedule be $f^*(.)$. If the actual values of p and q are jointly observable by principal and agent, Holmström's informativeness condition (Holmström 1979, 84–86), referred to earlier, in effect states that it is desirable to base the agent's compensation on p and q only if $E(x|f^*(p, q)) > E(x|f^*(x))$ (Baiman and Demski 1980b). From a motivational point of view it is worth disaggregating the actual value of x into the actual values of p and q only if this condition is met, that is, only if x is not a sufficient statistic for (p, q). If the condition is met, joint observation of p and q will better allow the principal to infer the extent to which the agent, rather than the environment, was responsible for x.

Baiman and Demski (1980a) remark that the reason for preferring the actual values of p and q to be jointly observable is the same as the reason for undertaking variance analysis, namely to isolate that part of the variance ("controllable variance") for which the agent is to be held responsible. It follows from the informativeness condition that if the actual outcome x has been disaggregated into its actual price and quantity components p and q (as when knowing p and q offers the principal more information on the agent's behavior than knowing x alone), there is no motivational value in computing the variances of p and q from their standard values, which are known to both principal and agent. The actual values of p and q serve as sufficient statistics for their variances.

In other agency research, Fama (1980) found the proposition that separation of security ownership and control can be explained as an efficient form of economic organization to be proved within an agency perspective, although he did not consider the objection raised by the markets and hierarchies viewpoint. Gjesdal (1981) and Atkinson and

Feltham (1981) have used an agency approach to gain insights into the stewardship role of published financial reports, that is, the role of public ex post financial reports in capital markets. Published financial reports can be regarded as serving two functions. The first is that of motivating managers (to maximize the stockmarket value of the firm in this context) under conditions of moral hazard. Second, together with dividend policy, alternative financial reporting systems serve as a basis for risk-sharing between managers and investors.

Guide to further reading

The list of references given in this chapter is formidable, and the reader interested in following up any of the topics discussed may like some guidance. The following is a short recommended reading list.

Behavioral theories of motivation	Hofstede (1972), ch. 3; Hopwood (1976), chs. 2-5; Lawler and Rhode (1976), chs. 2, 4-6
Evolution of motivation in theories of the firm	Cyert and March (1963), chs. 2-4, 6; Alchian (1965); Furubotn and Pejovich (1972)
Agency theory	Jennergren (1980); Baiman (1982); Tiessen and Waterhouse (1983); Namazi (1985)

11
Measurement

The idea of measurement, in the sense of "pinning numbers on things" (Stevens 1959), is so familiar that it is difficult to imagine life without it. Mathematics began with the concept of number, and hence with measurement in the everyday sense. Why, then, the reader may ask, has measurement been singled out to occupy such an exalted place among the key conceptual ideas involved in understanding management? That the concept of a measure is regarded as important in its own right both in scientific work and in everyday affairs is evidenced by the place accorded it in modern mathematics, and even in dealing with some classes of phenomena that may not be thought of as susceptible to quantification. In mathematics the topic of "measure theory" comes after the usual undergraduate degree program and courses in real analysis (theory of functions of a real variable) and general topology. We begin to get the impression, then, that there may be more to measurement than meets the eye, that the process used to answer the questions How many? and How much? may be conceptually deeper than appears at first sight. This much may already be familiar to students whose background is in the natural sciences or engineering, but it is less likely to be to arts and social sciences students. In what follows, *measurement* will be used interchangeably with *measure* as a noun, as well as describing the act of measuring. Measurement *theory* (Krantz et al., 1971) and measure *theory* (Halmos, 1950) contain a number of common themes but are distinct. While the latter is purely mathematical and abstract, the former is more concerned with adding to our understanding of empirical situations.

To understand the significance of measurement as part of the conceptual framework needed in studying the management of organizations, it will be our aim in the text of this chapter to steer a middle course between a superficial introduction to the subject and the deep problems of modern abstract analysis, in which measure theory forms part of the modern theory of the integral (we have to integrate with respect to some "measure"). For the latter, the reader could consult Halmos (1950), Carathéodory (1963), Royden (1968), Munroe (1968), Krantz et al. (1971), and Kirman (1981), and on probability measure Kolmogorov (1950), Loève (1963), and Moran (1968). A middle course of readings would be represented by Stevens (1959), Suppes and Zinnes (1963), and Roberts and Schulze (1973, ch. 3).

After discussing what is involved in measurement from the viewpoint of measure theory, we will ask what special problems may arise in making measurements in the social sciences and business administration.

What is measurement?

Measurement may be broadly defined as the process of mapping empirical properties or relations into a formal model. Historically, two distinct stages of development are discernible. Under what is now referred to as the classical view, which prevailed until at least the 1930s, measurement was restricted to the empirical operation of addition. That is, it was considered permissible to measure only if the things or properties concerned could be physically added together. The modern view, by contrast, defines *measure* in terms of invariance or uniqueness under various classes of transformations. Scales of measurement are classified in terms of the class of transformations that will leave the scale form-invariant. The modern theory is thus much more general than the classical theory; it is not limited to one restricted class of empirical operations (addition). Consequently, many things are now considered measurable that would not have been under the classical definition.

Terminology of measure theory

Before proceeding to consider the problem of measurement, it is necessary to define certain terms, namely *space, relational system, mapping (function, transformation), isomorphism* and *homomorphism, set function,* and *measure function* (or simply *measure*). In keeping with the character of this book, every endeavor will be made to keep the text as free of symbols as possible, but some will have to be introduced in this chapter. A formal statement of the main concepts of measure theory and some associated ideas is presented in the Mathematical Appendix.

First we introduce the concept of a *space*. Ω will denote the space under consideration, the totality of all the elements (points) that may appear in our investigation. We will be concerned with points in this space (denoted by lower-case letters x, y, . . .), sets of these points (denoted by capital letters A, B, . . .), and classes of these sets (denoted $\mathscr{A}$, $\mathscr{B}$, . . .). The symbol R will be used as the general symbol for a relation. Thus R may stand for $<$, $+$, and so on. The only other new notation is confined to the Mathematical Appendix.

The kind of space on which various types of measures are defined may be described as metric, pseudo-metric, or nonmetric. *Metric* is to be understood here as meaning the "distance" between two points of a space. The inclusion of nonmetric spaces, on which "distance" is not defined, shows the increased generality of the modern theory of measurement compared with the classical theory. Points in a nonmetric space, while not based on an addition operation, may nevertheless yield measurements on a ratio scale (defined below). An example of a nonmetric space might be the space of feelings, or of management styles.

A *relational system* consists of a set A and a number of specified relations R_i, $i = 1, 2, \ldots, m$. If the set A is the set of real numbers, the system is called a *numerical relational system*. If the set A represents anything other than the real number system (e.g., A may represent persons, commodities) the system is called an *empirical relational system*. The measurements we make and encounter in a business organization include both kinds of relational system.

A *function f* is a particular kind of relation in which all the members are *ordered pairs*, and such that if $\langle x, y \rangle$ and $\langle x, z \rangle$ are members of f, $y = z$. Part of the problem of measurement consists in mapping an empirical relational system onto a numerical relational system by showing that certain aspects of an appropriately chosen numerical relational system have the same structure as the empirical system. The mapping f results in numerical assignments to things or properties of things in the empirical system. If the function f satisfies certain conditions to be stated in a moment, it is called a *measure function*, or simply *measure*. In the case just described it would lead to a *fundamental measure*. If the mapping is not from an empirical relational system directly, but instead depends on other numerical assignments, it results in a *derived measure*. Thus weight is measurable in a direct or fundamental way, whereas density is measured by the ratio of two fundamental measures, mass and volume.

Reference was made above to setting up a correspondence between the structure of an empirical system and a set of numbers, usually the real number system or the extended real number system (including $-\infty$ and $+\infty$). This means that the function f must be order-preserving relative to some ordering relation such as the partial ordering $\leqslant$. It is intuitively obvious that if we wish to measure by a simple number a certain property of the elements of an empirical system, the mapping f must preserve the structure of the empirical system. Transformations that satisfy this condition are either isomorphic or homomorphic. An *isomorphic* transformation means that f is one to one—the empirical system and the number system have the same number of elements. A *homomorphic* transformation allows some elements of the empirical system to be assigned the same number (e.g., two people may have the same income). A mapping $f: A \rightarrow B$ is said to be *onto* if the range of f is all of b; otherwise f is said to be from A *into* (or to) B.

A *set function* is a numerically valued function that is defined for every set in some class of sets. That is, it assigns a real number to each such set. Roughly speaking, a measure function is a set function that is additive and nonnegative. If the set function $f(A)$ is a measure function, it may be regarded intuitively as the amount of "mass" contained in the set. Note that we are using the same symbol, f, to denote functions whose domains are point sets, such as the point function $f(x)$, and functions whose domains are classes of point sets, such as the set function $f(A)$. It is hoped that this will not cause any confusion.

The two basic properties of a measure, then, are that it is a function of sets, not of points, and that (except in the case of measures defined on nonmetric spaces) it satisfies an additivity condition; it also must always be nonnegative. In the Mathematical Appendix one particular kind of measure much encountered in business administration, probability measure, is defined as a special case. Subjective (or personal) probability as discussed in Chapter 5 meets the requirements of a measure as well as probability in the objective, relative frequency sense.

Over time the number of classes of set functions regarded as measures has grown considerably. To qualify as a measure, a set function need not now always correspond to the empirical operation of addition (measures defined on nonmetric spaces do not do so), but only meet the weaker condition that it is invariant under some class or classes of transformations.

The representation problem

We are now ready to address the two main problems in the theory of measurement. They are the problem of representation and the problem of uniqueness. The representation problem is to show that certain characteristics of the real number system (or the extended real number system) have the same structure as an empirical system being investigated, the latter consisting of things or properties of things. More precisely, a relation that measures (assigns a simple number to) a given set of things or the properties of a given set of things in the domain of an empirical system must be isomorphic, or at least homomorphic, to an appropriately chosen numerical relational system. This is what we mean by "having the same structure as." By "appropriately chosen numerical relational system" we mean that the numerical relations are familiar ones like addition and multiplication, not unnatural ones.

So the representation problem has to do with the mapping from a set of objects or properties of objects to a set of numbers. There are no restrictions on this mapping (measurement procedure) (i.e., on the way numbers are assigned), *except* that the assignments

(i) must not be random
(ii) must be isomorphic (one-to-one) or homomorphic (many-to-one), and
(iii) should be meaningful to the user of the measurement.

In order to establish a numerical assignment for the empirical system, it is sufficient to find one numerical relational system that is homomorphic to the empirical system. In the case of multidimensional measurements, relating to an empirical system that encompasses more than one domain, the numerical assignment f becomes a vector (or n-tuple) rather than a single number.

The uniqueness problem

The second basic problem of measure theory is to determine the kind of scale that results from the measurement procedure (i.e., from the mapping f). The type of scale specifies the degree to which the numerical assignment given by f is unique. That is, *uniqueness* is defined in terms of invariance under some specified type of transformation.

A measurement *scale* is defined in terms of an empirical relational system, a numerical relational system, and the function f, which maps the former homomorphically onto the latter. It is important to note that a scale and the mapping or numerical assignment f are two different things. Often there are several different mappings that would serve as a scale. In fact, we can conceive of an infinity of types of measurement scales that might be constructed, defined by various classes of numerical transformations. Most of these, however, would not be of practical use because they do not (at least in our present state of knowledge) bear any relation to empirical reality. The types of scale that remain can be arranged in a hierarchy of usefulness, ranging from a nominal scale (least useful) up to a ratio scale (most useful). One scale is more useful than another if it gives us more information about the empirical system under study. The type of scale that can be used in measuring any empirical phenomenon is determined by the relative uniqueness of the numerical assignment f. Uniqueness or invariance is always relative: it refers, explicitly or implicitly, to the admissible numerical assignments relative to some scale. For a given scale, the mapping f is called an *admissible transformation*.

Examples of the different types of measurement scales will help to make this clearer. The simplest types of scale are *classification scales* (e.g., the numbers appearing in certain positions in a sequence of numbers on a particular credit card of all holders living in the same area) or a *nominal scale* (numbers arbitrarily assigned to objects or names, such as the numbers assigned to members of a football team). At the same time it should be recognized that an operation of determining equality between an object and a number is at the very root of systematizing and conceptualizing our environment. In each of these cases the numbers merely identify something; they are useless in numerical operations. A nominal scale at first sight seems to contradict our earlier condition that the numerical assignments should be nonrandom, that is, not arbitrary. A nominal scale qualifies as a measurement scale if we say that measurement is the assignment of numbers to objects *according to rule*, the rule in this case being "don't assign the same number to different classes or different members of the same class" (Stevens 1959, 25). An *absolute scale* is exemplified by counting, which was the origin of number systems.

At a slightly more useful level an *ordinal scale* enables one to determine greater or lesser values. In other words, it preserves a ranking. For example, in the theory of consumer behavior in economics the satisfaction derived by a consumer from two different commodity bundles may be compared in terms of the relations of preference and indifference. A *difference scale* determines equality of differences. This type of scale is less common than the others discussed here. It apparently has been used in psychology (Suppes and Zinnes 1963, section 4.2). An *interval scale* determines equality of intervals. Here numbers are assigned to intervals, with the value of an interval taken to be the difference between its end points. Examples of such a scale are the measurement of temperature by thermometer readings, and von Neumann-Morgenstern utility, discussed in Chapters 4 and 5. Finally, a *ratio scale* determines the equality of ratios. The measurement of weight or of per capita income afford examples. The significance of "ratio" will be apparent from table 11.1. In practice we use a ratio scale wherever possible because it is the most powerful.

Table 11.1 gives definitions of the various scales of measurement and

TABLE 11.1. Definition and classification of measurement scales.

Scale	What it Does	Class of Admissible Transformations*	Degree of Uniqueness
Classification	Identifies	One-to-one transformation: $x' = x$ within any given class	Unique up to the identity transformation for distinct classes, otherwise arbitrary.
Nominal	Determines equality	One-to-one: $x' = f(x)$, f any one-to-one transformation	Unique up to the identity transformation.
Absolute	Determines equality (equivalence)	Identity transformation (a one-to-one mapping onto itself): $x' = x$	Unique up to the identity transformation. No arbitrary choice of unit or zero.
Ordinal	Determines greater or less	Monotone (increasing or decreasing) transformation	Unique up to a monotone transformation (preserves a ranking relation). Arbitrary except for order.
Difference	Determines equality of differences	Translation transformation: $x' = x + b$	Unique up to an additive constant. Unique unit, arbitrary origin.
Interval	Determines equality of intervals	Positive linear transformation: $x' = ax + b$, $a > 0$, $b >$, $=$, or < 0. Every linear transformation with $b = 0$ is a similarity transformation.	Unique up to a positive linear transformation. Unit and zero both arbitrary.
Ratio	Determines equality of ratios	Similarity transformation: $x' = cx$, $c > 0$	Unique up to a similarity transformation (i.e., up to multiplication by a positive constant). Unit arbitrary, origin unique.

*Any number x on the scale at left can be replaced by another number, x', where x' is the transformation (function) of x shown in this column.
Source: Compiled by the author.

a hierarchical classification of them. The third column is to be understood as cumulative, in the sense that the admissible class of transformations for a given scale includes the transformation shown against that scale and all transformations for scales appearing above it in the table. For example, to construct an interval scale we need a procedure for equating intervals, plus a procedure for equating differences, one for determining greater or lesser values, and one for determining equality (Stevens 1959, 24). A ratio scale is more powerful and useful than an interval scale, which is in turn more useful than an ordinal scale. The fourth column shows the degrees of uniqueness of the scales. Here the expression "unique up to (some transformation)" is to be understood as meaning that, of all the possible mappings that would serve as a scale, the admissible set of mappings that leaves the structure of the scale invariant (i.e., which results in a unique measure) is restricted to the class of transformation shown in column 3 of the same row. Each class of transformation mentioned in column 3 contains the one above it; for example, a "similarity" transformation (ratio scale) contains a linear transformation (interval scale).

Stevens (1959, 27) has classified some statistical measures by their invariance under admissible transformations. Some of the statistics appropriate to nominal and ordinal scales (e.g., mode, median) are called nonparametric or distribution-free statistics. The *cluster* concept is peculiarly suited to the needs of statistical scaling (and to those of statistical inference in general).

Meaningfulness

In addition to the two basic problems of representation and uniqueness there is a third technical problem involved in measurement, the problem of meaningfulness. The question here is: Given a mapping from an empirical set to the set of real numbers which qualifies as a measure, what numerical statements have a clear empirical meaning? This question is important because it affects how measurements may be used. From what has been said earlier it is fairly clear that the meaningfulness of any empirical statement about an empirical set will depend on the uniqueness of the scale that is used in making the statement. The following examples from Suppes and Zinnes (1963) will illustrate the point. Suppose we have two numerical statements about temperature: (1) The ratio of the maximum temperature today to the maximum temperature yesterday is 1.10 and (2) The ratio of the difference between today's and yesterday's maximum temperatures to the difference between today's and tomorrow's maximum temperatures is 0.95. Statement 1 has no clear meaning unless a measurement scale (Fahrenheit, Celsius, Kelvin) is specified. The statement is true if we use a Fahrenheit scale, untrue for a Celsius scale (the ratio would then be 1.15). So the choice of a specific numerical assignment is critical in this case. Statement 2 is true (meaningful), provided only that the same temperature scale is being used, and it is Fahrenheit or Celsius (but not Kelvin). This is because the F and C scales are interval scales (the Kelvin scale is a higher-order ratio scale) and the admissible class of transformations is a linear transformation. We know that to convert from the F to the C scale involves such a transformation: $C = 5 (F - 32)/9$. In other words, the specification of a measurement scale (unless it is Kelvin) is not critical in this case and the statement is meaningful. More generally, we say that a numerical statement about an empirical set is meaningful if its truth or falsity is constant under admissible scale transformations of any of its numerical assignments. The meaningfulness of numerical statements is thus determined by the uniqueness properties of their numerical assignments.

Measurement in the social sciences and in business administration

Before proceeding to examine the applicability of measure theory to the social sciences and business administration, it may be well to recapitulate the main points of the foregoing technical discussion.

Measurements may be made by the human senses and brain with or without the aid of measuring instruments. The latter are essential in measuring quantities to which the human senses do not respond (e.g., magnetism) or quantities that are not accessible. Instrumental measurement often improves on human capabilities, for example, by providing greater range, accuracy, or speed. The measurement process starts with a definition of the quantity, property, condition, or other characteristic that is to be measured. If this definition of the characteristic is conceptual in nature, it must be converted to an operational definition. To measure an object or characteristic is to assign it a unique position along some kind of numerical scale. Measure theory attempts to understand which qualitative relationships lead to numerical assignments that reflect the structure of these relationships, to explain the ways in which different measures relate to one another, and to examine the problem of error in the measurement process.

Leaving the last of these aside for the moment, the basic problems of measure theory are, first, to justify the assignment of numbers to objects or characteristics, that is, to go from relations in an empirical system to a numerical representation of these relations. This involves characterizing the formal properties of the empirical relations and showing that there are numerical assignments in which familiar mathematical relations and operations such as ⩾ and + correspond structurally to the relations found to exist in the empirical system. This is the representation problem. The second problem concerns the uniqueness of the representation provided by the numerical assignment: How close is it to being the only possible representation of its type? For example, a representation of mass is unique in all respects except choice of unit; the representation is different for pounds than for grams, and so on. The third problem mentioned earlier concerned the meaningfulness of the numerical assignments to users: Do they have unambiguous meaning empirically? A fourth basic problem, that of measurement error, will be taken up later.

That measurement problems are taken seriously in the social sciences can be judged by glancing at the literature. There has, for example, been a journal called *Annals of Economic and Social Measurement* since 1972. And a number of books by social scientists have addressed the theory and problems of measurement as applied to psychology, sociology, and economics (e.g., Kirman 1981; Blalock 1982, 1974; Krantz et al. 1971).

One of the problems that commonly arises, which is not peculiar to the social sciences, is that the social scientist will strive for a measure on the "highest" scale possible in the hierarchy of scales, at the same time being careful to ensure that her variables are linked with mathematical representations in such a way that the use of specific mathematical operations such as addition or multiplication are justified by the chosen scale. For example, only a very restrictive set of mathematical operations can be applied to an ordinal scale if the operations are to correspond to some real world counterpart. One set of numbers may be arbitrarily transformed into another, provided only that a numerical order is preserved among them. This extreme flexibility in the admissible transformations means that the researcher cannot expect very powerful mathematical conclusions to result. The mathematics will not carry her anywhere near as far as if greater restrictions had been imposed on the admissible transformations. The researcher will therefore try to define her concepts and the variables by which they are represented in such a way that the conditions for a ratio scale are fulfilled.

A problem faced in fundamental measurement (other than probability measurement) that is much more formidable in the social sciences than in the natural sciences is due to the absence of suitable empirical "concatenation" operations. This may be explained by reference to measuring length. If we have two objects, we can compare their relative lengths by aligning one of their end points and putting them side by side. This process yields only an ordinal scale, however (corresponding to the mathematical operation ⩾). But by using a ruler to measure length (or standard weights on one side of a balance to measure an unknown mass) we are able to make unique numerical assignments. These are justified by a physical operation, called concatenation, which is the counterpart of addition as a mathematical operation, and it yields a ratio scale. The former (noninstrumental) process is called *intensive measurement,* the latter *extensive measurement.* In the social sciences we cannot yet measure extensively such characteristics as utility, intelligence, and so on. It has been observed, however, that many of the attributes we wish to measure belong to objects having at least two independent components, each of which affects the attribute. For example, preference among gambles is affected by both the outcomes and the probabilities of occurrence. This has led to *conjoint measurement theory.* The way in which each component affects the attribute is studied by finding what changes have to be made in one component to compensate for changes in the other.

In the natural (physical) sciences, a number of derived concepts that make sense when applied to physical phenomena have been found to depend on homogeneity properties (or empirical constants) of a small number of fundamental concepts. Thus Cohen and Nagel (1955) noted that the remarkable progress achieved in the measurement of physical phenomena has involved the process of substituting derived measures for possible fundamental measurement operations that would have yielded only ordinal properties at best. In fact, over 100 basic variables in physics can be defined in terms of six fundamental measures (length, mass, time, temperature, charge, angle). In the social sciences there is a lack of such empirical constants. Human beings differ along many dimensions, and attempts to categorize or group individuals are therefore unlikely to produce sufficiently homogeneous units. In the same way there is a problem in determining the boundaries of a unit act in human behavior because behaviors merge imperceptibly into one another. Specific behaviors may need to be given differential weights depending on their intensity, duration, motivation, location within a sequence, and so on. Acts of different individuals at a given time, or even of the same individual at different times, are not interchangeable (homogeneous).

Many of the measures used by researchers in the social sciences and in practical business affairs are indirect, in the sense of being derived measures. They are obtained by combining in some way fundamental measures made by someone else or for a different purpose. A somewhat similar problem arises in connection with "auxiliary" measures when we want to be able to compare measures across different persons or different situations. Whenever this is the case it is incumbent upon the researcher to satisfy himself that he understands the basis of the fundamental measures or auxiliary measures. For example, to compare the mass of a body on the surface of the earth with that of a body on the surface of Mars we need a theory explaining the corrections (auxiliary measures) that must be made for the different gravitational constants near the surface of the two bodies. As Blalock (1982) notes, if a given indicator is of the form $Y = a + bX$, it may have different meanings in different contexts (e.g., over persons, time periods, geographically, etc.) if (i) b has opposite signs; (ii) the value of b (slope) differs from one setting to another; (iii) the intercept a differs; (iv) the relationship is linear in one setting and nonlinear in another; or (v) if the behavior represented by the indicator has different consequences in different settings.

Another way in which measures may be indirect which is often used in the social sciences is when measures on some population of objects are inferred on the basis of a statistical sample. Yet another sense in which measurement may be indirect occurs in psychology in the form of measurement by inference. Some very complex attributes such as intelligence or degree of introversion are inferred from measurements of observable behavior.

The results of any measurement must "make sense" in the real world. Essentially, this means that conceptual variables must be defined in such a way that zero points and measurement units have a well-understood meaning, to other researchers or empirically. If they do not, the validity of the mathematical or statistical analyses in which they are employed, and which presuppose that they do make sense, might be cast in doubt.

The multi-attribute nature of human beings may lead to a confounding of variables and oversimplified interpretations. People are exposed to a large number of influences/pressures/stimuli that are empirically interrelated and difficult to isolate from one another. If the researcher uses only a small number of these stimuli as indicators of the entire set in explaining some kind of individual behavior, the results may be misleading. And if he groups individuals by sex, race, age, religion, occupation, and so on, it may not be valid to assume (as he would be doing) that members of a group are sufficiently homogeneous on one of these dimensions with respect to a particular stimulus.

Most measures with which we are concerned in the social sciences and business administration are unidimensional, taking the form of a simple number. Multidimensional measures are not uncommon, however. The idea of a multidimensional measure, called *geometric measurement* in measure theory, dates back to the introduction of analytical geometry by Descartes in the seventeenth century. Geometric points are represented by a pair of numbers (coordinates) in the case of a plane, by a triple, and so on, in the case of a space. The only distinguishing feature here is that the representation is made in terms of pairs, triples, or n-tuples of numbers rather than by a simple number.

In the natural sciences it has long been recognized that the numerical value assigned to the object being measured (the latter is called the *measurand*) is not the same as that when the object is not being measured. This is because measurement always involves a comparison of the measurand with a reference quantity of the same kind, or of signals that represent them, and a transfer of energy occurs during this process. If the effect of the energy transfer is large enough to be significant, the exact value of the measurand must be inferred from knowledge of the disturbing process. Somewhat analogously, it has been noticed (first by Elton Mayo in the 1930s) that individual human behavior (and performance) in the workplace varies when individuals or groups know they are being observed. It was also noted in Chapter 9 that performance is not unaffected by the nature of the reference indicator (e.g., budget or standard) with which it is compared. Besides the question of how objects or characteristics are measured, there is also the question of frequency of measurement. If the dynamic behavior of the measurand oscillates or has a seasonal pattern, for example, the frequency with which measurements are made will have a decided effect on the resulting measures and their interpretation.

Another kind of problem encountered in economics, psychology, and sociology is concerned not so much with measurement per se as with *aggregation* to provide representative measures for larger units (an industry, economy, community). Basic to the process of aggregation is the notion of similarity. But, as Blalock (1982) observes, "similar to what?" The commonality of the measures being aggregated should have some theoretical or conceptual basis (e.g., the measures should have common causes or effects in causal analyses) or less restrictively, possess some conceptually common characteristic making them at least partially homogeneous. Items that are aggregated haphazardly (e.g., on the basis of administrative convenience) will generally yield misleading or meaningless aggregates (we would be confounding other causal variables with the ones being studied). The aggregation of items on a balance sheet, having been measured on different bases, affords an example of aggregation yielding misleading results. (The nature and role of measurement in accounting have been studied by Ijiri 1965b, 1967, 1975; Vickrey 1970; and Tippett 1978, among others.)

An aggregation procedure needs to be justified; before proceeding we should ask ourselves why the measures should *not* be aggregated. If undertaken, aggregation requires linear models; and the methods used to construct the aggregates must necessarily be relatively simple and explicit. Besides the problem of comparability or equivalence, some aggregates such as a wholesale price index, cost-of-living index, or index of gross national product (GNP) involve statistical sampling, with its attendant problems.

Errors

No discussion of measurement would be complete without mention of errors, because measurement in practice is always subject to error. There are many different possible sources of error, but it is probably fair to say that in research in the social sciences most attention is paid to one of them, namely, errors due to sampling, and very little to measurement error.

A comprehensive list of sources of possible error would include, first, errors of observation. These include inaccuracies in measuring instruments, personal errors due to human observers, systematic errors (such as making an incorrect adjustment for height above sea level in measuring atmospheric pressures), and random error, due to causes unknown or not understood. In practice, the last-mentioned receives most attention through the application of probabilistic methods. Errors due to sampling are a second source. Unlike the first type, these are of course expected, with the safeguard that they are likely to be smaller for larger samples. Sampling errors receive considerable attention in statistics and econometrics. Errors in fundamental measures used to construct derived measures are a third category. They are of course subject to errors of observation and possibly of sampling. A fourth source of error is that due to unjustified interpolation or extrapolation.

Conclusion

The theory of measurement has made marked progress since the 1950s. Up to that time measurement was considered justifiable only if there existed an empirical operation in the measurand similar to the mathematical operation of addition. In other words, only the measurement of quantities, not of qualities, was considered appropriate. The advent of Stevens' work in the late 1950s changed that; measurement was henceforth to be understood in terms of the relative uniqueness or invariance of the numerical representation. Modern measurement theory applies to quantities and qualities alike, and qualities are characterized by an absence of an empirical operation corresponding to addition. Hence measurement is no longer limited to one restricted class of empirical operations. There are still many qualities and "imponderables" that have not been measured; but there is no reason to suppose that in time many of these will not become measurable.

12

Causation and Explanation

Chapters 2 through 10 identified the areas in which conceptual matters are considered vital to an understanding of the management of organizations. In Chapter 11 we recognized that very few investigations can be carried out without the introduction of quantitative methods at some point. Both theoretical and practical considerations make it imperative that we be able to replace qualitative distinctions with quantitative ones; we need to be able to measure qualitative as well as quantitative differences. Investigations would be of limited value if they did not go beyond description of organization phenomena, however. We must explain as well as describe. We could say that description is prior to explanation, although in another sense description might be regarded as a first, superficial pass at explanation. Moreover, we should like to know whether there are any regularities (*general* hypotheses, laws) revealed by our explanations, for this would obviate the need for further investigations (observations or experiments) of the same class of phenomena. This final chapter addresses the question of what constitutes a valid explanation, and whether it needs to be causal.

The general notion of explanation may be stated as being any proper answer to a why question. A proper answer would exclude an answer that merely repeated the question without the *why,* or involved errors in reasoning (more on this later). The answer to the why? must intellectually satisfy the questioner, partially or completely. The key notion behind explanation is understanding. The questioner may already be in possession of part of the explanation and merely be seeking to complete it (so that a partial explanation may satisfy him); and of course an explanation that intellectually satisfies one person completely may not satisfy another person who is more advanced intellectually. In philosophical language, what is to be explained is called the *explicandum,* and the proposition (hypothesis) offered in explanation of it is called the *explicans,* the latter being required to be different from the former.

As we shall see in the sequel, there are different kinds of explanations, all of them perfectly valid. Different kinds of phenomena frequently call for different kinds of explanations. In science, the phenomena to be explained are empirical facts; scientific explanation seeks to make reality intelligible, or to explain already established scientific laws in terms of more general (higher-level) laws.

By no means do all of the proper answers to why? involve a cause–effect relation. In fact, even in the natural sciences, explanations and even laws are not all causal in the strict sense, to be defined shortly. Students of management, as of any other field of knowledge, should therefore recognize that explanation does not have to be causal to be valid. The first task, then, is to provide a list of some of the main types of explanation that may be used, and which are encountered, in relation to organizational phenomena.

Categories of Determination and Explanation

In view of the foregoing, let us replace the causal relation by the broader relation, "is determined by." Thus we will say, "*B* is determined by *A,*" where *A* is not necessarily the cause of *B*. For the present we will merely say, that what it means to state that *B* is *determined* by *A,* is that *B* becomes intelligible, understandable, by relating it to *A* in some way.

In this broad sense, determination is called "general determinism" or "neodeterminism" by Bunge (1979a), and is defined by saying that "everything is determined in accordance with laws by something else, this something else being the external as well as the internal conditions of the object in question" (p. 26). Thus two ideas are involved. The first is that the dependence of *B* on *A* must be in accordance with laws; it must be regular and conform to definite patterns, although the patterns may change and the regularity need not be universal (a small percentage of individual cases may not conform to the law). The second idea is that of productivity, the idea that nothing comes out of nothing or passes into nothing (the genetic principle). This principle says that *B* is *produced* by *A.* Hence, "*general determination*" *means* "*lawful production*", or production in accordance with some law or regular pattern, rather than arbitrarily. The necessary and sufficient components of determination in the general sense are productivity and lawfulness. This applies to all categories of determination.

So the explanation of B or of a change in B must rest on some notion of determination. A and B may be things, the states of things, the qualities of things, or they may be events. The nature of the determination, the way in which B is determined, may be unique (as in causal or mechanical determination) or stochastic (as in statistical and teleological determination), all of which will shortly be defined. The only case ruled out is where the relation between A and B is *completely* indeterminate. (In view of what was said earlier, it should be added that B is determined by some thing or things, but not by A.) To each of the categories of determination listed below there corresponds a different type of valid explanation, a proper answer to the question, Why B?. None of these categories of determination (and their associated explanations) is likely to occur as a pure type in the real world. Hence no single type of explanation is likely to offer a *complete* explanation, although certain natural and social phenomena may be predominantly determined and explained in a single way.

The following are thought to be the main categories of determination:

1. *Self-determination*: The distinguishing feature here is that B is *quantitatively* determined by inner rather than external processes. Thus some organisms tend to maintain a constant body temperature, and the higher forms of living system (human beings, organizations) can use inputs of energy and information from their environments to reverse increasing entropy and become negentropic (Chapter 2). In each case B has intrinsic activity of its own that takes it from one state to another that differs in quantitative respects only. This is not to deny that B may undergo qualitative variations; the latter fall in another category (see 8, below).

2. *Causal determination* (causation): In calling B the effect and A the cause, the essential idea is that B is not merely accompanied by A but is produced or generated by A, and that this relation is constant *and unique*. The associated explanation takes the form "B because A." In a subsequent section this kind of relation will be explored further.

3. *Interaction* (reciprocal causation): B is determined by mutual action—the action of A and the reaction of B. This kind of determination was discussed in Chapter 3. Causation as defined in 2, above, cannot be regarded as a special case of interaction because causation implies unidirectionality (the relation between A and B is asymmetrical). We might be tempted to think of interaction as having a functional representation, $y = f(x)$, provided the function is single-valued, because this relation can be inverted to yield $x = f^{-1}(y)$. A functional view of reciprocal causation is inappropriate, however, because (a) functions express *constant* invariable relations, and (b) they do not reflect the fact that x

produces y. In causal determination the essential feature of productivity is irreversible.

4. *Mechanical determination*: A combination of quantitative self-determination (category 1) and interaction (category 3). The present state of B is quantitatively determined by B's previous state, by external forces, and by internal interactions. (This would be sufficient to explain human behavior only if human beings were not purposeful and were always completely rational.)

5. *Statistical determination*: Many explanations occurring in the natural sciences, and especially in the social sciences, are not of the form of universal hypotheses stating that B is lawfully produced by A in 100 or 0 percent of cases, but rather that the relation is expected to hold in a certain proportion of cases between these limits. Statistical determination is accorded a separate category, rather than saying A causes B with probability p, because causal determination, as strictly defined here, is unique and nonstochastic. In statistical determination we understand that A belongs to a *class* of instances (events, properties, states, things) and that B belongs to *another* class of instances. In the formalization of statistical laws the causal relations implicit in them hold between probability distributions (of events, etc.) rather than between individual events. Some of the most far-reaching theories in physics (e.g., the quantum theory), as well as many of those in the biological and social sciences, offer statistical explanations. Some of these explanations appear to be irreducibly statistical in form; others describe the (average) behavior to be expected over a large number of instances, where isolated instances may be determined in other ways (e.g., mechanically or teleologically). The importance of statistical explanations is such that Braithwaite (1960, 116) is able to say, "it will be safer . . . to take statistical hypotheses as being the normalcy, and to regard universal (i.e., non-statistical) hypotheses as being extreme cases of statistical hypotheses when the proportions in question are 100 or 0%."

6. *Structural (or holistic) determination*: This is determination of the parts by the whole, as for example when the functioning of an organ is partly determined by the needs or purposes of the whole organism. Alternatively, determination (and explanation) may here be in terms of another part of the whole of which the thing to be explained is part—thus actions of the body are controlled by the brain. The latter case is called *functional determination* by Braithwaite (1960, 335). Structural determination is a special case of interaction, since the behavior of the parts is (partly) determined by the whole, whose behavior is, in turn, (partly) determined by the parts.

7. *Teleological determination*: This is determination of the means by the ends (goals). We briefly referred to this in Chapter 2. Here

explanation takes the form "*A* in order that *B*." In other words the Why? is answered by specifying a goal (*B*), toward the attainment of which the event or activity (*A*) is a means. The activity is described as goal-directed. Teleological determination should be understood in a statistical sense for, as Bunge notes (1979a, 275), "human action is too often unsuccessful." Behavior that is goal-directed (i.e., teleological) may be conscious (intentional) or unconscious (unintentional).

This kind of determination (and explanation) has been the subject of a great deal of controversy among philosophers, the difficulty of course being the *apparent* determination of the present by the future. Braithwaite (1960, ch. 10) argues that teleological explanations of intentional goal-directed behavior are always reducible to causal explanations with intentions as causes; the intention does not produce the goal, but starts a causal chain of events whose final stage is attainment of the goal. The distinguishing feature of this causal chain is persistence toward the goal under varying conditions. Usually teleological explanations make no reference to the length of time taken in attaining the goal. Braithwaite states that teleological explanations that are not reducible to explanations in terms of a *conscious* intention to attain a goal (i.e., the explanation relates to unconscious goal-directed behavior) are still perfectly acceptable *first-stage* explanations. His feeling is that as science (notably biochemistry and biophysics) advances, "there is less and less reason to suppose that there will be any teleological action (or at any rate any teleological action in which consciousness is not involved) that will not be explicable by means of the concepts and laws" of science alone (1960, 327). In other words, he believes such explanations must be accepted as irreducible to causal explanations at present, but not as irreducible in principle. (Braithwaite defines "causal" in a broader sense than that adopted here.) In view of the fact that human goal-seeking is often unsuccessful, and that the laws governing the determination of such behavior are hence nonunique, it seems more reasonable to believe that explanations of intentional or unintentional teleological behavior will always remain statistical in nature rather than causal as here defined, reducible in most cases only to more refined and tested teleological laws expressed as statistical tendencies.

8. *Dialectical determination*: Also known as qualitative self-determination (see category 1), this is determination of a whole process by the inner opposition and subsequent synthesis of its components, as in the eventual agreement that is reached after a struggle between opposing human groups. The thing to be explained (e.g., a society), however homogeneous it may seem, is to some extent nonhomogeneous in some respect. This leads to inner stress which, augmented by external forces, may eventually bring about a qualitative change in the society. Thus

conflicting economic interests of different social groups within a society may determine changes in the social structure of these groups.

The principle of causality

To make the definition of causal determination more precise, we begin by saying that every concrete thing is in some state at any time relative to a given frame of reference, and that nothing stays in the same state forever (see the Mathematical Appendix for Chapter 2). We define an "event" to be a change in state. Then in saying that thing A causes thing B to do C, we mean that a certain event or events in A induced the change C in the state of B, the events and times being taken relative to the same frame of reference (Bunge 1979a, xx). The event occurring in thing A is a *cause* and the event in thing B, the change C, is the *effect*.

We have seen that determination does not necessarily imply causation, the latter being only one among several interrelated categories of determination. In the real world, determination is never exactly or exclusively causal. Traditionally, scientific explanation was regarded as causal explanation—the explanation of a fact was not usually considered to be scientific unless proximate and ultimate causes were assigned. This view is no longer held. It is now recognized that the causal principle has a limited range of validity. At best it is a first-order approximation. The degree of approximation is satisfactory in explaining some facts but not others.

The essential elements of causation, then, are (1) *production*, that is, an event occurring in one thing producing an event in another thing (a statistical correlation between two things is not causal; it merely shows that changes in the things are regularly associated); hence causation is more than just a relation, it is a coupling (see Chapter 3); (2) *unidirectionality*, meaning that the production is not reversible (A produces B, but not vice versa); (3) *uniqueness*, meaning that B follows from A in an unambiguous way—there is a one-to-one correspondence between A and B (a single A for every B, and vice versa), compared with statistical determination, where the connections between causes and effects are many-to-one; (4) *constancy*, this says that the relation between A and B must hold *almost* always (not necessarily always); at some point (strict) causation becomes statistical determination; (5) *conditionality*, represented by "if" in the "if—then almost always" statement of the causal principle, although this way of stating the principle fails to make clear that the relation is irreversible. The cause, A, need not exist, but if it did B would result in most cases. In other words, the emphasis is not on A and B but on the relation between them.

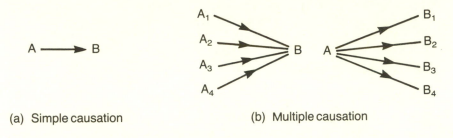

(a) Simple causation   (b) Multiple causation

FIGURE 12.1. Simple and multiple causation.

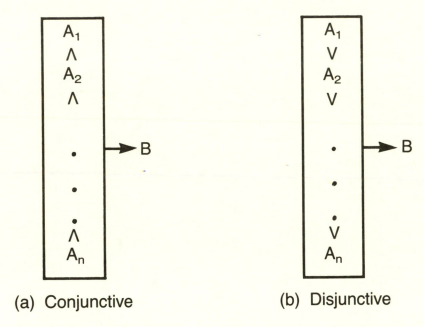

(a) Conjunctive   (b) Disjunctive

FIGURE 12.2. Conjunctive and disjunctive plurality of causes.

As thus defined, causation does not allow for the possibility of many causes and a single effect, or for a single cause and many effects. Together, these two cases are loosely referred to as multiple causation, compared with simple causation, in which there is a single cause and effect. This is illustrated in Figure 12.1.

A plurality of causes is defined as a single-effect case that subdivides into a conjunctive and disjunctive plurality of causes. The former involves *joint* determination of an effect by a number of causes. In the disjunctive case, by contrast, there is *alternative* rather than joint operation of the causes. Effect B is produced by A_1 *or* A_2 . . . , and if more than one cause is operating, the result is still B. This is illustrated in Figure 12.2, where the connective "$\lor$" denotes "and/or" and "$\land$" denotes "and." Conjunctive plurality of causes reduces to simple causation (i.e., $A_1 \land A_2 \land \ldots \land A_n = A$, the total cause), because the various causes, A_1, A_2, . . . , A_n, must all be present and acting jointly to produce B.

In this interpretation the term *multiple causation* relates only to disjunctive plurality of causes. But as Bunge points out (1979a, 124–25), even here it is a misnomer, because it does not conform to any of the accepted formulations of the causal principle, including the one given here. It is nonunique, and nonadditive—the joint action of several causes does not change the result. In the real world, explanations in the form of multiple (disjunctive) causation are often more enlightening than those expressing simple causation. How then should disjunctive multiple causation be treated? If we encounter a situation like that in Fig. 12.2 (b), with several possible alternative causes and a single effect, Bunge (1979a, ch. 5) says that we should try to break these multiple relations down into further, eventually noncausal, relations (the effect may not have been analyzed very carefully). As the set of causes becomes larger and more complex and the individual causes are roughly of equal influence, however, multiple causation degenerates into statistical determination.

To sum up, multiple causation, meaning disjunctive plurality of causes, may often provide a more complex explanation than simple causation, but strictly it is not a causal explanation. Discussion of plurality of effects (single cause, many effects) proceeds along lines similar to that of plurality of causes.

Scientific explanation

Science seeks to establish uniformities, *laws*. A scientific law is a *conditional general* hypothesis, stating what would happen if certain conditions are met. Scientific laws do not hold for individual instances, only for *classes* of facts or events. For such classes, scientific laws are statements of constant conjunction, or generalizations; but they are more than this. A scientific law offers an explanation, not in terms of generalizations that are only factually (or accidentally) true, although empirical observations were necessary in order to establish the law, but rather in terms of other laws in a scientific theory from which this law can be deduced. That is, in scientific explanation what serves to explain is usually a law that is consistent with other laws, rather than just an empirically established generalization. A *complete* scientific explanation involves explanation of classes of empirical phenomena in terms of a law, and explanation of the law in terms of other laws.

Thus we can speak of first- and second-stage explanation. A first-stage explanation is an explanation of particular empirical facts in terms of scientific laws, empirical propositions that hold if certain conditions are met and which are testable by experience. Second-state explanation consists of explanation of the scientific laws. The *why* is here answered by citing an established deductive system in which the law in question is a lower-level hypothesis deducible within that system from a set of higher-level laws (Braithwaite 1960, 342–43). Since scientific laws provide perfectible (and refutable) answers to *why*-questions (i.e., anticipate eventual extension of their domain of validity), there is no end to the hierarchy of scientific explanation—no completely final explanation.

A word should be added about the *disconfirmation of laws.* As already noted, laws are perfectible explanations; they may be discarded and replaced by improved laws. Here we note a difference between the way deterministic and probabilistic (or statistical) laws are disconfirmed. A deterministic scientific law or hypothesis is disconfirmed directly if it fails to be verified empirically. When a reliable observation conflicts with the prediction of a deterministic scientific law, some change must be made in the law. The validity of other scientific laws may also be affected. In addition, a deterministic scientific law may be disconfirmed indirectly if it is not consistent with some given body of scientific theory, that is, if there is no logical connection between it and other laws. If the scientific law is probabilistic, on the other hand, its disconfirmation requires not just a single disconfirming observation, but a sufficiently large number of such observations so as to show that the predicted distribution does not hold.

Scientific explanation and causation

Although causal explanation often forms an important part of scientific explanation, the answers to *why*-questions need not be causal in order to be scientific. To regard the two as identical amounts to assuming that *reason* and cause are the same, which they are not. Every kind of explanation described earlier involves giving a reason or reasons, providing an intellectually satisfying answer to a *why*-question. To equate reason and cause would be to insist that the only acceptable form of explanation is causal explanation. This mistaken identity was embodied in Leibniz's Principle of Sufficient Reason (1714) (nothing happens without sufficient reason), now discredited by all except orthodox rationalists. Incidentally, the Principle of Insufficient Reason (Jacob Bernouilli, seventeenth century), which says that chance events can be considered to be equally probable if we know of no reason why one of them should be expected rather than another, does not contradict the Principle of Sufficient Reason because it is a hypothesis, to be confirmed or refuted by empirical test of its consequences, not an ultimate explanation.

All explanations contain a reason or reasons; but some reasons may strike the *why*-questioner as dubious, suspect interpretations. Others may satisfy the questioner but will in fact mislead him; the explanation may therefore contain errors in reasoning. Some of the more common examples of these are classified below. More detailed accounts will be found in books on logic and scientific method, such as Cohen and Nagel (1955).

Errors in reasoning

Logical fallacies

Logical fallacies involve invalid inferences. Many important advances in knowledge have come from questioning propositions previously regarded as self-evident. Evidence is needed for what we believe or question. Usually we are satisfied with a preponderance of evidence. Logic is concerned with the adequacy of different kinds of evidence, more particularly with what constitutes conclusive evidence.

There are many kinds of logical fallacy. One results from the misuse of analogical reasoning. For example, it was once fashionable to draw certain conclusions in economics by analogy with processes in human biology. For the explanation of one series of events to serve by analogy to explain another, very different series of events, there must be some reason for believing that the two series of events have enough in common for the explanation of one to provide at least a partial explanation of the other. Reasoning in economics, psychology, and sociology by analogy with biology is invalid if the biological behavior is nonmotivated, that is, does not involve choice and purposiveness. And even in the case of motivated biological behavior, care must be taken in concluding that what is true for individuals is also true for groups of individuals. Recall from Chapter 2 that organizations are of a higher order of complexity than human systems; the parts as well as the whole are purposeful.

Verbal (or semilogical) fallacies

These involve ambiguities in the form of inference, such as use of the same word to mean two different things. Examples of this include the fallacy of composition (asserting that what is true of properties of elements of a whole is true of the whole); the fallacy of division (reasoning that the properties of a whole always apply to each of its elements); the fallacy of accident, deducing from some absolute principle (moral, social, legal) the answer to a specific human problem in which there are other considerations present that may more than offset it; and the converse fallacy (trying to refute a universal proposition by arguing that it does not hold in a certain individual case). What is true of individuals in certain specific cases (the "accidental" truth or exception referred to in the fallacy) is not necessarily true of them in general or in abstract relations. Science seeks to avoid all such ambiguities by defining all terms precisely and, through empirical testing, persistently trying to find counter-examples that falsify a conclusion.

Material fallacies

In everyday speech any argument that leads to a false conclusion is said to be fallacious. The false conclusion may have come about through errors in reasoning (logical fallacies) or ambiguities in the form of inference; "the logical kernel of explanation is generalization, the process of showing that the fact in question fits a general pattern" (Bunge 1979a, 291). In the present context we mean by logic the admissible procedures by which we go from an explicandum (the fact about which the *why*-question is asked) to an explicans (a general proposition or hypothesis, including the statement of a scientific law). But logic on its own does not tell the whole story of explanation any more than it does of the way in which our empirical knowledge is organized and advanced. We digress now to show why this is so.

Suppose we are asked to explain a certain fact. This may be done in two different ways. In the first we would explain the fact by reference to a law, that is, by demonstrating the inclusion of the fact in a class of the same or related facts that are governed by the law. This is the logical part of explanation, and the logical structure of this demonstration is that of *deduction:* the conclusion is a *logical* consequence of the premises (the law), and cannot be false if the premises are true. This method of explanation does not include a direct, explicit reference to facts, only to a proposition believed to be true of a wide class of facts. The second method of explaining would be by reference to a further fact, by showing that the second fact is *materially plausible.* The fact to be explained, for example, might be shown to have been caused by the second fact. This kind of explanation, while perhaps more immediately satisfying than the first, is incomplete, because reference to a law or general hypothesis is implicit in it. In other words, this second way masks the role of *inductive inference* in explanation.

In the empirical sciences (whether natural or social), by contrast with mathematics and formal logic, explanation and proof involve both deduction, going from a law to a particular instance or from a higher-level to a lower-level law, and induction, the inference of an empirical generalization from its instances or of a law (hypothesis) from empirical evidence for it. That is, the ground for believing a particular scientific law proceeds from the beginning (a general hypothesis) to the end (it applies in a particular instance) logically *and* from the end to the beginning epistemologically (confirming the general hypothesis by confronting it with experience). In mathematics and formal logic, on the other hand, the method of explanation and proof is one-way, from beginning to end, both logically and epistemologically. Braithwaite (1960, 257–58) describes this by saying that in deduction the reasonableness of belief in the premises overflows, providing reasonableness for the belief in the conclusion, whereas in induction there is no such automatic overflowing of reasonableness—it is no longer logically impossible for the premises to be true and the (inductive) conclusion false.

What are here called material fallacies, then, are errors in answers to *why*-questions which are not due to mistakes in reasoning or to semantics. The digression was designed to show that an explanation may lead to a false conclusion because logic alone cannot guarantee the material truth of all conclusions. With impeccable logic a conclusion may still be false because the premises (law, general hypothesis) from which it was deduced were false or because testing of the premises by experience was based on faulty observations.

Material fallacies come in many different forms, some of which are as follows:

post hoc, ergo propter hoc fallacy: that whatever follows an event is therefore caused by it. Whether the B that follows A was caused by A is a matter of fact, not merely of logic.

ex post theorizing: The converse case, which consists in inferring from objective, observable, realized events (*ex post* data) the subjective, *ex ante* forces (such as motivation) which led to them.

question begging: Including in what is to be explained or in the premises of an argument, in a disguised form, that which is to be explained or proved.

circular reasoning: Introducing into the premises of an argument a proposition that depends on the one at issue. In order to avoid reasoning in a circle, scientific method recognizes the logical necessity of beginning with a set of *unexplained* concepts (unexplained, at least, in the given context), which are regarded simply as hypotheses or assumptions, not as self-evident truths. The justification for their use is provided by the consequences that are deduced from them and by their consistency with other established hypotheses. Together, these describe the hypothetico-deductive inductive method of science. The logical necessity referred to extends to explanation in general, either directly or indirectly, as has been shown.

false question: For example, the question, Why was *A* wrong to leave his job with company *B*? falsely *assumes* already that he *was* wrong.

self-evidence: Explanations that rely entirely on intuitively revealed truth are no proof against their falsity; the intuition must be put to the test.

appeal to authority: It is no kind of valid explanation to appeal to a higher, expert authority. All humans are fallible.

sophistry: This kind of explanation, generally a refutation of an argument, confuses the issue. That is, the explanation (or refutation) involves using words or raising issues of an emotive or exaggerated nature that are logically irrelevant to the question at issue.

Other fallacies or failures to offer a valid explanation spring from misuses of the scientific method. Only one will be referred to here, the confusion between necessary and sufficient conditions for some proposition or result to hold. Formally, proposition p_1 is a sufficient condition for another proposition p_2 if "p_1 implies p_2" is true, while proposition p_1 is a necessary condition for proposition p_2 if "p_2 implies p_1" is true. Necessary and sufficient conditions are sometimes expressed in the form "*A* if and only if *B*," where "only if" is the necessary condition and the first "if" the sufficient condition. Example: for $x + 4 \geqslant 14$ to be true it is necessary that $x \geqslant 0$ (no negative value of x would do). $x \geqslant 100$, on the other hand, is sufficient, but not necessary. $x \geqslant 10$ is both necessary and sufficient. In the calculus, necessary and sufficient conditions are termed first-order and second-order conditions, respectively.

Statistical fallacies

Most fallacious types of reasoning can be carried over into statistics. Apart from the general point that statistical statements refer to characteristics of a group of items and do not provide any information about any one item in the group, some of the more common types of fallacy encountered in statistical explanations are:

ignoring the "exposure base": For example, because traffic deaths are reported after public holidays, it is sometimes concluded that it is more dangerous to drive on public holidays than on other days. While the conclusion may or may not be correct, the reasoning is fallacious, since it ignores the fact that more people drive on public holidays, hence more people are exposed to the possibility of an accident. The same kind of fallacy is evident in comparison of fatalities in aircraft accidents with those associated with other forms of transport.

precision fallacy: Exact methods often produce exact answers to the wrong questions. For example, the use of an average without reference to dispersion may be misleading, especially when the sample is small.

suppression of information: As when the response rate to a postal questionnaire is low, and no analysis is made of the nonrespondents. Suppression of the uninteresting is another illustration: published statistics are biased in favor of what is interesting (to politicians and civil servants).

biased (nonrandom) sample

sample too small

misleading use of graphs or pictures

regression fallacy: This may arise in what are called cross-sectional studies, such as studies of a number of firms in a given year. Johnston (1960, ch. 6) gives the following example: Suppose a firm produces a product, the demand for which has a known two-year cycle, so that it plans to produce 100 units in year 1, 200 in year 2, 100 in year 3, and so on. Further suppose that it plans to make identical outlays for hired factors in each year, so that there are no variable costs. If outlays are regarded as total costs, average cost per unit will be twice as large when output is 100 as when it is 200. Now if instead of years 1 and 2 we substitute firms 1 and 2, a cross-sectional study would show sharply declining average costs. When firms are classified by actual output, this kind of bias is likely to arise. The firms with the largest output are unlikely to be producing at an unusually low level. On the average, they are likely to be producing at an unusually high level, and conversely for those firms which have the lowest output. The results of such a cross-sectional study give a misleading impression because they generalize over firms of different size. Conditions favorable to the occurrence of this "regression fallacy" are likely to be the rule rather than the exception in cross-sectional studies that do not allow for this fact. To avoid the regression fallacy in this example we would have to incorporate output capacity as a variable in the statistical analysis or alternatively classify firms on the basis of plant size.

implicit assumption of independence of events (and their probabilities) when they are interdependent.

correlation and causation: positive correlation does not imply causation. A correlation is called spurious if it holds between two variables that are not causally related. Since the causal ordering among variables can be determined only within the context of a scientific theory, it is only within such a context that a correlation can be shown to imply causality.

For a more detailed discussion of fallacies involving statistical statements, see Good (1959) and Huff (1954).

Before leaving this section the question may be asked, Are there any circumstances in which only a *causal* explanation would do? The question of course implicitly assumes that the answer to a *why*-question is at least partly causal. The answer would appear to be that we would require a causal explanation, or the causal part of an explanation of a relationship or process in which several different kinds of determination were present, if we wished to intervene and control the relationship or process.

The reader is reminded that throughout this chapter causal determination and explanation are defined in a restricted technical sense, following Bunge (1979a), as referring only to single cause–single effect relationships, and that in the literature "causal" will often be used more loosely to include multiple as well as simple causation. Also, we did not call the determination causal, even though cause–effect relations were present, unless it was deterministic, applying in almost 100 percent or almost 0 percent of cases.

Causation and Prediction

It has sometimes been asserted that prediction is the overriding purpose of science. Is this indeed the case, and how is prediction related to causality?

It was earlier suggested that causation could usefully be replaced by the broader relation of general determination, or lawful production, and that valid explanations could be yielded in terms of any of the categories of determination there discussed.

We can learn a good deal about the world around us from description alone, even more from explanation. Like explanation, prediction may be associated with any of the categories of determination previously discussed. We may define prediction as the deduction of propositions concerning facts that are as yet unknown on the basis of general hypotheses (laws) and specific information. In this way we distinguish predictions from prophecies and crystal balls. Causality and prediction are not necessarily related, any more than causality and explanation are related.

Prediction has the same logical structure (namely deduction) as explanation; for example, a theory can predict to the degree that it can describe and explain. But epistemologically, prediction differs from description and explanation, for while description and explanation are never complete or exact, prediction involves a further uncertainty associated with the emergence of novel facts or events. Bunge (1979a, 311) argues that, since prediction rests on description and explanation, it cannot be a more important part of the business of science than they are, merely as important.

Prediction has two functions: to forecast the unknown, and to test hypotheses. The latter are confirmed or disconfirmed by means of prediction. In both cases predictions are usually statistical; they predict what is *likely* to occur in the vast majority of cases whenever certain conditions are met. In other words, when we make a forecast or use a forecast to test a hypothesis, usually there will be a statistical element involved. We predict what is likely to happen, or whether the hypothesis is confirmed, in a large percentage of cases if certain conditions are met. The forecast does not apply without exception to every individual event of a certain kind, but only for a given percentage of a large number of events. This is not to suggest that predictions containing a statistical element are not useful. It is possible to make inaccurate predictions on the basis of (deterministic) causal laws, while statistical laws sometimes permit near-certain predictions. They can, in general, be as certain or uncertain as predictions based on any other kind of law of determination. Laws (general hypotheses) are a prerequisite for any kind of prediction.

A prediction may turn out to be wide of the mark as a result of (1) errors in the general hypothesis on which it was made, or of choice of the wrong law; (2) errors in specific information (about singular facts such as the present state of the system or value of the variable whose future (or past) state (value) is being predicted; (3) the emergence of novel features or events (e.g., the mutation of a species, a major technological breakthrough, a natural disaster, or a large-scale war).

This completes the discussion of the relation between causation, on one hand, and determination, explanation, reason, scientific laws, and predictability on the other. The general conclusion is that the principle of causality is only one among many categories of determination, explanation, and scientific law; nor do the scientific laws on the basis of which predictions are made need to be causal. Predictions may be based on teleological, statistical, or other noncausal laws.

Explanation in the social sciences

In the social sciences causal explanation as here defined occupies a less prominent place at present than in the natural sciences. Many explanations occurring in the social sciences are statistical (this is also true of the natural sciences). Teleological and dialectical explanations are also common. Since these sciences are concerned with living beings rather than with natural objects or artifacts, explanation in terms of self-determination is also common. So is explanation based on structural determination, since one of the distinguishing features of human beings and social groups is the partial subordination of the parts to the whole (see Chapter 2).

We saw in Chapter 2 that human beings and human organizations occupied the two top rungs of the ladder of system complexity. It should not be altogether surprising, therefore, that the explanation of human and social phenomena is often fraught with great difficulties, that the advancement of knowledge and the establishment of laws has been much slower in the social sciences than in the natural sciences. The social scientist is less often able to explain things by subsuming a phenomenon under a known law. More frequently his explanation must be in terms of retrospectively applicable patterns which, however, have a limited area of validity and a tendency to change over time with infuriating frequency. Many features of human behavior (e.g., motivation) vary not only from individual to individual, but in the same individual at different times or with reference to different problems at a given time, and are not yet well understood. And the relations between members of an organization such as a business enterprise are often a strange mixture of cooperation and noncooperation. There are also, as we have seen in the previous chapter, difficulties in measuring social phenomena. Social scientists sometimes assume that scaling and measuring make it more likely that useful laws can be discovered. But a scale may disguise as well as reveal the existence of regularities. The descriptive value of a scale and its theoretical utility are independent considerations, which may lead in different directions.

MATHEMATICAL
APPENDICES

2

Systems

Every system should be viewed as a three-tiered hierarchy of systems. Let σ denote a particular system with subsystems or components s_i, $i = 1, \ldots, n$, and let Σ denote the universe, the totality of systems. Then $(s_i, \forall_i) \in \sigma \in \Sigma$.

Couplings

In concrete systems, couplings comprise matter–energy–information transfers and any behavior-influencing relations that exist between two objects or two physical qualities that are representable by mathematical functions or operators. The term *coupling* (or *connection*) is sometimes reserved for relations by which one component of a system alters the behavior of another (cf. Bunge 1979b, 6). It is more customary not to distinguish between *relation* and coupling, but the distinction is useful, as we shall see in Chapter 3.

Most mathematical representations of coupling are interpreted as relations between *qualities,* few as relations between *objects.* The relations we are concerned with in "system structure" consist of relations between system components (objects) and between system components and the environment (objects). We therefore need a way of representing relations between objects mathematically. In mathematical functions the variables, denoting qualities, not objects, are the arguments of a function and sometimes the function itself. For example, in the representation $y = f(x)$, x and perhaps y are variables.

A coupling is best represented mathematically either by the composition of two or more functions, or by a function of two or more variables, namely by either

$$F = f \circ g \qquad\qquad 2.1$$

or by

$$G = h(x, y) \qquad\qquad 2.2$$

where G takes a constant value and $\circ$ and h represent couplings. To show how two variables, x and y, coupled as in Equation 2.1, may be construed as belonging to different components (or one belonging to a system component and the other to the environment) and $\circ$ as thus representing a coupling between two objects rather than two qualities, decompose 2.1 into

$$F = f(y)$$
$$y = g(x)$$

and interpret y to be both an output of the component represented by g and an input to the component represented by f. In this sense a coupling becomes a common variable to two components, or to a component and the environment.

It makes sense to speak of variables in a system only when they are representable mathematically. It follows that not all couplings between concrete objects are formally representable. By contrast, all couplings between conceptual objects are so representable—by logical connectives, if not by mathematical functions or operators. For example, in the conceptual system p consisting of propositions q and r and the logical operator of conjunction, that is, $p = q \wedge r$, the operator $\wedge$ is a coupling.

Minimal model of a system

A system σ at time t is minimally modeled by the ordered triple $\sigma_t = \langle C, E, S \rangle$, where C denotes composition, E environment, and S system structure. We also require C and E to be mutually disjoint sets: $C \cap E = \emptyset$, and S to be a nonempty set of relations on the union of C and E.

System state

System σ at time t is represented by a number of state variables F_i, $1 \leqslant i \leqslant n$, each representing a general property of the system associated with a particular reference frame. A process is a sequence of different states.

State variables (or total state function)

The state variables of system σ at time t associated with a set of reference frames are $F(t) = \langle F_1(t), \ldots, F_n(t) \rangle$.

State space

If the ranges of the various components of F are denoted by $V_1, \ldots, V_n$, the (lawful) state space of σ is the range, V, of F, where $V = V_1 \times V_2 \times \ldots \times V_n$.

The state space of a single concrete object, an aggregate, and a concrete system

Every thing is in some state at a given time relative to a given reference frame. In fact, it has at least two different states, because at a given time it either possesses the particular property associated with the given reference frame or it does not. A single conceptual element, on the other hand, is in no state at all. If x is a thing and y a conceptual element, and denoting state space by $S(.)$, $|S(x)| \geqslant 2$, while $|S(y)| = \emptyset$. An aggregate of things or conceptual elements, α, is a set of independent components. Suppose α is made up of r noninteracting components, the partial state spaces of which are $S(c_i)$, $i = 1, \ldots, r$. Then the state space of the aggregate is

$$S(\alpha) = \bigcup_{i=1}^{r} S(c_i), r \geqslant 2$$

For example, if the aggregate is made up of three independent items, each of which can be in two states denoted by 0 or 1, the state space of the aggregate is $S(\alpha) = \{\langle 0, 0, 0 \rangle, \langle 1, 0, 0 \rangle, \langle 0, 1, 0 \rangle, \langle 0, 0, 1 \rangle, \langle 1, 1, 0 \rangle, \langle 1, 0, 1 \rangle,$ $\langle 0, 1, 1 \rangle, \langle 1, 1, 1 \rangle\}$. The state space has 2^r points, where r is the number of components or elements.

The state space of a system σ with r components relative to a given reference frame, on the other hand, is not equal to the union of the partial state spaces:

$$S(\sigma) \neq \bigcup_{i=1}^{r} S(c_i)$$

because (a) some or all of the r components are interrelated, so that their values are mutually restricted (the states of some or all components are at least partly determined by the states other components are in) and (b) the system possesses certain emergent properties that none of its components has.

Degree of complexity expressed in terms of degrees of freedom

Now suppose system σ has r components, $r \geqslant 2$, each of which could, if it were able to act independently of other components, take on two values associated with a given reference frame. If all components were independent, the state could range over 2^r different points in the state space. But at least two components are interacting, otherwise σ is not a system. Suppose at a given time only m actual behaviors ($m < 2^r$) are observed related to the given reference frame. That is, the actual variety of behavior is less than when the state of each component takes on its full range of values independently of the values taken on by the other component states. We then say the system's behavior is constrained to the degrees of freedom, m, of the full set of behaviors. The possible (as distinct from conceivable) state space of the system associated with the given reference frame at a given time will contain the following number of different points:

2^r

$-k_1$ excluded by mutual restriction of values due to interrelatedness of components

$-k_2$ excluded by other constraints not due to interrelatedness

$+k_3$ representing emergent behaviors of the system

m

The actual degree of complexity of the system σ in terms of the single given reference frame could then be expressed as m. To make this into a complete measure, we would have to include all possible reference frames.

Comparing the degrees of complexity of an ordinary machine, the human body, and a social organization in terms of a single reference frame, as above:

System	Degree of complexity
social organization	$m \rightarrow (2^r - k_1 + k_3)$, the arrow here meaning "approaches"; many of the k_2 constraints may be treated as soft constraints
human body	$m \ll (2^r - k_1 + k_3)$
ordinary machine	$m = 2$; in relation to a reference frame for activity, for example, the machine either operates or does not operate.

Closed and open systems

Denoting entropy by ε, the total change in entropy in a closed system is

$$d\varepsilon = d_i\varepsilon \qquad\qquad 2.3$$

where subscript i denotes the production (increase) of entropy due to irreversible processes within the system. In the case of an open system the total change in entropy is

$$d\varepsilon = d_i\varepsilon + d_e\varepsilon \qquad\qquad 2.4$$

where subscript e denotes the change in entropy made possible by net matter–energy–information inflows from the environment. The first term on the right of Equation 2.4 is always positive by the second law of thermodynamics, hence the entropy change in a closed system is always positive. The second law holds only when $d\varepsilon > 0$. The second term on the right of Equation 2.4 may be negative or positive, and consequently the total entropy change in an open system may be negative as well as positive. An open negentropic system is one in which $d\varepsilon < 0$. Denoting the system's environment by E, $E(\sigma, t) \neq \emptyset$ is sufficient to characterize an open system, but not to show that an open system may become negentropic. For this we must require that $d\varepsilon < 0$ for finite t (*all* concrete systems eventually cease to exist).

The universe is defined as the only system that is closed at all times in the sense of having no exchanges with its environment, in fact being without environment: $E(\Sigma, t) = \emptyset, \forall t$.

Steady state

To illustrate the meaning of the term *steady state,* consider the firm as represented by a production function. Suppose the firm has two inputs, K (capital) and L (labor), and a single output, Q. Rates of output and input per unit of time are related in the production function:

$$Q = \alpha L^{\beta_1} K^{\beta_2} \qquad 2.5$$

If constant rates of input L and K yield a constant rate of output Q this is equivalent to saying that

$$\frac{dL}{dt} = \frac{dK}{dt} = \frac{dQ}{dt} = 0 \qquad 2.6$$

The system is then in a steady state with respect to all its input and output variables, for as long as this condition holds (i.e., a steady state means stable stationary values of the variables concerned).

Note that *steady state,* although much used in physics and biology, is not a well-defined term. To make it precise we would have to specify which features of the system are being considered (sometimes the term *steady state* is applied to all system variables, other times only to some of them), how these features are measured, and with what frequency they are measured (e.g., "stationary" value may imply, not constancy over time, but behavior that is periodically repetitive over time, as it is sometimes understood in economics).

Integration

Although, as indicated in the text, we cannot measure a system's degree of integration in those cases (social organizations certainly, human beings probably) where information links play at least as important an integrating role as pure energy, because the units for energy and information are incommensurate, it may be useful to illustrate the idea of integration for a system (physical, chemical) which depends on energy alone to bind it together. Bunge (1979b) shows how this might be done.

Suppose two objects, 1 and 2, form a linear system represented by the equations $\dot{F}_1 = a_{11}F_1 + a_{12}F_2$ and $\dot{F}_2 = a_{21}F_1 + a_{22}F_2$, the dot denoting time derivative. Assuming the a_{ij} are time-invariant, the degree of integration of this system could be defined as

$$w = \frac{|a_{12}|}{|a_{11} + a_{12}|} + \frac{|a_{21}|}{|a_{21} + a_{22}|}$$

If $a_{12} = a_{21} = 0$, the components 1 and 2 do not form a system; in every other case they do. If all the $a_{ij} = 1$, $w = 1$, and the system is maximally integrated.

3

Types of Interdependence

Relations and couplings (bonding relations)

The set of relations within a system, and between system and environment, consists of simple relations (e.g., $x > y$) and couplings or bonding relations (e.g., y depends on x, or y is influenced by x). Bunge (1979b) describes these in the following terms. Let $\{R_i | 1 \leqslant i \leqslant n\}$ be the total set of relations just referred to for system σ at time t, defined on $C(\sigma, t) \cup E(\sigma, t)$, where C and E stand for system composition and environment, respectively, as in Chapter 2. Couplings are denoted by $B(\sigma, t)$, nonbonding relations by $\bar{B}(\sigma, t)$. The structure of system σ can now be defined as $S(\sigma, t) = \{R_i \in B(\sigma, t) \cup \bar{B}(\sigma, t) | B(\sigma, t) \neq \emptyset; 1 \leqslant i \leqslant n\}$, provided it is understood that couplings with the environment are unidirectional: $E(\sigma, t) \rightarrow (\sigma, t)$.

Actions and interactions

The couplings may be one-way or reciprocal (actions or interactions). For two different things x and y, if F is the state function of x and G the state function of y relative to a common reference frame, and H is the state function $H = g(F, G) \neq G$, then denoting the history of x by $h(x)$ and the history of x when acted on by y by $h(x|y)$, x acts on y if and only if $h(y|x) \neq h(y) \neq \emptyset$; x and y interact if, in addition, $h(x|y) \neq h(x) \neq \emptyset$. The effect of x acting on y is $A(x, y) = h(y|x) \cap \overline{h(y)} \neq \emptyset$, where $\overline{h(y)}$ denotes the autonomous action of y alone. Similarly, the effect of y reacting to x is $A(y, x) = h(x|y) \cap \overline{h(x)} \neq \emptyset$, and the total effect of the interaction between x and y is $I(x, y) = A(x, y) \cup A(y, x)$ (Bunge 1977, 258–60). It should also

168

be noted that, if A depends on B, it depends on any collection that contains B: $B \rightarrow A$ and $B \subset B'$ implies that $B' \rightarrow A$. Many dependence relations are possible (i.e., there are many interpretations of "A depends on B"); for example, the relation may or may not be symmetric (interdependence), transitive, idempotent, conditional, and so on.

Externalities

In terms of the last section, x must take into account the externality $h(y|x) - \overline{h(y)}$, and y the externality $h(x|y) - \overline{h(x)}$, in each case if it is significantly greater than zero, at the margin or in total, depending on the problem.

Dynamic interdependence

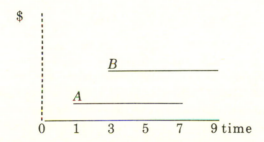

A and B represent the net cash flows from the same investment project started in year 1 (A) or in year 3 (B). The problem is which of these mutually exclusive projects to select, that is, when to start the project. If the firm's investment criterion is maximization of net present value (NPV), it pays to postpone the project as long as the reduction in the PV of the investment outlay is greater than the PV of the lost net operating receipts.

More particularly, comparison of the projects depends on whether or not it is intended, before the initial decision is taken, that the assets comprising the project will eventually be replaced. It is usually assumed that they will be unless expressly stated otherwise. If the assets are to be replaced, the two out-of-phase cash flow streams will be repeated indefinitely. One means of ensuring comparability between them is to calculate the net present value (NPV) of each stream, convert each to a constant annual equivalent, and continue this constant annual series to infinity. Thus if the cash inflows (end of year) are identical in each stream for all years except that they are displaced two years, and the investment outlay is at the beginning of the first year of the project, both streams could be represented by the series $(-c_1, c_2, c_3, c_4, c_5, c_6, c_7)$, where $c_2 = \ldots = c_7 = c_r$ for simplicity, and $c_1 \neq c_r$ (e.g., $\text{NPV}_A = -c_1 v + c_r a_6 v = X$, $\text{NPV}_B = -c_1 v^3 + c_r a_6 v^3 = X v^2 = Y$).

The constant annual equivalent of NPV_A is X/a_7, and that of NPV_B is Y/a_7. The PV of each of these constant annual streams to infinity is $X/i a_7$ and $Y/i a_7$, respectively, where i is the effective rate of interest per period; $v = (1 + i)^{-1}$ and $v^n = (1 + i)^{-n}$; $a_n = (1 - v^n)/i$ is the PV of a series of n equal payments of 1 per period at rate i per period; and $a_\infty = 1/i$ is the PV of an infinite series of equal payments of 1 per period at rate i per period

$$a_\infty = \lim_{n \to \infty} \frac{(1 - v^n)}{i}.$$

Comparing the projects, we can then calculate

$$\text{PV}_{A-B} = \frac{X(1 - v^2)}{1 - v^7} \text{ or } \frac{X - Y}{1 - v^7}$$

The same result could be obtained by comparing the two cash flow streams at a common date, the most convenient probably being the end of the earlier project (here the end of year 7), and taking their PVs. Before discounting, the only differences between the two streams are the first three terms of A, the first term and the last two terms of B. But under our assumption of asset replacement, these terms will recur every seven years.

If, on the other hand, it is known before taking the initial decision that the assets will not be replaced, PV_{A-B} is simply $X - Y$. For a detailed example, see Amey and Egginton (1979, problem 11.9) and the solutions manual to this text.

Serial interdependence

The nature of serial interdependence as it occurs in the asset replacement problem is illustrated in the following diagram. Suppose for simplicity we are concerned with a single asset for which the optimal replacement policy (under NPV) is periodic (i.e., the asset is retired and replaced every L years). We abstract from uncertainty. Retirement/replacement dates are denoted by T and machines by M:

M_0	M_1	M_2	$M_3 \ldots$
T_0	T_1	T_2	T_3
Past	Future		

The set of problems making up the optimal replacement problem (determination of optimal replacement period, whether to replace, when to replace) between them involves interdependencies between the characteristics (discounted net operating cash flows, etc.) of the existing machine (M_0) and of the entire chain of future replacements $M_1, M_2, \ldots$, theoretically stretching to infinity. The problem will not be pursued further here. Interested readers will find a full discussion of it in Amey and Egginton (1979, ch. 12).

Cost interdependence

For two products X_1 and X_2 whose costs are interrelated, the cost equation will be of the form $C = c_1(x_1, x_2)x_1 + c_2(x_1, x_2)x_2 + k$, where c_1, c_2 are variable cost functions and k denotes fixed costs. Marginal costs are

$$\frac{\partial C}{\partial x_1} = c_1 + x_1 \frac{\partial c_1}{\partial x_1} \boxed{+ x_2 \frac{\partial c_2}{\partial x_1}}$$

$$\frac{\partial C}{\partial x_2} = c_2 + x_2 \frac{\partial c_2}{\partial x_2} \boxed{+ x_1 \frac{\partial c_1}{\partial x_2}}$$

The last terms on the right are the marginal externalities. The last term will be less than zero if the products are complementary in production, and greater than zero if they are competitive in production.

Demand interdependence

Let X_1 and X_2 be two products with interrelated demands. If p denotes price, the revenue function is then $R = p_1(x_1, x_2)x_1 + p_2(x_1, x_2) x_2$, and the marginal revenues are

$$\frac{\partial R}{\partial x_1} = p_1 + x_1 \frac{\partial p_1}{\partial x_1} \boxed{+ x_2 \frac{\partial p_2}{\partial x_1}}$$

$$\frac{\partial R}{\partial x_2} = p_2 + x_2 \frac{\partial p_2}{\partial x_2} \boxed{+ x_1 \frac{\partial p_1}{\partial x_2}}$$

Again, the last terms represent the marginal externalities. The last term will be greater than zero if the products are complementary in demand, and less than zero if they are substitutes.

Agency interdependencies

These are discussed in Chapter 10.

Consumption interdependencies

If there are two consumers and two products, and the utility level of each consumer depends on the consumption of the other, then if q_{ij} denotes the consumption of the jth product by the ith consumer, the utility functions of the two consumers will be of the form $U_1 = U_1(q_{11}, q_{12}, q_{21}, q_{22})$ and $U_2 = U_2(q_{11}, q_{12}, q_{21}, q_{22})$. For a formal treatment of interdependent utility functions in a welfare context, see Henderson and Quandt (1980, 297–98).

Statistical interdependence

Denoting probability by $P(\ )$, joint probability by $P(\ ,\ )$, and conditional probability by $P(\ |\ )$, if two events A and B are nonindependent, in the statistical sense that the probability of one's occurring is not unaffected by the probability of the other's occurring, then

$$P(A, B) = P(B)\, P(A|B) = P(A)\, P(B|A) \neq P(A)\, P(B);$$

$$P(A|B) \neq P(A)$$

$$P(B|A) \neq P(B)$$

$$P(A|B) = \frac{P(B|A)\, P(A)}{P(B)} \neq \frac{P(A, B)}{P(B)};$$

$$P(B) \neq 0$$

$$P(B|A) = \frac{P(A|B)\ P(B)}{P(A)} \neq \frac{P(A,\ B)}{P(A)}$$

$$P(A) \neq 0$$

from which the interdependence of the probabilities is clearly seen:

$$P(A) = \frac{P(A|B)\ P(B);}{P(B|A)}$$

$$P(B) = \frac{P(B|A)\ P(A).}{P(A|B)}$$

4

Objectives

Individual decision-making under risk

With the St. Petersburg Paradox, Bernouilli showed that, in the presence of risk (outcomes of action not known with certainty, but each outcome occurs with a known probability) it would be foolish for anyone to use expected monetary value of the outcome as the criterion of (rational) choice. Instead, in problems of risky choices he proposed the criterion of maximizing expected utility rather than expected monetary outcome. It is now recognized that in decision-making under risk, the value assigned by a decision-maker to a risky outcome may differ from its mathematical expectation, unless the decision-maker is risk-neutral. Denoting an alternative by x and the utility function by $U(\ )$, $U\{E(x)\}$ will not necessarily equal $E\{U(x)\}$. Often a risky outcome will be valued at less than its expected utility value: $U\{E(x)\} < E\{U(x)\}$.

Arrow's conditions on the group preference function and his Impossibility Theorem

It is felt that nothing would be gained by restating these conditions formally here. The interested reader is referred to Arrow (1951, chs. 2 and 3).

Von Neumann-Morgenstern axioms of rational choice under uncertainty

Von Neumann and Morgenstern show that, if the objects of choice have risky outcomes, and if individual preferences are consistent as prescribed by the following conditions, the individual's preferences can be represented numerically by a utility function. This utility measure has the important property that an individual will prefer lottery A to lottery B if and only if $E(U_A) > E(U_B)$. Consistency or rationality requires:

1. *Complete ordering and transitivity*: Between two alternatives x and y, either x is preferred or y is preferred or the individual is indifferent; and if x is preferred to y and y to z, then x is preferred to z.

2. *Continuity*: Denote a lottery offering outcome x with probability p and outcome y with probability $1 - p$ by (p, x, y). Then if x is preferred to y and y to z, this condition says that there exists some probability p, $0 < p < 1$, such that an individual will be indifferent between a certain y and the lottery (p, x, z).

3. *Independence*: Suppose there are three outcomes x, y, and z and that an individual is indifferent between x and y. If one lottery, L_1, offers outcomes x and z with probabilities p and $1 - p$, respectively, and another lottery, L_2, offers outcomes y and z with the same probabilities, the individual is indifferent between the two lotteries. And if the individual prefers x to y, he will prefer L_1 to L_2.

4. *Unequal probability*: Between two lotteries $L_1 = (p_1, x, y)$ and $L_2 = (p_2, x, y)$, $p_1 \neq p_2$, if the individual prefers x to y, she will prefer L_2 to L_1 only if $p_2 > p_1$.

5. *Reduction of compound lotteries*: Any compound lottery is indifferent to a simple lottery with x, y, z as prizes, their probabilities being computed according to the ordinary probability calculus. If $L_1 = (p_1, x, y)$ and $L_2 = (p_2, L_3, L_4)$, where $L_3 = (p_3, x, y)$, and $L_4 = (p_4, x, y)$ is a compound lottery in which the outcomes are lottery tickets, the individual is indifferent between L_1 and L_2 if $p_1 = p_2 p_3 + (1 - p_2)p_4$.

Multiple objective linear programming

There are a number of different approaches to this problem, with strong connections. Only one will be sketched here, the vector maximization approach (Geoffrion 1968). Let $f(x) = [f_1(x), \ldots, f_r(x)]$ be a vector-valued criterion function defined over a set X, where X is the set of feasible decisions and $f_k(x)$, $k = 1, \ldots, r$ is the value of the kth criterion at the point x. Let Y be the range of X: $y = f(x)$ for some $x \in X$. The decision-maker seeks an x-vector to maximize y, subject to certain constraints and nonnegativity conditions on x. It is assumed that higher values of y_k are preferred to lower values; any criteria (e.g., involving a cost) that demand the opposite are defined as their negatives, $-f_k(x)$. It is usually assumed that all the f_k are linear. A point $x^0 \in X$ is defined as *efficient* (or undominated) if $f_k(x) > f_k(x^0)$ for some $x \in X$ implies that $f_j(x) < f_j(x^0)$ for at least one other index j. The set of points $x \in X$ which are efficient is denoted X_E. A point $x^0 \in X_E$ is defined as being *properly efficient* if there exists a number $M > 0$ such that, for each k and each $x \in X$ satisfying $f_k(x) > f_k(x^0)$ there exists at least one other index j such that $f_j(x) < f_j(x^0)$ and

$$\frac{f_k(x) - f_k(x^0)}{f_j(x^0) - f_j(x)} \leqslant M$$

The set of points $x \in X$ which are properly efficient is denoted X_{PE}; $X_{PE} \subset X_E$. The vector maximization problem is then the problem of finding all elements of x_{PE}.

Geoffrion (1968) produced a theorem relating the vector maximization problem to the scalar maximization problem:

$$\underset{x \in X}{\text{Maximize}} \sum_{k=1} \lambda_k f_k(x)$$

subject to the same constraints, where the λ_k, $0 < \lambda_k \leqslant 1$, $\Sigma \lambda_k = 1$, are interpreted as weights representing the importance attached to objective k. Solution of this problem yields a properly efficient point for every λ_k. Parametric programming with respect to λ does not, however, necessarily generate all elements of X_{PE}. Geoffrion proves that if X is a convex set and all f_k are continuous and concave on X, $x^0 \in X_{PE}$ if and only if x^0 is optimal in the scalar maximization problem for some λ_k. This result allows parametric generation of all elements of X_{PE}. It also allows the decision-maker to search for a decision point $x \in X$ by varying the weights he assigns to the various criteria. The procedure terminates when the deicision-maker finds a decision that is satisfactory with respect to a vector of satisfaction levels on all the criteria values and feels that the chances of finding a decision offering a significantly higher vector of satisfaction levels are quite small.

Goal programming

This method assumes that all relationships in the model are linear and that, if management cannot set desired values for different goals, it can at least put upper and lower limits on them (depending on whether the goal is a cost or benefit, respectively). Instead of trying to maximize the weighted sum of goals as in the previous method, the aim here is to minimize the deviations, positive and negative (d_i^+ and d_i^- respectively,

$i = 1, \ldots, n$), between goals (which we assume are incompatible) and to achieve what it is possible within a given set of constraints. Note that the constraints must be satisfied before any attempt is made to meet the goals (Ijiri 1965a, ch. 3). The goals are ranked according to their priorities so that lower-order goals are considered only after higher-order goals have been achieved. This is done by assigning priorities P_j, $j = 1, \ldots, m$, to the deviational variables, such that $P_j >>> P_{j+1}$, the latter denoting a lower-level goal. It means that no number n, however large, can make $P_j \geqslant P_{j+1}$. We still need some way of allowing for tradeoffs between deviational variables in the same priority group, P_j, to reflect how much increases in one would be offset by a unit decrease in some other variable in the same priority group. This is done by attaching weights, w_{ij}^+ or w_{ij}^-, representing the relative penalty to be assigned to a positive or negative deviation, respectively, from the ith goal in the jth rank.

The general form of the problem with incompatible multiple goals is then:

$$\text{minimize} \quad \sum_j \sum_i P_j(w_{ij}^+ d_i^+ + w_{ij}^- d_i^-)$$

$$\text{subject to:} \quad \sum_j c_{ij}x_j - d_i^+ + d_i^- = g_i, \; i = 1, \ldots, n$$

$$\sum_j a_{kj}x_j \qquad \leqslant b_k, \; k = 1, \ldots, p$$

$$x_j, \, d_i^+, \, d_i^- \qquad \geqslant 0, \text{ all } i \text{ and } j$$

where the x_j are the decision variables, the c_{ij} are goal coefficients, g_i are the desired level of the ith goal, a_{kj} are technological coefficients, and b_k are resource limitations. The problem may be solved using a modified version of the simplex method. (The simplex method is an iterative procedure for solving any linear programming problem exactly in a finite number of steps, or for indicating that the solution is unbounded. In goal programming problems—where the cardinal objective function of linear programming is replaced by multiple, incompatible criteria, including perhaps some highly abstract criteria—a modified simplex method represents an ordinal rather than a numerical solution approach.)

Divisional and corporate goals

The problem here is to ensure that the behavior of subunits of the firm (such as departments, divisions) is consistent with achievement of the corporate goals, that subunit and corporate goals are effectively congruent. Suppose a firm has two divisions. These divisions interact; decisions taken by one affect the other, causing external economies or diseconomies. Assume for simplicity that the firm has a single objective, profit maximization, which it seeks to achieve subject to certain companywide constraints. Its objective function is $f(x)$, where $x = (x_1, x_2)$ are the decision variables. If the divisions each act autonomously, maximizing the objective functions $f_1(x_1)$ and $f_2(x_2)$, subject only to their own divisional constraints, this will not maximize $f(x)$ for the firm. For their behavior to be consistent with overall maximization, they must take into account their interdependency and include companywide constraints in their maximization problems.

An iterative procedure giving the divisions the illusion of autonomy would be for the central management to instruct division 1 to choose x_1 to maximize $f_1(x_1 | x_2 = b)$, subject to division 1 and companywide constraints, and division 2 to choose x_2 to maximize $f_2 | x_1 = a)$, subject to division 2 and companywide constraints. Each division optimizes and reports the results to central management, which changes the values of b and a until the divisional solutions are consistent with the optimal corporate solution. Alternatively, the divisions could each solve a maximization problem subject only to their own constraints, and central management would take the companywide constraints as well as the divisional interdependencies into account in determining the values of b and a.

5

Choice under Risk and Uncertainty

Determination of utilities in decision-making under risk

The method of approach used involves hypothetical reference lotteries, which the reader may recall were mentioned in discussing the von Neumann-Morgenstern axioms of rational choice in Chapter 4, and particularly in the Mathematical Appendix for that chapter.

Suppose a choice must be made from a set of acts $\{a_i, i = 1, \ldots, m\}$, the relative consequence (c_{ij}) of each act depending on which state of nature $(s_j, j = 1, \ldots, n)$ prevails. The decision-maker is able to assign probabilities to each of the states s_j; but by use of the word "risk" we are stipulating that the decision problem is such that EMV maximization is inappropriate. For example, suppose the act with the highest EMV has EMV = \$5,000, derived as follows:

State	Probability	Consequence ($)
s_1	.3	10,000
s_2	.5	8,000
s_3	.2	−10,000

The decision-maker's attitude, however, is characterized by the rule that he would *not* be willing to undertake any act in which there was an equal chance of making or losing \$10,000.

Select two reference consequences, one of which $(\bar{c})$ is at least as attractive as the best possible consequence of the real decision problem, and the other (c) is at least as unattractive as the worst possible consequence. Use these reference consequences to scale the decision-maker's preferences (utilities) and judgments ("probabilities"), by in-

179

venting a number of reference lotteries, each of which has a specified probability p of resulting in $\bar{c}$ and probability $(1 - p)$ of resulting in $\underline{c}$.

The decision-maker's preference for any possible consequence c_{ij} of the actual decision problem can now be scaled by specifying a number, call it $u(c_{ij})$, such that she would be indifferent to c_{ij} for certain and a lottery offering a chance $u(c_{ij})$ of winning $\bar{c}$, and hence a chance $1 - u(c_{ij})$ of winning $\underline{c}$. It is assumed that the decision-maker's preferences obey certain principles of consistent behavior, principally that they are transitive. A decision-maker's judgmental "probability" concerning any possible state s_j can be scaled by specifying a number p_j such that she would be indifferent to the choice between a lottery with consequence $\bar{c}$ if state j occurs, $\underline{c}$ if it does not (these being equally probable), and another lottery offering an objective probability p_j of winning $\bar{c}$ and $(1 - p_j)$ of winning $\underline{c}$. We then say that *for decision purposes* what we have called judgmental "probabilities" may be regarded in the same way as objective probabilities, and that the judgmental probability of s_j is p_j.

Identifying the function u above with utility, we can now say that the expected utility of act a_i, denoted by EU_i, is

$$EU_i = \sum_j p_j u(c_{ij})$$

The decision-maker should be indifferent to the choice between the real act a_i and a lottery giving a chance EU_i at $\bar{c}$ and a chance $(1 - EU_i)$ at $\underline{c}$. That is, to every act a_i, $i = 1, \ldots, m$, there is a lottery offering the *same* two consequences, $\bar{c}$ and $\underline{c}$, the lotteries differing only in the chances EU and $(1 - EU)$ of obtaining these two consequences. The most desirable of these reference lotteries is the one offering the greatest chance EU at $\bar{c}$ (and the smallest chance of $\underline{c}$). This enables us to choose between any two acts, a_j and a_k. If the associated expected utility indices are EU_j and EU_k calculated as above, the decision-maker should prefer a_j to a_k if and only if $EU_j > EU_k$. That is, she should maximize her expected utility.

An example, taken from Schlaifer (1959, 32–39), will make the method of analysis clearer.*

1. The real decision is between act P and act Q, the details of which are:

---

*From Robert O. Schlaifer. 1959. *Probability and Statistics for Business Decisions: An Introduction to Managerial Economics under Uncertainty* (New York: McGraw-Hill), pp. 32–39. Copyright by the President and Fellows of Harvard College. Used with the permission of the Harvard Business School.

State	P Probability	Consequence ($)	State	Q Probability	Consequence ($)
a	.30	9,000	r	.25	7,500
b	.45	7,500	s	.60	2,000
c	.25	−9,000	t	.15	−7,000

Act 0 (doing neither P nor Q) has an EMV of $0, compared with $3,825 for P and $2,025 for Q.

2. Select two reference consequences, $10,000 and −$10,000. In respect of real act P:

3. Invent a number of hypothetical reference lotteries, each with a specified probability u of resulting in 10,000, $(1 - u)$ of resulting in −10,000. Suppose we nominate five reference lotteries, with probability u in turn equal to 1, .75, .5, .25, and 0 of resulting in a 10,000 return, and complementary probabilities $(1 - u)$ of resulting in −10,000.

4. Ask the decision-maker to state the cash equivalent, in her opinion, of these reference lotteries. Suppose this gives:

Probability u of a 10,000 return	Cash equivalent
1	10,000
.75	−3,000
.5	−7,000
.25	−9,000
0	−10,000

(The decision-maker in question is a "risk-seeker".)

5. Diagram this information:

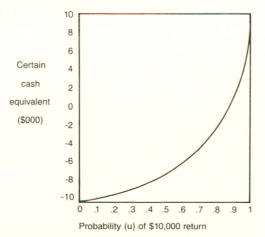

Probability (u) of $10,000 return

6. Take each possible consequence of the real act P and read off from this diagram the value of u that would make a reference lottery equivalent to it:

State	Consequence	Act P u of equivalent reference lottery
a	9,000	.99
b	7,500	.98
c	−9,000	.25

For the real act P substitute a reference lottery with $u = .99$ of gaining $10,000 for the $9,000 consequence in state a, and similarly for states b and c (in the case of c, a reference lottery with $u = .25$ instead of paying out $9,000), since the decision-maker has expressed indifference between these. Call the modified alternative P'; it has only two consequences, either $10,000 or −$10,000.

7. The desirability of act P' depends on the probability that it will result in $10,000. To compute this probability, draw a ball marked a from an urn containing the proportion p_a of balls so marked. Now represent the reference lottery associated with state a by the right to draw a ball from another urn in which the proportion of balls marked "win $10,000" is u_a. Do the same for states b and c and the corresponding reference lotteries. Then the overall probability of winning $10,000 under modified act P' is:

$$\text{EU}(P') = p_a u_a + p_b u_b + p_c u_c$$
$$= .3(.99) + .45(.98) + .25(.25) = .80$$

In respect of real act Q:

8. Repeating this procedure, the corresponding overall probability of winning $10,000 under modified act Q' will be found to be $\text{EU}(Q') = .86$.

9. Since the decision-maker is indifferent between P' and P, Q' and Q, he should choose real act Q over real act P. And Q is better than the null act 0: from the diagram above, the consequence $0 of the latter is equivalent to a reference lottery with $\text{EU}(0) = .85$, slightly less attractive than Q.

Bayes' formula or decision rule for the inference of probabilities from empirical evidence

Suppose our present belief as to whether B_i will be true is represented in the probability $P(B_i)$, where B_i might be a particular state of nature, one of a set of mutually exclusive states $B_1, \ldots, B_n$, one of which is bound to occur. Denote by $P(A|B)$ the probability that A is true given that B is true, and suppose that event A has occurred. Then the probability of B_i on the evidence A is given by:

$$P(B_i|A) = \frac{P(A|B_i)\, P(B_i)}{\sum\limits_{i=1}^{n} P(A|B_i)\, P(B_i)}$$

The a posteriori (or revised) probabilities $P(B_i|A)$ thus depend on the original a priori probabilities $P(B_i)$ of the various states and on the probabilities $P(A|B_i)$ of the occurrence of the observed event A under the various states. These latter probabilities are sometimes referred to as the likelihoods of the various states, given A.

The Bayes' formula for probability revision is not to be confused with Bayes' theorem or criterion, which says in effect that if we have no information at all on the probabilities of the various states, we should assign equal probabilities to them and choose the act with the highest expected payoff. *The Principle of Insufficient Reason* (Jacob Bernouilli, seventeenth century) states that in the absence of evidence that one of a set of mutually exclusive and exhaustive events is more likely to occur than another, the events should be judged equally probable. Bayes reasoned from his theorem that, in the absence of further evidence, the states B_i, $i = 1, \ldots, n$ above could be judged equiprobable. It then follows that the a posteriori probabilities $P(B_i|A)$ are proportional to the likelihoods of the various states.

Dynamic programming

Abstracting from uncertainty, denote by $X = (X_1, X_2, \ldots, X_N)$ the information available to the firm on the state of the system (in this case the state of the *firm*) at the beginning of periods $1, \ldots, N$, and by $Y = (Y_1, \ldots, Y_N)$ the vector of decisions to be taken for periods $1, \ldots, N$, and let p_t denote the vector (X_t, Y_t). Let N be the finite horizon of a sequence of decisions. Then the problem at time zero is to maximize

$$\sum_{i=0}^{N} G(p_t)$$

where $G(p)$ is a prescribed function. Let ϕ be the transformation whereby p_t is obtained from p_{t-1}. The sequence of functions $f_N(p)$ is then defined by the relation

$$f_N(p) = \max \sum_{t=0}^{N} G(p_t)$$

$$= \max \{G(p) + G[\phi(p)] + G[\phi^2(p)] + \cdots + G[\phi^N(p)]\}$$

with the maximization to be performed over Y and $X_1, \ldots, X_N$, with X_0 known, where the function G is called a policy or strategy. $f_N(p)$ is then the total return obtained, starting in state p, from using an optimal policy. Bellman's principle of optimality permits one to conclude that, whatever the initial decision Y_0, for $N \geqslant 1$ $f_N(p)$ satisfies the recurrence relation $f_N(p) = \max \{G(p) + f_{N-1}[\phi(p)]\}$, $f_0(p) = G(p)$. The idea of a "policy" in the above sense is the main feature of dynamic programming. The policy is structured in such a way as to enable the decision-maker, by successive approximations, to make decisions that are optimal over the horizon N with a knowledge of only the current state of the system p.

Possibilistic decision-making

This topic is rather marginal to the discussion of this chapter; it does not have quite the history and standing of the other topics as yet. It could be a dawning truth or end in oblivion. The fact remains that a great deal of decision-making in the real world involves communication of information that is extremely vague (e.g., statements such as "it is cold," "it is raining," "stocks are getting low"); and decisions that turn out to have been not too irrational are taken routinely on such information. Zadeh (1978) has proposed a way of quantifying such imprecise information, using the idea of "fuzzy sets." Only a very brief indication of the approach will be given here.

A distinction is made between a fuzzy subset and an ordinary (Boolean) subset. Given an (ordinary) set of elements X, a fuzzy subset A of X is a subset of X whose characteristic function lies in $[0, 1]$ instead of $\{0, 1\}$ for an ordinary subset. That is, each $x \in X$ is assigned a number from $[0, 1]$ indicating the degree to which it belongs to A, the degree to which it satisfies the conditions specified by A (which might be "coldness"). (More precisely, a fuzzy subset is a mapping from an ordinary set

X to any lattice.) Thus if A and B are fuzzy subsets of X, the operations of union and intersection may be defined on these subsets as: $C = A \cup B$, where $C(x) = \max [A(x), B(x)]$, and $D = A \cap B$, where $D(x) = \min [A(x), B(x)]$. $A(x)$, $B(x)$, $C(x)$, and $D(x)$ are called the *membership functions* of x in A, B, C, and D, where C and D are also fuzzy subsets of X.

A statement such as, "It is cold today" can be represented in a form capable of organized manipulation by letting $X = \{0, 10, 15, 20, \ldots\}$ be a set of temperatures and defining "cold" as a fuzzy subset of X as follows:

$$\text{cold} = \left\{ \frac{1}{0}, \frac{1}{10}, \frac{0.9}{15}, \frac{0.8}{20}, \ldots \right\}$$

So much for the idea of fuzzy subsets and linguistic variables ("today's temperature" in the above example). The statement, "It is cold today" is an example of possibilistic uncertainty in that it gives some idea of the possible values of $x \in X$; for example, it would guide decisions to the extent that we probably would not go swimming outdoors.

If X is the set of all conceivable temperature readings, A the fuzzy subset of X defining "cold" as above, and y denotes today's temperature, a possibility distribution is a rule that assigns to each $x \in A$ a number $\pi(A)$ indicating the possibility of $y \in A$. If A is a fuzzy subset of X,

$$\pi(A) = \sup_{x \in X} [\min\{\pi(x), A(x)\}]$$

For an example of possibilistic decision-making, see Yager (1979).

6

Information

Information theory

If i is a particular value of a discrete variable ($1 \leqslant i \leqslant n$), and p_i is the probability that value i will be sent, the entropy measure of the expected amount of information in this message, $H(i)$, is the following function of the probability distribution on i:

$$H(i) = -\sum_{i=1} p_i \log_2 p_i, \; 0 \leqslant p_i \leqslant 1; \sum_i p_i = 1;$$

$$0 \leqslant H(i) \leqslant \log_2 n \qquad\qquad 1$$

(A "bit" is the unit of information in discrete information theory. The number of bits in a message is the number of yes-no questions that have to be asked to obtain the information contained in the message, or the amount of information gained when the number of possible outcomes is halved.) A similar definition serves for continuous i, an integral sign replacing the summation sign and the logs being to base e. Similarly, for a number of variables $S = I_1, I_2, \ldots I_n$, the entropy of the system of variables is defined as

$$H(S) = -\sum_s p_s \log_2 p_s \qquad\qquad 2$$

where the summation is over all possible values s of the vector $S = I_1, I_2, \ldots I_n$ and p is the distribution on the n-tuples.

Conditional entropies such as $H_{I_1 I_2}(I_3)$ may be defined, either through the conditional distribution:

$$H_{I_1 I_2}(I_3) = -\sum_{i_1, i_2} p(i_1 i_2) \sum_{i_3} p(i_3 | i_1 i_2) \log_2(i_3 | i_1 i_2)$$

$$= -\sum_{i_1, i_2, i_3} p(i_1 i_2 i_3) \log_2 p(i_3 | i_1 i_2) \qquad\qquad 3$$

or equivalently through entropies:

$$H_{I_1 I_2}(I_3) = H(I_1, I_2, I_3) - H(I_1, I_2), \qquad\qquad 4$$

with the quantities on the right defined by Equation 2. $H_{I_1 I_2}(I_3)$ measures the average uncertainty of I_3 if one knows I_1 and I_2—that is, the variability of I_1, I_2, I_3 not accounted for in $I_1 I_2$. $H_{I_1 I_2}(I_3)$ will be in the interval $[0, H(I_3)]$; and equal zero if I_3 is determined by I_1, I_2 in the sense that $p(i_3 | i_1 i_2) = 0$ or 1; and equal $H(I_3)$ if I_3 is independent of I_1, I_2 in the sense that $p(i_3 | i_1 i_2) = p(i_3)$ for all i_1, i_2.

Although not of direct use in economic analysis, the information theory measure of (the amount or expected amount of) information, besides being essential to engineers in designing communication systems (which is where it originated), has been suggested as a means of measuring information loss through aggregation, a type of processing much engaged in by accountants (Theil 1968–69).

Another suggestion is that it could be used to measure the strength of interdependencies within a system. Here the amount by which two variables are related (i.e., not statistically independent) would be measured by the amount of communication between them. If x_1 and x_2 are the two variables, the communication ("transmission") is defined by

$$T(x_1 : x_2) = H(x_1) + H(x_2) - H(x_1, x_2)$$
$$= H(x_1) - H_{x_2}(x_1) = H(x_2) - H_{x_1}(x_2)$$

The measure is symmetric and measures the amount by which knowledge of one variable reduces uncertainty about the other, or the amount by which the joint uncertainty $H(x_1, x_2)$ is smaller than if x_1 and x_2 were independent. $T(x_1 : x_2)$ is defined in the interval $[0, \min \{H(x_1), H(x_2)\}]$; it is zero if the variables are statistically independent and a maximum if one variable determines the other.

The analysis is extended to dynamic systems by defining the entropy rate $\bar{H}(x)$, the entropy of x conditional on all its prior values, and the transmission rate $\bar{T}(x_1 : x_2)$. The strength of the causal relations are then quantified in terms of these information transmission rates between variables. In this way information theory can be used in the analysis of constraints or dependencies (Conant 1976). Conant claims that information theory as a tool for the statistical analysis of n-variable systems has advantages over other techniques of statistical analysis in that (i) it is applicable to systems whether they are linear or nonlinear, metric or nonmetric, discrete or continuous; (ii) it allows measures of *rates* of constraint between dynamic variables; and (iii) the measures have the property of additivity, which allows decomposition of constraints. The analysis, of course, makes no claim to measure the *economic* effects of interdependencies between variables (the marginal externalities discussed in Chapter 3).

The economics of information

Notation:

$X = \{x\}$ Set of possible states of the world, assumed finite (e.g., a set of price changes)

P Decision-maker's probability distribution on X

$A = \{a\}$ Set of possible actions ("terminal acts", decisions); we assume here that only one action is being considered (i.e., this is a single-period model)

$H = \{\eta\}$ Set of possible information structures, an information structure being a particular way of partitioning X; this includes the degenerate case of X partitioned into itself, representing no information

$Y = \{y\}$ Set of potential messages (signals) generated by H, based on observations of past events; $y = \eta(x)$

u Payoff (utility measure); if utility is linear in money (decision-maker risk-neutral), u would also represent cash flows

ω Payoff function; $u = \omega(x, a)$

α Decision rule, a function associating a message y with an action a: $a = \alpha(y)$

U Expected utility: $U = \underset{x}{E}\, u = E\omega\{x, \alpha[\eta(x)]\} = \Sigma_x p_x \omega\{x, \alpha[\eta(x)]\}$. U can be expressed as $U = U(\alpha, \eta; \omega, P)$, the semicolon separating the functions the decision-maker can choose (α and η) from those he cannot (ω and P).

The objective is to maximize U by choosing the optimal decision rule $\alpha = \alpha^*$, the rule that maximizes U over all messages y. That is,

$$U(\alpha^*, \eta; \omega, P) = \max_{\alpha} U(\alpha, \eta; \omega, P)$$

$$= V(\eta; \omega, P)$$

where $V(\ )$ denotes the value of information structure η. Note that V depends on the payoff function ω, which is a function of the decision taken and the state of the world.

If the existing information structure (which could also be the "no information" member of the set H) is denoted η^0, the maximum value of U achievable with this structure is

$$U_0 = \max_{\alpha} \underset{x}{E}\omega\{x, \alpha[\eta^0(x)]\}$$

$$= V(\eta^0; \omega, P)$$

If η^1 is some other information structure leading to a different (finer) partition of X with greater information value, and the decision-maker can change to this new structure before selecting his action a, the maximum value of U achievable with this new structure is

$$U_1 = E \max_{\alpha} \omega[x, \alpha(\eta^1(x))]$$

$$= V(\eta^1; \omega, P)$$

It will pay to change information structures if $U_1 - U_0 = E \max_{\alpha} u - \max E \max u - \max Eu \geqslant 0$. Assuming the optimal action $a = a^*$ is taken with the information structure available in each case, the upper bound on the value, $U_1 - U_0$, of any additional information for the decision under consideration is reached if the new structure U_1 provides perfect information on x, that is, if $\eta^1(x) = \eta^*(x) = x$.

Use of general functional forms in the above formalization results in a considerable simplification, as will be seen by consulting the references (e.g., Feltham 1972). Also, the value of an information structure in the foregoing means value net of the cost of the information structure. Treatments in the literature often assume that the payoff (utility) is linear in the cash flows and that it is separable into a value component and a cost component, the value component being denoted by ω^+ and the cost component by ω^-, where $\omega^+ + \omega^- = \omega$. If this distinction is made, the value of using information structure η^1 compared with the existing structure η^0, as above, is $V(\eta^1, \eta^0) = E(\omega^+|\eta^1, a_{\eta^1}) - E(\omega^+|\eta^0, a_{\eta^0})$ and the cost of using structure η^1 compared with structure η^0 is $C(\eta^1, \eta^0) = E(\omega^-|\eta^0, a_{\eta^0}) - E(\omega^-|\eta^1, a_{\eta^1})$. Information structure η^1 is more valuable than η^0 if $V(\eta^1, \eta^0) > C(\eta^1, \eta^0)$.

The analysis becomes more complex when extended to a number of actions (periods).

Note finally that whether a particular information structure offers a greater expected payoff than another depends in general on the form of the payoff function. As a result, the ranking of information structures according to their value depends on the usefulness of information to a given user, and is accordingly subjective (Marschak 1959).

The amount and value of information

The information theory definition of information is of limited value in economic analysis because different pieces of information, equal in "amount," usually have quite different benefits and costs, different decision-relevance. An example will illustrate this point (the example, although not the analysis, is taken from Feltham, 1972).

Example

Suppose a decision-maker may take either action a_1 or a_2. The payoff from the action chosen depends on whether event b_1 or b_2 has occurred and on whether event c_1 or c_2 has occurred. The payoffs are:

		a_1		a_2	
		b_1	b_2	b_1	b_2
c_1		10	4	4	10
c_2		9	5	5	9

The decision-maker may observe either event b or event c, but not both. He attaches the following probabilities to these events: $p(b_1) = 1/3$; $p(b_2) = 2/3$; $p(c_1) = p(c_2) = 1/2$. Events b and c are statistically independent. Which event is the more uncertain (i.e., yields the greater amount of information) and which is the more valuable (i.e., offers the largest expected payoff)?

Expected amount of information:

$$H(b) = \qquad\qquad -\tfrac{1}{3}\log_2\tfrac{1}{3} - \tfrac{2}{3}\log_2\tfrac{2}{3}$$

$$= 0.9179$$

$$H(c) = -\tfrac{1}{2}\log_2\tfrac{1}{2} - \tfrac{1}{2}\log_2\tfrac{1}{2}$$

$$= 1.0000.$$

So even c is more uncertain (yields the greater expected amount of information).

Value of information:

Note first that with *no* information the expected payoffs are:

$$Ep(a_1) = Ep(b_1|a_1) + Ep(b_2|a_1)$$

$$= 9(1/6) + 10(1/6) + 4(2/6) + 5(2/6) = 37/6$$

$$Ep(a_2) = 4(1/6) + 5(1/6) + 10(2/6) + 9(2/6) = 47/6$$

The expected payoffs for $EP(c_1|a_1) + Ep(c_2|a_1)$ and for $EP(c_1|a_2) + EP(c_2|a_2)$ will be the same as those above. With no information the best expected payoff is 47/6.

Information on b:

Given b_1 : $Ep(a_1) = 10(1/2) + 9(1/2) = 19/2$ $\qquad\qquad$ $p(b_1) = 1/3$

Given b_2 : $Ep(a_1) = 4(1/2) + 5(1/2) = 9/2$ $\qquad\qquad$ $p(b_2) = 2/3$

Given b_1 : $Ep(a_2) = 4(1/2) + 5(1/2) = 9/2$

Given b_2 : $Ep(a_2) = 10(1/2) + 9(1/2) = 19/2$

$$Ep(b) = \tfrac{19}{2}\cdot\tfrac{1}{3} + \tfrac{19}{2}\cdot\tfrac{2}{3} = 9.5$$

Information on c:

Given c_1 : $Ep(a_1) = 10(1/3) + 4(2/3) = 18/3$ $\qquad\qquad$ $p(c_1) = 1/2$

Given c_2 : $Ep(a_1) = 9(1/3) + 5(2/3) = 19/3$ $\qquad\qquad$ $p(c_2) = 1/2$

Given c_1 : $Ep(a_2) = 4(1/3) + 10(2/3) = 24/3$

Given c_2 : $Ep(a_2) = 5(1/3) + 9(2/3) = 23/3$

$$Ep(c) = \tfrac{24}{3}\cdot\tfrac{1}{2} + \tfrac{23}{3}\cdot\tfrac{1}{2} = 7.83$$

Therefore information on c has no value (because the best expected payoff, 7.83, is no better than with no information). Hence information on b is the more valuable, although event c is the more uncertain.

8

Value and Cost

The incremental and total approaches to decision-making under uncertainty

The following example from Ekern and Bøhren (1979) illustrates the case where a decision is subject to uncertainty, the utility function is linear, but shared amounts are not constant within states (case (iii) (a) in the text).

Example

Suppose the estimated costs of two alternative advertising campaigns, where costs depend on (output and hence on) demand levels, are:

Total costs for alternatives

		Event (Demand)		
		Low	High	EMV
Act	A_1	$60 (.9)	$100 (.1)	$64
(Advertising				
campaign)	A_2	$50 (.2)	$ 80 (.8)	$74

Therefore choose A_1

Incremental costs for alternatives

	Low	High	EMV
A_1	$50 (.9)	$60 (.1)	$51
A_2	$40 (.2)	$40 (.8)	$40

Therefore choose A_2

193

The conditional probabilities in parentheses refer to *events*: .9 is the conditional probability of finding a low demand if campaign A_1 is chosen.

Notice that a different decision is indicated by the two tables. Also, by comparing the tables, we see that the shared amount z is $10 in the case of low demand and $40 for high demand.

With this knowledge the first table can be presented in more detail:

Total costs for alternatives

		Event		
		Low	High	EMV
				$[E(x_i) = E(y_i + E(z)]$
	A_1	50 + 10	60 + 40	51 + 13 = 64
Act				
	A_2	40 + 10	40 + 40	40 + 34 = 74

The first figure under each event is the incremental amount y_i, $i = 1, 2$ denoting the decision alternative, the second is the shared amount z. z is constant within events (column) but not across events (row). In this formulation, where probabilities are associated with events, the relationship between the decision variables that appears in the text of Chapter 8 is $x_{ik} = y_{ik} + z_k$, where the subscript k denotes an event.

We now reformulate the problem in terms of states instead of events, where by *state* we mean the description of the decision-maker's relevant environment, in this example the state of demand. In other words, we recast the problem in the framework of *statistical* decision theory, in which probabilities are assigned to states. Such probabilities are not influenced by the act that is chosen, whereas event probabilities may be.

There are four possible states: L_1L_2, L_1H_2, H_1L_2, H_1H_2, each completely describing the state of the world with respect to demand, where H_1L_2 denotes high demand if action A_1 is taken and low demand if action A_2 is taken. Let p be the probability of state L_1L_2. Then the other state probabilities are:

L_1H_2	$.9 - p$
H_1L_2	$.2 - p$
H_1H_2	$p - .1$

These are calculated as follows:

Probability of L_1 = .9; therefore probability of H_1 = .1

Probability of $L_1L_2 + L_1H_2$ = probability of L_1 = .9

Probability of $L_1L_2 = p$, by definition; therefore probability of L_1H_2 = .9 − p

Probability of $H_1L_2 + L_1L_2$ = probability of L_2 = .2

Probability of H_1L_2 therefore = .2 − p

Probability of $H_1H_2 + H_1L_2$ = probability of H_1 = .1

Probability of H_1L_2 = .2 − p (as above); therefore probability of H_1H_2 = .1 − (.2 − p) = p − .1

In terms of states the last table will appear as below:

State

		L_1L_2	L_1H_2	H_1L_2	H_1H_2	Expected value $[E(x_i) = E(y_i) + E(z_i)]$
	A_1	50 + 10	50 + 10	60 + 40	60 + 40	64
Act						
	A_2	40 + 10	40 + 40	40 + 10	40 + 40	74

Notice that in states L_1H_2 and H_1L_2 the shared cost varies within states. Looking at column L_1H_2, if action A_1 is chosen and demand is low, the shared cost is 10, while if action A_2 is chosen and demand is high, the shared cost is 40. This means that because of the two middle columns (L_1H_2 and H_1L_2) the equation of the state formulation may no longer be written as $x_{ij} = y_{ij} + z_j$ (where subscript j denotes state), as it could have been if shared cost had been constant within states, but must be replaced by $x_{ij} = y_{ij} + z_{ij}$, because the shared cost varies over alternatives within states. The result is that $E(z_1) \neq E(z_2)$, where the subscript denotes act. Thus, for states L_1H_2 and H_1L_2:

$$E(z_1) = 10(.9 − p) + 40(.2 − p)$$
$$E(z_2) = 40(.9 − p) + 10(.2 − p)$$

Consequently, the relevant expected cost to consider is not $E(y_i)$ but $E(x_i)$; we should follow the total approach if the shared amount varies within states.

9

Control and "Performance"

Feedback system

Consider a system with a single feedback, illustrated in the diagram below:

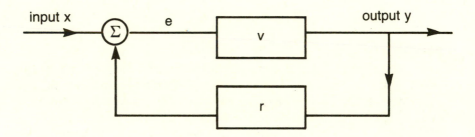

The system has input (control instruments) x, forward transformation v, output (observed results) y, feedback transformation r, and Σ denotes a summation point. The ratio of output to input, called the system's *transfer function*, is y/x before the feedback is activated. Now let the feedback operate. The output of the feedback transformation is ry. Hence, the new input to the forward transformation is $e = x + ry$ (previously e was equal to x), and output becomes ev. So after the feedback has operated the system's transfer function is:

$$\frac{ev}{e - ry} = \frac{v}{1 - \dfrac{ry}{e}}$$

and since $y = ev$,

$$= \frac{v}{1 - vr}$$

It is reasonable to assume that $v > 0$, that is, that the work done by the system always has a positive value. If $r = 0$ (nil deviations from desired results), the feedback has no effect:

$$\frac{y}{x} = \frac{v}{1 - v \cdot 0} = v$$

If $r > 0$, vr is > 0, and $1 - vr$ is < 1. Hence $y/x > v$, and the feedback is positive. If $r < 0$, $vr < 0$, and $1 - vr > 1$. Hence $y/x < v$, and the feedback is negative.

Error-correcting feedbacks are necessarily negative if deviations from a desired result are measured as absolute values, that is, regardless of sign (whether favorable or unfavorable, the deviation is a positive discrepancy). If absolute values of deviations are transmitted over the feedback network, the resulting input to the forward transformation becomes $e = x - ry$ instead of $x + ry$ as above, because we know that the absolute value of the feedback transformation must be subtracted from (oppose) the original input. The transfer function then changes to $v/(1 + vr)$. If deviations are measured in absolute terms, this transfer function will always have a value less than v, reflecting negative feedback, because r will always be greater than 0.

In accounting, the usual convention is to give unfavorable cost variances a negative sign. The transfer function is then of the first form, $v/(1 - vr)$. With this first form of the transfer function, the output of the feedback transformation is always added to the original input, as indicated by the summation point Σ in the diagram. The effect of the feedback then depends on the sign of r, as shown above.

If inputs and outputs are both vectors, then $y = Tx$, where the matrix T is the total system transformation. More precisely, if T is made up of forward transformation A and feedback transformation B, A and B being matrices, then when deviations are measured with due regard to sign,

$y = Ax + (AB)\,y$; $(I - AB)y = Ax$, I being the identity matrix; and the transfer matrix [corresponding to the transfer function $v/(1 - vr)$ in the scalar case] is $x^{-1}y = (I - AB)^{-1}A$.

The law of requisite variety

Let D, R, and V denote, respectively, sets of environmental disturbances, control system responses, and outcomes. Then if "variety" is denoted by b with an appropriate subscript (e.g., b_D is the variety in environmental disturbances), when "variety" is measured in absolute terms the law states that min $b_V \geqslant b_D/b_R$ or min $(\log_2 b_V) \geqslant \log_2 b_D - \log_2 b_R$ when "variety" is measured in "bits."

Modern control theory

The state–space model of the system to be controlled is here represented by equations of the general form shown below. (These particular equations are for a discrete, time-invariant, linear system.)

$$v_{t+1} = Av_t + Bu_t$$
$$y_t = Cv_t + Du_t$$
$$u_t = \tfrac{1}{\varepsilon} y_t$$

Small letters denote vectors, capital letters matrices. The state vector is denoted by v, the control vector by u, and the output vector by y; t denotes time. The third equation has been included to show that the system has output feedback control. If $\varepsilon = 1$, the feedback consists of the actual outputs, while if ε is a small positive number ($0 < \varepsilon < 1$), these are amplified ("high gain" feedback).

Statement of the control problem under the state–space approach

Let J denote the sum of the costs referred to in the text. Then, using the same symbols as above, the problem is to choose the values of u at each point in time to minimize $J_t = f(u_t, v_t)$, subject to:

$$v_{t+1} = Av_t + Bu_t$$
$$y_t = Cv_t + Du_t$$
$$u_t = \tfrac{1}{\varepsilon} y_t$$

$$v_0 \text{ given}$$

10

Motivation, Risk-Sharing, and Incentives

The basic agency model

We consider a single principal-single agent relationship in which the agent takes action $a \in A$ on behalf of the principal, where "action" will also be interpreted as the effort level supplied by the agent and A is the set of all possible actions (effort levels). An action a together with a random state of the world θ determines the monetary payoff x resulting from the action; $x = x(a, \theta)$. The problem is to determine how x should be optimally shared between principal and agent. Both parties are assumed to be rational expected utility (EU) maximizers. The principal selects a fee schedule $f(x, \theta, a)$ specifying the share of x that goes to the agent. The principal receives the remainder, $x - f(x, \theta, a)$. The principal's utility function is defined over money alone: $G(x - f(\ ))$. The principal is usually assumed to be weakly risk-averse (i.e., either risk-averse or risk-neutral). Denoting the principal's share by x_P, $\partial G/\partial x_P > 0$, $\partial^2 G/\partial x_P^2 \leqslant 0$. The agent's utility is defined over money and action (effort): his utility function is denoted $H(f(x, \theta, a), a)$. It is assumed that this function is separable into pecuniary and nonpecuniary elements: the agent's net utility $H(\ ) = U(f(\ )) - V(a)$. The agent is assumed to be strictly risk-averse and to experience disutility from increased effort. Denoting the agent's share of the payoff by x_A, where $x_A + x_P = x$, $\partial U/\partial x_A > 0$, $\partial^2 U/\partial x_A^2 < 0$; $\partial V/\partial a > 0$, and $\partial x/\partial a > 0$ (greater effort leads to increased payoff). (Both G and H are assumed to be twice continuously differentiable.)

Agency theory restricts the feasible set of fee schedules to those that are self-enforcing in the sense of the perfect Nash equilibrium concept (i.e., the theory assumes the agent does not engage in "strategic" behavior to influence the principal's choice of fee schedule; the principal limits his

199

choice of fee schedules to that set for which the agent, acting in his own self-interest, will supply what he promises to supply, and the agent will choose to supply that level of effort that maximizes his EU given the fee schedule selected). The fee schedule is chosen by the principal from the set of self-enforcing schedules by applying the Pareto-optimality criterion, that is, all schedules that are Pareto-inferior to at least one other are eliminated from consideration. A Pareto-optimal schedule will then be selected from the remaining subset, subject to the agent's EU being not less than that of his opportunity wage, the highest earnings he could get in other employments (H^0), and subject to the agent taking that action that maximizes his EU given the fee schedule selected.

Formally, this amounts to solving the following problem:

$$\max_{f(\ ),\, a} E\{G(x - f(x, \theta, a)\} \tag{1}$$

subject to:

$$E\{H(f(x, \theta, a), a)\} \geqslant H^0 \tag{2}$$

$$a \in \operatorname*{argmax}_{a' \in A} E\{H(f(x, \theta, a'), a')\} \tag{3}$$

where E is the expectation operation, argmax denotes the set of arguments that maximizes the objective function that follows (i.e., constraint 3 expresses the self-seeking behavior of the agent, who is expected to maximize his own EU over a' for any given fee schedule $f(\ )$), and the inclusion symbol $\in$ before argmax is used because $E(H)$ need not be concave in a, with the result that there may be multiple solutions.

An approach to solving this problem that results in a more intuitive interpretation of an optimum was suggested by Mirrlees (1974, 1976). Suppress θ and view x as a random variable with distribution function $F(x, a)$, parameterized by the agent's action. Assume that F has density function $\phi(x, a)$, with ϕ_a and ϕ_{aa} well defined for all (x, a), where subscripts denote partial derivatives with respect to the corresponding variable.

As formulated in expressions 1–3, there is a possibility that the agent's optimal choice of a will not be unique. The problem can be reformulated to ensure that the optimal a exists and is unique by restricting the range of $f(\ )$ and replacing constraint 3 with its corresponding first-order condition. Making these two changes, and assuming that principal and agent have homogeneous beliefs $[\phi_P(x, a) = \phi_A(x, a) = \phi(x, a)]$, the problem may be restated as:

$$\max_{f(\ )\in J;\ a} \int G(x - f(x,\ a))\ \phi(x,\ a)\ dx \qquad\qquad 4$$

subject to:

$$\int (U(f(x,\ a)) - V(a))\ \phi(x,\ a)\ dx \geqslant H^0 \qquad\qquad 5$$

$$\int U(f(x,\ a))\ \phi_a(x,\ a)\ dx = V'(a) \qquad\qquad 6$$

where the subscript again denotes partial derivative, a prime denotes derivative, and f is restricted to the closed interval J to avoid nonexistence of a solution.

A fuller statement of the problem would include explicit reference to the monitoring system (post-decision information system) used by the principal. Suppose monitoring system $\eta\varepsilon\Xi$ provides a signal y. The principal's problem is to choose the fee schedule and monitoring system that will maximize his own EU subject to inducing the agent to work for him, and subject also to the agent maximizing his own EU, given the fee schedule and monitoring system. With this addition, the problem may be stated as follows:

$$\max_{\substack{\eta\varepsilon\Xi \\ f(y)\in J \\ a\in A}} \int\int G(x - f(y))\ \phi(x,\ y|a,\ \eta)\ dx\ dy \qquad\qquad 7$$

subject to:

$$\int H(f(y),\ a)\ \phi(y|a,\ \eta)dy \geqslant H^0 \qquad\qquad 8$$

$$\int U(f(y))\ \phi_a(y|a,\ \eta)\ dy = V'(a) \qquad\qquad 9$$

Reverting now to the earlier formulations, a solution described as first-best is obtained by solving expressions 1 and 2, or expressions 4 and 5, ignoring expressions 3 or 6. This is the case discussed in the text where the principal can observe x and a and employ a "forcing" contract, where the agent's fee schedule is $f(x)$, more precisely $f(x|a)$.

Constraint 3 or 6, on the other hand, reflects the fact that the principal can observe x but not a. In this case let λ and μ be the Lagrangean multipliers for constraints 5 and 6, respectively. Holmström (1979) has shown that pointwise optimization of the resulting Lagrangean expression yields an optimal sharing rule

$$\frac{G'(x - f(x))}{U'(f(x))} = \lambda + \frac{\mu\ \phi_a(x,\ a)}{\phi(x,\ a)} \qquad\qquad 10$$

for almost every x for which expression 10 has a solution $f(x) \in [J]$; otherwise $f(x)$ is a limit of this closed interval. This Pareto-optimal *payoff-sharing* solution will result in Pareto-optimal *risk-sharing* between the principal and the risk-averse agent if the right-hand side of Equation 10 equals k, a constant (Borch 1962), that is, only if $\mu = 0$. [The principal may or may not be risk-neutral $(G'' \leqslant 0)$]. But this is shown by Holmström (1979) to lead to a contradiction. Hence expression 10 represents a second-best solution, so-called because it is inferior to a first-best solution with respect to risk-sharing. A second-best solution is Pareto-optimal with respect to payoff-sharing but not to risk-sharing. That is to say, under a second-best contract both principal and agent are better off in terms of EU, but risk-sharing will not be Pareto-optimal because the agent is required to bear more of the risk than he would wish.

Where the principal can observe the payoff but not the agent's effort level, there are two exceptions to the conclusion that only a second-best contract is possible. The first is where the agent is risk-neutral. In this case the optimal (although unlikely) arrangement would be for the agent to rent the firm from the principal, paying the principal a fixed fee and keeping the rest of the payoff as his own remuneration. The fee schedule for this case is of the form $f(x, \theta, a) = x - k$, where k is the fixed fee paid to the principal. The second exception is where the principal can observe x and θ. In this case the principal has sufficient information to infer the agent's effort, and a fee schedule based on x and θ will yield a first-best solution. This contract will be Pareto-superior to any contract that also includes the agent's effort, because such a contract provides no additional information and involves increased monitoring costs.

Pareto-optimality

As stated in the text, the P-optimality criterion says that it is not possible to make one party better off without making the other (or others) worse off or, putting it another way, a contracting arrangement is P-optimal as regards payoff-sharing and expected utilities if each party's EU is a maximum, given the EU level of the other party. The purpose of this note is to explain that, while P-optimal payoff-sharing always leads to P-optimal EUs, the latter do not invariably mean P-optimal risk-sharing.

In agency theory the principal is assumed to be the dominant party. Hence the Pareto criterion means that maximizing the principal's EU must not be at the expense of reducing the agent's EU. The set of *P-optimal fee schedules* for the agent is obtained by solving the problem

$$\max_{f(x)} EG(x_P) + \lambda E[H(x_A) - H^0] \quad \lambda \geqslant 0 \qquad\qquad 11$$

for all feasible sharing arrangements $f(x) = x_A$; for example, the feasible sharing rules may be $x_A = 20$, 25, 30, or 35 percent of x.

If the principal can observe a as well as x, he can select the fee schedule $f(x)$ that yields P-optimal EUs. If he cannot observe a, the principal selects from the set of P-optimal fee schedules $f(x)$ the one satisfying constraint 6, which assumes that the agent's optimal (EU maximizing) act, a^*, will be unique for the fee schedule so selected. That is, when the principal cannot observe a the *P-optimal EUs* are obtained by solving the problem

$$\max_{f(x)} EG(x_P) + \lambda E[H(x_A) - H^0] \qquad\qquad 12$$

subject to *EH* being maximized over a and being unique; in other words, the solution to expressions 4, 5, and 6. The validity of the assumption that the agent's optimal choice of action, a^*, is unique for the fee schedule $f^*(x)$ found by solving this problem has not been established in general (Holmström 1979, 78n).

Before formulating expression 12, the solution to Equation 6 is incorporated in the principal's objective function: $x_P = x - f(x, 0, a^*)$, that is, the principal is assumed to know the agent's utility function (and, in the case of the model stated in expressions 4–6, the agent's information also) and hence can infer how the agent, acting in his own self-interest, will respond to any given fee schedule.

The condition for *P-optimal risk-sharing* has already been stated in expression 10. Essentially, if the principal is risk-neutral ($\partial^2 G/\partial x_P^2 = 0$), P-optimal risk-sharing means that he should bear all the risk, while if both principal and agent are risk-averse ($\partial^2 G/\partial x_P^2 < 0$, $\partial^2 H/\partial x_A^2 < 0$), P-optimal risk-sharing requires the agent to bear some of the risk.

P-optimal EUs and P-optimal risk-sharing coincide only when a first-best solution is possible, that is, a solution to expressions 4 and 5 only (see Holmström, 1979, and Shavell, 1979, for a demonstration and proof).

Example: Suppose first that the principal is risk-neutral with $G(x - x_A) = x - x_A$, and the agent is risk-averse with $U(x_A) = x_A^{1/2}$, and that they have homogeneous beliefs. Here there is no risk for the agent to share because, provided he can observe a, the principal can use a dichotomous forcing contract, based formally on x alone, solving expressions 4 and 5 only to yield a first-best solution. Expression 6 is superfluous and hence $\mu = 0$ in expression 10. From the Lagrangean expression 11, we obtain the first-order condition

$$\frac{\partial L}{\partial x_A} = -1 + \frac{\lambda}{2x_A^{1/2}} = 0$$

whence the optimal sharing rule is $x_A = \lambda^2/4 = k$. P-optimal payoff-sharing and EUs here satisfy the Borch condition (that the right-hand side of expression 10 = k), and are consistent with risk being borne P-optimally (all by the principal).

Now suppose the principal is also risk-averse with a utility function in the same class as the agent's: $G(x - x_A) = (x - x_A)^{1/2}$. In this special case principal and agent have identical risk attitudes, meaning that they will agree on what should be done in any decision situation (Wilson 1969, 293–95). The principal does not have to monitor the agent's actions; the principal observes only x. We can therefore again dispense with expression 6. From the Lagrangean expression the first-order condition for the optimal payoff-sharing rule is

$$\frac{\partial L}{\partial x_A} = (x - x_A)^{-1/2} + \lambda x_A^{-1/2} = 0$$

whence

$$x_A = \frac{\lambda^2}{1 + \lambda^2} x \neq k$$

The Borch condition tells us that in this case, P-optimal payoff-sharing and EUs do not coincide with P-optimal risk-sharing.

Incidentally, it has been shown (Ross 1973; Wilson 1969) that if principal and agent both have utility functions belonging to the same class, and that class is exponential or logarithmic utilities or power function utilities with the same power (as in the example above), the P-optimal payoff-sharing rule will be linear in form, meaning the agent's remuneration will consist of a fixed fee plus a share of the payoff. The optimal sharing rule stated above is not inconsistent with this conclusion, being expressible as $x_A = k + bx$, with $k = 0$.

11

Measurement

Space

Let Ω be the space (or set) under consideration. Ω denotes the totality of all the elements of this space that may appear in our investigation.

Ω is a *pseudo-metric space* if there is a real-valued distance function (or metric), ρ, of all pairs of points on $\Omega \times \Omega$ such that:

(i) $\rho(x, x) = 0$ for every element (point) $x \in \Omega$
(ii) $\rho(x, y) \leqslant \rho(z, x) + \rho(z, y)$ for every three points $x, y, z \in \Omega$ (the triangle inequality).

The (distance) functions ρ have two other basic properties:

(iii) $\rho(x, y) \geqslant 0$
(iv) $\rho(x, y) = \rho(y, x)$

A *metric space* is a pseudo-metric space in which ρ satisfies the additional condition, $\rho(x, y) = 0$ implies $x = y$. In any pseudo-metric space $\rho(x, y) = 0$ is an equivalence relation; and the set of equivalence classes forms a metric space. A relation R in a set X is an equivalence relation if it is reflexive (i.e., if xRx for every $x \in X$), symmetric (if xRy implies yRx), and transitive (if xRy and yRz implies xRz).

A *nonmetric space* is a space in which no real-valued (distance) function ρ is defined. Sets of points in a nonmetric space yield measures that are not based on an addition operation, but which may lead to a ratio scale (and hence to an interval or ordinal scale; see below).

Relational system

A relational system is a finite sequence of the form $\langle A, R_1, \ldots, R_n \rangle$, where A is a nonempty set of elements called the domain of the relational system and $R_1, \ldots, R_n$ are relations on A. An *empirical relational system* is one in which A is a set of objects or properties of objects. A *numerical relational system* is one in which A is a set of real numbers. We will use U and N to denote empirical and numerical relational systems, respectively, where $U = \langle A, R_i \rangle$ and $N = \langle \mathbf{R}^n, S_i \rangle$, $i = 1, \ldots, n$, $\mathbf{R}^n$ is the nth Cartesian product of the set of real numbers, $\mathbf{R}$, and S_i are familiar relations on the set of real numbers.

Ordered pair

An ordered pair is a two-element set with one of the elements distinguished as first. If A and B are two sets, the product set $A \times B$ is the set of all ordered pairs $\langle a, b \rangle$ where $a \in A$ and $b \in B$ (the two-element set is here $\{ \{a\}, \{a,b\} \}$), and the notation $\langle \ , \ \rangle$ denotes the order of a sequence. A binary relation is a set, each of whose members is an ordered pair; an n-ary relation a set of ordered n-tuples. Two relational systems are said to be "similar" (of the same type) if they are both binary, both n-ary, and so on.

Function

A function from A to B is a subset, f, of $A \times B$ such that every element of A appears as a first entry in exactly one element of f. A, the set of all first entries in the ordered pairs of f, is called the *domain* of f. The subset of B consisting of all second entries in the ordered pairs of f is called the *range* of f. If the range of f is all of B, f is from A *onto* B, otherwise it is *into* (or to) B. (Sometimes what is called a function above is called a *mapping*, the term "function" being restricted to the case where the elements of A and B are numbers. Usually, however, the terms *mapping* and *function* are used interchangeably.) Formally, f is a function if (i) the members of f are ordered pairs and (ii) if $\langle a, b \rangle$ and $\langle a, c \rangle$ are members of f, then $b = c$.

Isomorphism, homomorphism

The concept of isomorphism relates to ordered sets. The function f: $X_1 \to X_2$ is an isomorphic mapping relative to ordering relations R_1 for X_1

and R_2 for X_2 if and only if xR_1y implies $f(x)$ $R_2f(y)$. The mapping is one-to-one and onto, and is such that both it and its inverse mapping f^{-1} are order-preserving. In an isomorphic mapping each element of the range of f appears as the second entry in exactly one ordered pair of f. In a homomorphic mapping an element of the range of f may appear as the second entry in more than one ordered pair of f, that is, f is no longer one-to-one but many-to-one.

Set function and measure function

A set function is a numerically valued function that is defined for every set in some class of sets. It associates with each such set a real number. Not every function of sets meets the requirements for a measure function, however. If Ω is any space, in most cases of practical importance the domain of the measure function is smaller than the class of all subsets of Ω. Before defining "measure" we must therefore examine some of the properties that are demanded of the domain of a set function that qualifies as a measure function.

Restating this in formal terms, it is not possible in general to define a measure on the set, $\mathscr{P}(\Omega)$, of all subsets of a space Ω but only on certain subclasses of $\mathscr{P}(\Omega)$; see Munroe (1968, 42) for an exception. As will be described in the sequel, in most cases of interest the domain of the measure function is some completely additive, smaller class than $\mathscr{P}(\Omega)$. Specifically, the measurability of a set function is restricted to σ-algebras, often to an even more restrictive class, Borel σ-algebras (also called the class of Borel sets). The terms *algebra, σ-algebra*, and Borel σ-*algebra* will now be defined.

An *algebra*, $\mathscr{F}$ is a nonempty class of subsets of any space Ω such that if $A \in \mathscr{F}$ and $B \in \mathscr{F}$ so also are $A \cap B$, $A \cup B$, A^C, B^C, and Ω, where $A^C = \Omega - A$ is the complement of A with respect to Ω. In other words, $\mathscr{F}$ is the class of all closed subsets of Ω. (A set is said to be closed if it contains all its limit points, if any. Thus in one-dimensional space an interval $a \leqslant x \leqslant b$ which contains its end points is closed. An open set is defined as the complement of a closed set.)

A σ-*algebra*, $\mathscr{S}$ is an algebra with the additional property that if a sequence of disjoint sets $A_i \in \mathscr{F}$ then

$$\bigcup_{i=1}^{\infty} A_i \in \mathscr{F}$$

Also

$$\bigcap_{i=1}^{\infty} A_i \in \mathscr{S}$$

$$\emptyset \in \mathscr{S}$$

$$\text{if } A \in \mathscr{S}, A^C \in \mathscr{S}$$

For a given space Ω, the smallest σ-algebra containing the class of all open sets of Ω (which will also contain all closed sets of Ω) is called the *class of Borel sets,* denoted by $\mathscr{B}$. This is sometimes also referred to as the Borel field; Loève (1963) and Moran (1968) use the term *field* where we have used algebra. This completes the review of terms needed in defining the domain of measure functions.

One further requirement must be imposed before defining a measure function (more precisely, a measure function on a metric or pseudo-metric space). It concerns additive classes. If Ω is any space and $\mathscr{A}$ is a class of subsets of Ω (i.e., $\mathscr{A} \subset \mathscr{P}(\Omega)$, $\mathscr{A}$ is said to be a *finitely additive class of sets* if

$\emptyset \in \mathscr{A}$ (where $\emptyset$ denotes the null set)

if $A \in \mathscr{A}$ and $B \in \mathscr{A}, A - B \in \mathscr{A}$

if $A \in \mathscr{A}$ and $B \in \mathscr{A}, A \cup b \in \mathscr{A}$

A class of sets $\mathscr{A}$ is *completely (or countably) additive* if it satisfies the stronger conditions:

$\emptyset \in \mathscr{A}$

if $A \in \mathscr{A}, A^C \in \mathscr{A}$

if A_i is any sequence of sets from $\mathscr{A}$,

$$\bigcup_{i=1}^{\infty} A_i \in \mathscr{A}$$

A set function $f: \mathscr{F} \to$ the extended real line is *σ-additive* if

$$f(\emptyset) = 0$$

for any sequence A_i of disjoint sets of $\mathscr{F}$

$$f(\bigcup_{i=1}^{\infty} A_i) = \sum_{i=1}^{\infty} f(A_i)$$

Now consider a space Ω and a σ-algebra $\mathscr{S}$ of its subsets. The couple $(\Omega, \mathscr{S})$ defines a *measurable space.* A set function $\mu: \mathscr{S} \to \mathbf{R}_+$, or more commonly, $\mu: \mathscr{B} \to \mathbf{R}_+$, is called a *measure function* (or measure) if μ is σ-additive (or $\mathscr{B}$-additive) and nonnegative. In other words, a measure function is a nonnegative (therefore nondecreasing), completely additive, set function whose domain is a σ-algebra, or in most cases of interest, a Borel σ-algebra.

More formally, a set function $\mu: \mathscr{B} \to$ the real line (or the extended real line) is a measure if:

$\mu(\emptyset) = 0$

$\mu(A_i) \geqslant 0$, all i, where A_i is a sequence of subsets of $\mathscr{F}$

$\{A_i\} \in \mathscr{B}$ and $A_i \cap A_j = \emptyset$, all $i \neq j$, implies:

$$\bigcup_{i=1}^{\infty} A_i \in \mathscr{B}$$

$$\mu(\bigcup_{i=1}^{\infty} A_i) = \sum_{i=1}^{\infty} \mu(A_i), \text{ and}$$

$\sum_{i=1}^{\infty} \mu(A_i)$ not bounded as n increases implies

$$\sum_{i=1}^{\infty} \mu A_i \to \infty$$

Probability measure

In probability theory and statistics, an "event" is defined as a set of states, and a probability measure the assignment of a numerical probability to an event. For example, the event that exactly one day in a given week will be rainy in a particular city is a set having seven states as elements. In statistical decision theory, an act is a measurable function from the measurable space of events to the measurable spaces of outcomes, where "measurable space" is confined to a σ-algebra or Borel σ-algebra.

Given a space Ω and $\mathscr{F}$, an algebra of subsets of Ω, a countably additive function $\mu: \mathscr{F} \to [0, 1]$ with $\mu(\Omega) = 1$, is called a *probability distribution*. If $A \in \mathscr{F}$ then $\mu(A)$, $0 \leqslant \mu(A) \leqslant 1$ for every $A \in \mathscr{F}$ is called a *probability measure*.

Being defined on a σ-algebra or an even more restricted class of sets (a Borel σ-algebra), measures in general are assumed to be countably additive (compare the earlier definitions of a σ-algebra and a completely additive class of sets). Probability measures are also generally assumed to be countably additive. By "countably (or completely) additive" we mean that if each of an infinite sequence, A_i, of disjoint sets is measurable, the probability of their union is the sum of their probabilities.

Subjective or personal probability in theory possesses all the mathematical properties attributed to probability in general (but see the qualification in Chapter 5). The only difference is that a subjective probability distribution is required to be only a finitely additive function, not in general countably additive (Savage 1954, 43).

The representation problem

In fundamental measurement what has to be represented by an assignment of numbers is a set of things or properties of things in an empirical relational system (ERS), $U = \langle A, R_1, \ldots, R_n \rangle$, where A is a set of things or properties. In derived measurement what has to be represented by an assignment of numbers is a set of properties within a derived measurement system (DMS). A DMS may be denoted by $B = \langle B, f_1, \ldots, f_n \rangle$, where B is a set of things possessing a certain property and $f_1, \ldots, f_n$ are measures of other properties of the elements of B.

Scale

A fundamental measurement scale is defined in terms of an ERS, a full numerical relational system (NRS), and a function that maps the former homorphically onto a subset of the latter. If $U = \langle A, R_i \rangle$ is an ERS, $N = \langle \mathbf{R}^n, S_i \rangle$ a full NRS, and f a homorphic mapping from the former onto the latter, a scale is the ordered triple $\langle U, N, f \rangle$. The type of scale (nominal, ordinal, etc.) is determined by the relative uniqueness of the mapping f.

In a DMS, $B = \langle B, f_1, \ldots, f_n \rangle$, a derived measurement scale is denoted by $\langle B, R, g \rangle$, where g is the derived numerical assignment defined on B or $B \times B$, and R is a relation between $f_1, \ldots, f_n$ and g. Thus $f_1, \ldots, f_n$ may refer to fundamental measures of mass (m) and volume (V) of the elements of the set B, and g to the derived measure of density, m/V.

Meaningfulness

Let $U = \langle A, R_1, \ldots, R_n \rangle$ be an empirical relational system, where A is any identifiable set of objects or properties, and let $N = \langle \mathbf{R}^n, S_1, \ldots, S_n \rangle$ be a specified numerical relational system, where $\mathbf{R}^n$ as before is the nth Cartesian product of the set of real numbers. Then a statement of an n-ary numerical relation S_i which is intended to correspond to the specified empirical relational system is meaningful if, for any two admissible mappings, $f_1: A \to \mathbf{R}^n$ and $f_2: A \to \mathbf{R}^n$, the relation S_i holds.

Bibliography

Ackoff, R. L. 1971. "Towards a System of Systems Concepts." *Management Science* 17: 661–71.

Ackoff, R. L. and F. E. Emery. 1972. *On Purposeful Systems.* (Chicago, IL: Aldine-Atherton).

Alchian, A. A. 1965. "The Basis of Some Recent Advances in the Theory of Management of the Firm." *Journal of Industrial Economics* 14 (November): 30–41.

Alchian, A. A. and H. Demsetz. 1972. "Production, Information Costs, and Economic Organization." *American Economic Review* 62 (December): 777–95.

Amey, L. R. 1973. "On Opportunity Cost and Decision-Making." In *Readings in Management Decision,* edited by L. R. Amey (London: Longman).

_____. 1979. *Budget Planning and Control Systems* (London: Pitman).

_____. 1984a. "Adaptive Control in Weakly Coupled Systems." Unpublished paper presented at the International Conference on Systems Research, Informatics and Cybernetics, Baden-Baden, West Germany, August 1–5. A modified version appears in Amey (1986), appendix to ch. 4.

_____. 1984b. "Joint Product Decisions, the Fixed Proportions Case: A Note." *Journal of Business Finance and Accounting* 11 (Autumn): 295–300.

_____. 1985. "Joint Product Decisions: The Variable Proportions Case." Working paper, McGill University Faculty of Management.

_____. 1986. *Corporate Planning: A Systems View* (New York: Praeger).

Amey, L. R. and D. A. Egginton. 1979. *Management Accounting: A Conceptual Approach* (London: Longman; first published 1973).

Anthony, R. N. 1965. *Planning and Control Systems: A Framework for Analysis* (Boston, MA: Harvard University Graduate School of Business Administration).

Argyris, C. 1952. *The Impact of Budgets on People* (Ithaca, NY: School of Business and Public Administration, Cornell University).

_____. 1964. *Integrating the Individual and the Organization* (New York: Wiley).

Arrow, K. J. 1951. *Social Choice and Individual Values* (New Haven, CT: Yale University Press).

————. 1958. "Utilities, Attitudes, Choices: A Review Note." *Econometrica* 26; reprinted in *Readings in Management Decision,* edited by L. R. Amey (London: Longman), ch. 3.

————. 1959. "Optimization, Decentralization, and Internal Pricing in Business Firms." In *Contributions to Scientific Research in Management* (Western Data Processing Center, Graduate School of Business Administration, UCLA), pp. 9–18.

————. 1964a. "Control in Large Organizations." *Management Science* 10 (April): 397–408.

————. 1964b. "Research in Management Controls: A Critical Synthesis." In *Management Controls: New Directions in Basic Research,* edited by C. P. Bonini, R. K. Jaedicke, and H. M. Wagner (New York: McGraw-Hill), ch. 17.

————. 1974a. "Limited Knowledge and Economic Analysis." *American Economic Review* 64 (March): 1–10.

————. 1974b. *The Limits of Organization* (New York: W. W. Norton).

Ashby, W. R. 1956. *An Introduction to Cybernetics* (New York: Wiley).

————. 1960. *Design for a Brain* (London: Chapman & Hall).

————. 1968. "Principles of Self-Organizing Systems." In *Modern Systems Research for the Behavioral Scientist,* edited by W. Buckley (Chicago, IL: Aldine).

Atkinson, A. A. and G. A. Feltham. 1981. "Information in Capital Markets: An Agency Theory Perspective." Unpublished working paper, University of British Columbia, January.

Atkinson, J. W. and J. O. Raynor (eds). 1974. *Motivation and Achievement* (New York: Wiley).

Baiman, S. 1982. "Agency Research in Managerial Accounting: A Survey." *Journal of Accounting Literature* 1 (Spring): 154–213.

Baiman, S. and J. S. Demski. 1980a. "Variance Analysis Procedures as Motivation Devices." *Management Science* 26 (August): 840–48.

————. 1980b. "Economically Optimal Performance Evaluation and Control Systems." *Journal of Accounting Research* 18, Supplement: 184–220.

Bar-Hillel, Y. and R. Carnap. 1964. "An Outline of a Theory of Semantic Information." In *Language and Information,* edited by Y. Bar-Hillel (Reading, MA: Addison-Wesley).

Baumol, W. J. 1959. *Business Behaviour, Value and Growth* (New York: Macmillan).

————. 1965. *Economic Theory and Operations Analysis,* 2d ed (Englewood Cliffs, NJ: Prentice-Hall).

Baumol, W. J. and T. Fabian. 1964. "Decomposition, Pricing for Decentralization and External Economies." *Management Science* (September): 1–32.

Bellman, R. and R. Kalaba. 1965. *Dynamic Programming and Modern Control Theory* (New York: Academic Press).

Berle, A. A., Jr. and G. C. Means. 1932. *The Modern Corporation and Private Property* (New York: Macmillan).

Bertalanffy, L. von. 1950. "The Theory of Open Systems in Phsyics and Biology." *Science:* 23–29; reprinted in *Systems Thinking,* edited by F. E. Emery (Hardmondsworth, England: Penguin, 1969).

Bierman, H., Jr. and T. R. Dyckman. 1976. *Managerial Cost Accounting,* 2d ed (New York: Macmillan).

Blalock, H. M., Jr. (ed). 1974. *Measurement in the Social Sciences* (Chicago, IL: Aldine).

_____. 1982. *Conceptualization and Measurement in the Social Sciences* (Beverly Hills, CA: Sage Publications).

Bonbright, J. C. 1965. *The Valuation of Property,* 2 vols (Charlottesville, VA: The Michie Co.; originally published 1937).

Boulding, K. E. 1956. "General System Theory—the Skeleton of Science." *Management Science* 2: 197–208.

_____. 1962. *Conflict and Defense* (New York: Doubleday).

Borch, K. 1962. "Equilibrium in a Reinsurance Market." *Econometrica* 30: 424–44.

Braithwaite, R. B. 1960. *Scientific Explanation* (New York: Harper and Brothers).

Buckley, W. 1967. *Sociology and Modern Systems Theory* (Englewood Cliffs, NJ: Prentice-Hall).

Bunge, Mario. 1977. *Treatise on Basic Philosophy,* vol 3, *The Furniture of the World* (Dordrecht, Holland: Reidel).

_____. 1979a. *Causality and Modern Science,* 3d revised ed (New York: Dover; first published 1959).

_____. 1979b. *Treatise on Basic Philosophy,* vol 4, *A World of Systems* (Dordrecht, Holland: Reidel).

Carathéodory, C. 1963. *Algebraic Theory of Measure and Integration* (New York: Chelsea Publishing).

Christensen, J. 1981. "Communication in Agencies." *Bell Journal of Economics* (Autumn): 661–74.

Coase, R. H. 1937. "The Nature of the Firm." *Economica,* n.s. 4 (November): 386–405; reprinted in *Readings in Price Theory,* edited by G. J. Stigler and K. E. Boulding (London: Allen and Unwin), pp. 331–51.

_____. 1960. "The Problem of Social Cost." *Journal of Law and Economics* 3 (October): 1–44.

Cofer, C. N. and M. H. Appley. 1964. *Motivation: Theory and Research* (New York: Wiley).

Cochrane, J. L. and M. Zeleny (eds). 1973. *Multiple Criteria Decision Making* (Columbia, SC: University of South Carolina Press).

Cohen, M. R. and E. Nagel. 1955. *An Introduction to Logic and Scientific Method* (London: Routledge & Kegan Paul; first published 1934).

Coleman, J. S. 1974. *Power and the Structure of Society* (New York: W. W. Norton).

Collard, D. A. 1973. "External Effects." In *Readings in Management Decision,* edited by L. R. Amey (London: Longman).

Conant, R. C. 1976. "Laws of Information which Govern Systems." *IEEE Transactions on Systems, Man, and Cybernetics,* SMC-6 (April): 240–55.

Cyert, R. M. and J. G. March. 1963. *A Behavioral Theory of the Firm* (Englewood Cliffs, NJ: Prentice-Hall).

Debreu, G. 1959. *Theory of Value* (New Haven, CT: Yale University Press).

Demski, J. S. 1967. "An Accounting System Structured on a Linear Programming Model." *Accounting Review* (October): 701–12.

_____. 1972. *Information Analysis* (Reading, MA: Addison-Wesley).

_____. 1976. "Uncertainty and Evaluation Based on Controllable Performance." *Journal of Accounting Research* (Autumn): 230–45.

Demski, J. S. and G. A. Feltham. 1978. "Economic Incentives in Budgetary Control Systems." *Accounting Review* 53: 336–59.

_____. 1976. *Cost Determination* (Ames, IA: Iowa State University Press).

Dillon, R. D. and J. F. Nash. 1978. "The True Relevance of Relevant Costs." *Accounting Review* 53 (January): 11–17.

Doeringer, P. B. and M. J. Piore. 1971. *Internal Labor Markets and Manpower Analysis* (Lexington, MA: D.C. Heath).

Edwards, W. 1961. "Behavioural Decision Theory." *Annual Review of Psychology* 12: 473–98; reprinted in *Decision Making,* edited by W. Edwards and A. Tversky (Harmondsworth, England: Penguin, 1967, ch. 2).

Ekern, S. 1981. "Time Dominance Efficiency Analysis." *Journal of Finance* 36 (December): 1023–34.

Ekern, S. and O. Bøhren. 1979. "Consistent Rankings Based on Total and Differential Amounts under Uncertainty." *Decision Sciences* 10: 519–26.

Emery, F. E. and E. L. Trist. 1965. "The Causal Texture of Organizational Environments." *Human Relations* 18: 21–32; reprinted in *Systems Thinking,* edited by F. E. Emery (Harmondsworth, England: Penguin, 1969).

Estes, W. K. 1954. "Individual Behavior in Uncertain Situations: An Interpretation in Terms of Statistical Association Theory." In *Decision Processes,* edited by R. M. Thrall, C. H. Coombs and R. L. Davis (New York: Wiley), pp. 127–38.

Fair, W. R. 1960. "The Next Step in Management Controls." In *Management Control Systems,* edited by D. G. Malcolm and A. J. Rowe (New York: Wiley).

Fama, E. F. 1980. "Agency Problems and the Theory of the Firm." *Journal of Political Economy* 82: 288–307.

Feltham, G. A. 1972. *Information Evaluation* (Sarasota, FL: American Accounting Association).

Forrester, J. W. 1975. "Counterintuitive Behavior of Social Systems." In *Collected Papers of J. W. Forrester* (Cambridge, MA: Wright-Allen Press), ch. 14.

Furubotn, E. G. and S. Pejovich. 1972. "Property Rights and Economic Theory: A Survey of Recent Literature." *Journal of Economic Literature,* 10 (December): 1137–62.

Galbraith, J. 1973. *Designing Complex Organizations* (Reading, MA: Addison-Wesley).

Geoffrion, A. M. 1968. "Proper Efficiency and the Theory of Vector Maximization." *Journal of Mathematical Analysis and Applications* 22: 618–30.

Gjesdal, F. 1981. "Accounting for Stewardship." *Journal of Accounting Research* 19 (Spring): 208–31.

Good, I. J. 1959. "A Classification of Fallacious Arguments and Interpretations." *Technometrics* 4: 125–32.

Gouldner, A. W. 1959. "Organizational Analysis. In *Sociology Today,* edited by R. K. Merton, L. Broom, and L. S. Cottrell Jr. (New York: Basic Books).

Groves, T. and M. Loeb. 1979. "Incentives in Divisionalized Firms." *Management Science* 25 (March): 221–30.

Halmos, P. R. 1950. *Measure Theory* (Princeton, New Jersey: Van Nostrand).

Hammond, K. R., D. A. Summer, and D. H. Deane. 1973. "Negative Effects of Outcome-Feedback in Multiple-Cue Probability Learning." *Organizational Behavior and Human Performance:* 31.

Harris, M. and A. Raviv. 1978. "Some Results on Incentive Contracts with Applications to Education and Employment, Health Insurance, and Law Enforcement." *American Economic Review* 68 (March): 20–30.

_____. 1979. "Optimal Incentive Contracts with Imperfect Information." *Journal of Economic Theory* 20: 231–59.

Hedberg, B. and S. Jönsson. 1978. "Designing Semi-Confusing Information Systems for Organizations in Changing Environments." *Accounting, Organizations and Society* 3: 47–64.

Henderson, J. M. and R. E. Quandt. 1980. *Microeconomic Theory: A Mathematical Approach,* 3d ed (New York: McGraw-Hill).

Herzberg, F., B. Mausner, and B. B. Snyderman. 1959. *The Motivation to Work* (New York: Wiley).

Hirshleifer, J. 1971. "Where Are We in the Theory of Information?" *American Economic Review* 61: 31–39.

Hofstede, G. H., 1972. *The Game of Budget Control* (London: Tavistock).

Holmström, B. R. 1979. "Moral Hazard and Observability." *Bell Journal of Economics* 10 (Spring): 74–91.

Hopwood, A. G. 1976. *Accounting and Human Behaviour* (Englewood Cliffs, NJ: Prentice-Hall).

Huff, D. 1954. *How to Lie with Statistics* (New York: Norton).

Ijiri, Y. 1965a. *Management Goals and Accounting for Control* (Amsterdam: North-Holland).

_____. 1965b. "Axioms and Structures of Conventional Accounting Measurement." *Accounting Review* 40 (January): 36–53.

_____. 1967. *The Foundations of Accounting Measurement* (Englewood Cliffs, NJ: Prentice-Hall).

_____. 1975. *Theory of Accounting Measurement* (Sarasota, FL: American Accounting Association).

Itami, H. 1977. *Adaptive Behavior: Management Control and Information Analysis* (Sarasota, FL: American Accounting Association, Study in Accounting Research, no. 15).

Jennergren, L. P. 1980. "On the Design of Incentives in Business Firms: A Survey of Some Research." *Management Science* 26 (February): 180–201.

Jensen, M. C. and W. H. Meckling. 1976. "Theory of the Firm: Managerial

Behavior, Agency Costs and Ownership Structure." *Journal of Financial Economics* 3 (October): 305–60.

Johnston, J. 1960. *Statistical Cost Analysis* (New York: McGraw-Hill).

Kaplan, R. S. 1982. *Advanced Management Accounting* (Englewood Cliffs, NJ: Prentice-Hall).

Katz, D. 1964. "The Motivational Basis of Organizational Behavior." *Behavioral Science* 9 (March): 131–46.

Keynes, J. M. 1949. *The General Theory of Employment, Interest and Money* (London: Macmillan; first published 1936).

Kirman, A. P. 1981. "Measure Theory with Applications to Economics." In *Handbook of Mathematical Economics,* vol 1, edited by K. J. Arrow and M. D. Intriligator (New York: North-Holland), ch. 5.

Kolmogorov, A. N. 1950. *Foundations of the Theory of Probability,* English ed. (New York: Chelsea Publishing; originally published 1933).

Krantz, D., R. D. Luce, P. Suppes, and A. Tversky. 1971. *Foundations of Measurement,* vol 1 (New York: Academic Press).

Kreps, D. M. and R. B. Wilson. 1981. "Sequential Equilibria." Unpublished working paper, Graduate School of Business, Stanford University, May.

Lawler, E. E., III and J. G. Rhode. 1976. *Information and Control in Organizations* (Pacific Palisades, CA: Goodyear).

Lawrence, P. R. and J. W. Lorsch. 1967. *Organization and Environment: Managing Differentiation and Integration* (Boston, MA: Harvard University Graduate School of Business Administration).

Lee, S. M. 1972–3. "Goal Programming for Decision Analysis of Multiple Objectives." *Sloan Management Review* 14 (Winter): 11–24.

Leibniz, G. W. von. 1954. *Principles of Nature and of Grace, Founded on Reason.* Edited by A. Robinet, 1714 (Paris: Presses Universitaires de France), section 7.

Littlechild, S. C. 1970. "Marginal-Cost Pricing with Joint Costs." *Economic Journal* (June): 323–34.

Loève, M. 1963. *Probability Theory,* 3d ed (New York: van Nostrand).

Luce, R. D. and H. Raiffa. 1957. *Games and Decisions* (New York: Wiley).

Machlup, F. 1962. *The Production and Distribution of Knowledge in the United States* (Princeton, NJ: Princeton University Press).

Madsen, K. B. 1974. *Modern Theories of Motivation* (Copenhagen: Munksgaard).

Malone, D. J. 1964. "An Analysis of the Cost and Value of Improvable Information for Quantitative Decisions." Doctoral dissertation, University of Pennsylvania.

March, J. G. 1976. "The Technology of Foolishness." In *Ambiguity and Choice in Organizations,* edited by J. G. March and J. P. Olsen (Bergen, Norway: Universitetsforlaget).

Marris, R. 1964. *The Economic Theory of Managerial Capitalism* (Glencoe, IL: Free Press).

Marschak, J. 1959. "Remarks on the Economics of Information." In *Contributions to Scientific Research in Management* (Los Angeles: Western Data Processing Center, UCLA), pp. 79–98.

Marshall, A. 1920. *Principles of Economics*, 8th ed (London: Macmillan).

Maslow, A. H. 1960. *Motivation and Personality* (New York: McGraw-Hill).

McClelland, D. C. 1961. *The Achieving Society* (New York: Van Nostrand-Reinhold).

McGregor, D. 1960. *The Human Side of Enterprise* (New York: McGraw-Hill).

Mesarovic, M. D., D. Macko, and Y. Takahara. 1970. *Theory of Hierarchical, Multilevel, Systems* (New York: Academic Press).

Mirrlees, J. A. 1974. "Notes on Welfare Economics, Information, and Uncertainty." In *Essays on Economic Behaviour under Uncertainty*, edited by Balch, McFadden, and Wu (Amsterdam: North-Holland).

————. 1976. "The Optimal Structure of Incentives and Authority Within an Organization." *Bell Journal of Economics* (Spring): 105–31.

Moran, P. A. P. 1968. *Introduction to Probability Theory* (London: Oxford University Press).

Mowshowitz, A. 1976. *The Conquest of Will: Information Processing in Human Affairs* (Reading, MA: Addison-Wesley).

Munroe, M. E. 1968. *Measure and Integration* (Reading, MA: Addison-Wesley).

Namazi, M. 1985. "Theoretical Developments of Principal-agent Employment Contract in Accounting: The State of the Art." *Journal of Accounting Literature* 4 (Spring): 113–63.

Neumann, J. von and O. Morgenstern. 1944. *Theory of Games and Economic Behavior* (Princeton, NJ: Princeton University Press).

Ouchi, W. G. 1980. "Markets, Bureaucracies and Clans." *Administrative Science Quarterly* 25 (March): 129–41.

Parsons, T. 1960. *Structure and Process in Modern Societies* (Glencoe, IL: Free Press).

Penrose, Edith T. 1958. *The Theory of the Growth of the Firm* (Oxford: Blackwell).

Peponides, G. M. and P. V. Kokotovic. 1983. "Weak Connections, Time Scales, and Aggregation of Nonlinear Systems." *IEEE Transactions on Systems, Man, and Cybernetics,* SMC-13 (July–August): 527–32.

Roberts, B. and D. L. Schulze. 1973. *Modern Mathematics and Economic Analysis* (New York: W. W. Norton).

Rosen, R. 1975. "Biological Systems as Paradigms for Adaptation." In *Adaptive Economic Models,* edited by R. H. Day and T. Groves (New York: Academic Press), pp. 39–72.

Ross, S. A. 1973. "The Economic Theory of Agency: The Principal's Problem." *American Economic Review Proceedings* 63: 134–39.

Royden, H. L. 1968. *Real Analysis,* 2d ed (New York: Macmillan).

Sahal, D. 1982. "Structure and Self-Organization." *Behavioral Science* 27: 249–58.

Savage, L. J. 1954. *The Foundations of Statistics* (New York: Wiley).

Schlaifer, R. 1959. *Probability and Statistics for Business Decisions* (New York: McGraw-Hill).

Scott, W. R. 1981. *Organizations: Rational, Natural, and Open Systems* (Englewood Cliffs, NJ: Prentice-Hall).

Shavell, S. 1979. "Risk Sharing and Incentives in the Principal and Agent

Relationship." *Bell Journal of Economics* 10 (Spring): 55–73.

Shubik, M. 1961. "Approaches to the Study of Decision-Making Relevant to the Firm." *Journal of Business* (April): 101–17.

Simon, H. A. 1957a. *Administrative Behavior,* 2d ed (New York: Macmillan).

———. 1957b. *Models of Man* (New York: Wiley).

———. 1957c. "Rationality and Administrative Decision Making." In Simon, *Models of Man* (New York: Wiley).

———. 1959. "Theories of Decision Making in Economics and Behavioral Science." *American Economic Review* (June): 253–83.

———. 1962. "The Architecture of Complexity." Proceedings of the American Philosophical Society, December, pp. 467–82; reprinted in Simon, *The Sciences of the Artificial,* ch. 4 (Cambridge, MA: MIT Press, 1969).

———. 1973. "Applying Information Technology to Organization Design." *Public Administration Review* 33 (May–June): 268–78.

———. 1978. "On How to Decide What to Do." *Bell Journal of Economics* (Autumn): 494–507.

Simon, H. A. and A. Ando. 1961. "Aggregation of Variables in Dynamic Systems." *Econometrica* 29 (April): 111–38.

Stedry, A. C. 1960. *Budget Control and Cost Behavior* (Englewood Cliffs, NJ: Prentice-Hall).

Steiner, G. A. 1969. *Top Management Planning* (New York: Macmillan).

Stevens, S. S. 1959. "Measurement, Psychophysics, and Utility." In *Measurement: Definitions and Theories,* edited by C. W. Churchman and P. Ratoosh (New York: Wiley), ch. 2.

Suppes, P. and J. L. Zinnes. 1963. "Basic Measurement Theory." In *Handbook of Mathematical Psychology,* vol 1, edited by R. D. Luce, R. R. Bush, and E. Galanter (New York: Wiley).

Theil, H. 1968–69. "On the use of Information Theory Concepts in the Analysis of Financial Statements." *Management Science* 15: 459–80.

Tiessen, P. and J. H. Waterhouse. 1983. "Towards a Descriptive Theory of Management Accounting." *Accounting, Organizations and Society* 8: 251–67.

Tippett, M. 1978. "The Axioms of Accounting Measurement." *Accounting and Business Research* (Autumn): 266–78.

Varian, H. R. 1978. *Microeconomic Analysis* (New York: W. W. Norton).

Vickrey, D. W. 1970. "Is Accounting a Measurement Discipline?" *Accounting Review* (October): 731–42.

Vroom, V. H., 1964. *Work and Motivation* (New York: Wiley).

Vroom, V. H. and E. L. Deci (eds). 1970. *Management and Motivation* (Hardmondsworth, England: Penguin).

Wald, A. 1950. *Statistical Decision Functions* (New York: Wiley).

Whitehead, A. N. 1947. *Adventures of Ideas* (London: Cambridge University Press).

Whitmore, G. A. and M. C. Findlay (eds). 1978. *Stochastic Dominance* (Lexington, MA: Lexington Books).

Williamson, O. E. 1963. "A Model of Rational Managerial Behavior." In *A*

Behavioral Theory of the Firm, edited by R. M. Cyert and J. G. March (Englewood Cliffs, NJ: Prentice-Hall), ch. 9.

_____. 1964. *The Economics of Discretionary Behavior* (Englewood Cliffs, NJ: Prentice-Hall).

_____. 1975. *Markets and Hierarchies: Analysis and Antitrust Implications* (New York: Free Press).

_____. 1979. "Transaction-Cost Economics: The Governance of Contractual Relations." *Journal of Law and Economics* 22 (October): 233–61.

_____. 1981. "The Modern Corporation: Origins, Evolution, Attributes." *Journal of Economic Literature* 19 (December): 1537–68.

Williamson, O. E., J. Harris and M. Wachter 1975. "Understanding the Employment Relation: The Analysis of Idiosyncratic Exchange." *Bell Journal of Economics* (Spring): 250–78.

Wilson, R. B. 1968. "The Theory of Syndicates." *Econometrica* 36 (January): 119–32.

_____. 1969. "The Structure of Incentives for Decentralization under Uncertainty." In *La Decision,* edited by M. Gilbaud (Paris: Centre Nationale de la Recherche Scientifique).

Yager, R. R. 1979. "Possibilistic Decision-Making." *IEEE Transactions on Systems, Man, and Cybernetics,* SMC-9 (July): 388–92.

Zadeh, L. A. 1977. "Pruf and Its Application to Inference from Fuzzy Propositions." In *Proceedings of IEEE Systems on Fuzzy Sets,* New Orleans, pp. 1359–60.

_____. 1978. "Fuzzy Sets as a Basis for a Theory of Possibility." *Fuzzy Sets and Systems* 1: 3–28.

Zimmerman, J. L. 1979. "The Costs and Benefits of Cost Allocations." *Accounting Review* 54: 504–21.

Author Index

Subject Index

About the Author

Lloyd R. Amey is Professor and Head of Accounting at McGill University, Montreal. He received his Ph.D. in economics from the University of Nottingham, England, and is a CPA (Australia). He has taught in England, the United States, and Canada. In addition to *Corporate Planning*, Professor Amey is the author of *The Efficiency of Business Enterprises, Budget Planning and Control Systems*, and numerous journal articles. He is the coauthor, with D. A. Egginton, of *Management Accounting: A Conceptual Approach* and the editor of *Readings in Management Decision.*